ON DEMOCRACIES
AND DEATH CULTS

**ALSO BY
DOUGLAS
MURRAY**

The War on the West

The Madness of Crowds

The Strange Death of Europe

ON DEMOCRACIES AND DEATH CULTS

Israel and the Future of Civilization

DOUGLAS MURRAY

BROADSIDE BOOKS

HarperCollins books may be purchased for educational, business, or sales promotional use. For information, please email the Special Markets Department at SPsales@harpercollins.com.

Broadside Books™ and the Broadside logo are trademarks of HarperCollins Publishers.

FIRST EDITION

Library of Congress Cataloging-in-Publication Data

Names: Murray, Douglas, 1979– author.
Title: On democracies and death cults : Israel and the future of civilization / Douglas Murray.
Other titles: Israel and the future of civilization
Description: New York, NY: Broadside, [2025] | Includes bibliographical references.
Identifiers: LCCN 2024058955 (print) | LCCN 2024058956 (ebook) | ISBN 9780063437135 | ISBN 9780063437159 (ebook)
Subjects: LCSH: October 7 Hamas Attack, Israel, 2023. | Arab-Israeli Conflict—History.
Classification: LCC DS119.77 .M87 2025 (print) | LCC DS119.77 (ebook) | DDC 956.9405/5—dc23/eng/20250121
LC record available at https://lccn.loc.gov/2024058955
LC ebook record available at https://lccn.loc.gov/2024058956

ISBN 978-0-06-343713-5

25 26 27 28 29 LBC 5 4 3 2 1

Someone might ask: "Why write about this, why remember all that?" It is the writer's duty to tell this terrible truth, and it is the civilian duty of the reader to learn it.

—Vasily Grossman

CONTENTS

INTRODUCTION

Sometimes a flare goes up and you get to see exactly where everyone is standing.

The morning of October 7, 2023, was just such a moment. That morning air-raid sirens went off all across Israel. This was no unusual thing in itself. Certainly not in the south of the country that had for seventeen years been within rocket range of Hamas. Nor in the north of the country into which Hezbollah had fired rockets since the 1980s. But in Tel Aviv and Jerusalem the sirens sounded too. People woke up that Saturday morning to the realization that something very unusual was happening.

Soon social media and various messaging platforms began blowing up with people relating the unimaginable. Reports from people in the south suggested that there had been a major terrorist breach from Gaza into Israel. This strip of land had been dominated by the terrorist group Hamas almost immediately after Israel withdrew from the territory in 2005. There had been terrorist incursions over the years since, including the cross-border raid and kidnap of the young soldier Gilad Shalit in 2006. But here were reports of hundreds, perhaps thousands of terrorists streaming through the communities of southern Israel. The fighting seemed to be everywhere. As well as entering the communities (called "kibbutz") in the south they had also entered major towns and were attacking the young people who had been dancing at the Nova festival—a rave party that had been arranged on the eve of the Jewish festival of Simchat Torah.

The fact that it was the Sabbath—and a major religious festival—meant that many religious people were off their phones that morning. Many Jews do not use electronic devices on the holy day. But for everyone who was on their phones they were soon seeing the horror in real time.

Across the south of Israel first responders rushed to the scene and found sights of butchery and chaos. The volunteer group United Hatzalah has volunteers all across Israel. Their citizen members are trained to respond to road crashes and other emergencies. Members of the public call in and a volunteer in the area will get there as soon as possible. That morning, as the head of the group would later tell me in their control room in Jerusalem, their situation screens started to light up with incidents. Indicating the huge map in their control room, Eli Beer told me that thirty years of incidents all combined didn't add up to an hour of what happened that morning.

One of the many volunteers from Hatzalah got an alert and thought he was going to the scene of an accident. He spotted a car on the roadside, saw some dead bodies, and slowed down. But something was not right. The people by the car were dressed in the uniforms of Israeli soldiers. They started shooting at him. Incidents like this caused utter confusion on top of the terror. *Why would they be shooting at me?* was his first thought. But some of the Hamas terrorists had come into the country wearing versions of the uniforms of Israeli soldiers. Others had taken them off the bodies of the dead in the military bases Hamas had already overwhelmed.

Within hours the sheer scale of the assault started to become apparent. The terrorists had come into Israel not just by land vehicles and on foot but by boat and on hand gliders; perhaps as many as six thousand in total. Wherever they arrived they brought death—with rifles, grenades, incendiary weapons, rocket-propelled grenades, machine guns, and more. It would take weeks—in fact months—to identify the number of people killed that day. The final body count was not identified until ten months later. The death toll turned out to be just short of 1,200 people.

The victims were mainly civilians. At the Nova dance party near Kibbutz Re'im, just a couple of miles from the Gaza border, 364 attendees were slaughtered as they hid or tried to flee. Many of them called their families. In the age of videophones the scale and brutality of the slaughter swiftly became clear across the country and then the world. Children called their parents—asking for help, asking for advice, or just telling their parents that they loved them.

An additional horror soon became clear. Videos started to emerge showing Israelis of all ages being taken into Gaza, on motorbikes, in pickups and cars, and on foot. It soon became clear that roughly 250 people ended up being kidnapped that day. The world started to learn this, and more, because many of the terrorists recorded their acts as they did them. Using GoPro cameras and mobile phones the terrorists broadcast their acts of violence with pride. By late in the day on October 7, it was already clear that these acts included burning people alive, shooting innocent people, cutting off people's heads, and raping men and women. Sometimes before killing them. Sometimes after.

Israel is a country with a population of just 9 million people. America is a country of some 333 million people. To put it in perspective, the death toll on October 7 was the equivalent of some 44,400 Americans being killed by terrorists on a single day. Or around fifteen 9/11s. The kidnap toll if it had happened by ratio in the US would have been almost 10,000 Americans taken from their homes as hostages. It would be the equivalent of some 5,000 Canadians being killed in a single day and a thousand taken hostage. Or 8,400 French or British people being slaughtered in a single day and another 1,750 taken hostage.

These figures are almost too much for anyone in any of these countries to comprehend. They were for the people of Israel too. But it happened to them.

The massacre of October 7 came almost exactly fifty years to the day since Israel's neighbors—including Egypt—had last tried to annihilate it. In that war, known as the Yom Kippur War, an identical tactic had been used by Israel's enemies. That war also started with a surprise attack on a religious holiday in which Israel's enemies expected to find her sleeping.

***

Like many people around the world I was sleeping in another time zone on the morning of the 7th, and so caught up late with what was happening. First I saw the news and messages about rocket fire into Israel, and I remember thinking that this was nothing special. I had sat in many bomb shelters in Israel since my first visit there during the 2006 war with Hezbollah in Lebanon. On one occasion I did so with the citizens of Sderot after agreeing, curiously, to open a skateboard park donated by a British charity for the town's beleaguered children. Sderot was one of the major cities in which it was clear that some of the worst fighting on the 7th was occurring. The attack from Gaza was a brigade-sized one, which happened in several waves of people. Terrorists from Hamas and Islamic Jihad came first, then came citizens of Gaza intent on joining in the looting and killing. But it was only when I saw footage of a Hamas truck heading down the main street in Sderot—a street I knew—and saw Hamas firing a rocket-propelled-grenade down the street that I realized this was something of a different order.

I was at my home in New York when—like the rest of the world—I started trying to absorb the news. Though not Jewish myself, I had visited Israel many times since the 2006 war. I had friends there, and as the day went on I did what many people around the world did, and tried first to find out if they were all right.

The next day I heard news of a major demonstration that was due to take place in Times Square. It had been swiftly organized and hastily publicized. But it was not a protest against the horrors of the previous day. It was not a protest against the terrorists of Hamas. It was instead a protest against the State of Israel and the citizens of the world's only Jewish state.

Hundreds of people were gathered in Times Square that lunchtime. Some came with homemade signs. One headscarf-covered woman was smiling gleefully, waving a sign that said "Zionist nightmares. 10/6/73 Egyptians. 10/7/23 Palestinians. #Long Live Intifada." As I photographed her with my phone she punched the air and screamed with joy. Another participant held a sign saying "Land Back"—an American movement that seeks to give the land of America and other Western countries over to their "indigenous peoples," and which is also used as an attack on Israel.

However, most people in the crowd carried banners handed out by the organizers. They read "From the River to the Sea," "Resistance Is Justified," "Resistance Is Not Terrorism," "Fight White Supremacy," and "Long Live the Intifada." One of the most chilling signs read "By Any Means Necessary." This was at a time when the world already knew that these "means" included the mass sexual abuse of women and the burning alive of whole families in their homes. While this protest was going on in New York, the massacres were still going on in the south of Israel and the terrorists had still not yet been pushed back.

This pattern was repeated in cities across the West. In Germany and France (which have Europe's largest Muslim and Jewish communities), anti-Israel protests erupted. But there the authorities tried to clamp down on people shouting anti-Jewish slogans. In London on the night of the 7th, huge crowds gathered near the Israeli embassy and began setting off flares. Amid the violent disorder and a breakdown of policing, these hundreds of impromptu protesters were gleeful. They were there to celebrate the massacres. In London and other British cities these protests grew and grew, with hundreds of thousands of people soon coming out on the streets of London. All before Israel had even responded to the Hamas attacks. Similar protests occurred across North America, on the streets and on the most elite college campuses. Open support for Hamas and their actions was explicit and only grew.

In Canada alone, after October 7, synagogues were firebombed and shot at, Jewish schools were shot at, Jewish shops were fire-bombed, and Jewish-owned bookshops were vandalized.

Throughout this period, from the moment news of the massacre in Israel emerged, one thing in particular is worth noticing: there was not a single major protest against Hamas in any Western city. Not one. The people who carried out the massacre and started a war did not find themselves the object of criticism on the streets of one Western city. Some people will say that this is because Hamas would not listen to protesters on the streets of America or Europe. Or that Western countries have no control over Hamas.

But the governments of all these countries had been funding the Palestinians in Gaza for years. They had given billions of dollars in foreign aid direct to the Hamas government there, through UN organizations among many others. This money had been used by Hamas's leaders to either enrich themselves (the group's leaders became billionaires) or to build the infrastructure of terror inside Gaza that allowed the group to carry out the October 7 attack, steal Israelis, and hold them hostage inside Gaza.

With all of this going on, I decided that I should get to Israel as soon as I could. Several things persuaded me. The first was that sight in Times Square. The knowledge that if there was celebration of these attacks in New York, then there would soon be celebration around the globe. A second was a certainty that the scale of the atrocities carried out that day would soon be passed over. Not just because on that day, the 7th, long before the scale of the attack was understood, Western media were already focusing not on what had just happened but on what Israel might do in response. Having covered many of these wars, I already knew that the question "What will the Israelis do in retaliation?" was soon going to be the main story. I also feared—correctly, as it turned out—that a great wave of denial would sweep across the world, that what turned out to be the biggest massacre of Jews anywhere in the world since the Holocaust would swiftly be denied just as surely as neo-Nazis and others chose to try to deny the Nazi Holocaust after it had happened.

In my native London I would later be shown—along with other journalists—the forty-six-minute edited footage of the October 7 massacres. This footage had been put together from the terrorists' own recordings from the day, from the footage taken by first responders arriving at the scenes, and from footage that victims had taken on the day which had been found on their phones. In the coming months I would see many such videos, from people who had been at the Nova party, from relatives who showed me the last moments in the lives of their loved ones, and from the organizations like Hatzalah whose brave Jewish, Muslim, and Druze volunteers had all driven toward the disaster that day.

But none of it compared with the impact of that first, bludgeoning viewing of portions of the massacre. The murders and bodies seen in the footage seemed to go on endlessly. Scene after scene after scene.

There was footage of terrorists using a shovel to try to remove the head of a young man lying on the floor. With each strike they shouted "Allahu Akbar." There was footage of the young women on an Israeli army base cowering in a corner as the armed male terrorists walked in. There was the footage of young people running for their lives from the Nova party—or hiding wherever they thought was safe. And then the footage of the first responders going in among heaps of dead bodies shouting desperately to see if anyone was still alive. The footage felt like it had gone on for hours, but the number of victims shown in that film included barely 10 percent of the victims of that day.

It takes a lot to silence a roomful of British journalists, but three-quarters of an hour of this did it. I left with an old friend of mine from the British media, a journalist in his seventies who has seen his share of war. It took a long while for either of us to find any words as we walked along the gray, leaf-covered streets of London. Eventually he did manage to say something. "Bastards," he said. "Bastards," I agreed.

Of course that didn't do justice to what we had just seen. Nothing could. But as I started to grapple with it there was one thing in particular I just couldn't fathom. From writing about and covering wars on three continents I have seen my share of horrors. But there was something unusual about this atrocity. As I tried to put my finger on it, I couldn't help reflecting on the fact that in all this footage of the terrorists—taken by them and broadcast to their supporters (who would first celebrate and then deny these acts)—there was something uncommon even in the long history of violence. It was that the terrorists of October 7 did what they did with such relish. Not just the endless shouting of their war cries. Or the visible glee you could see in their faces and hear in their voices. It was the fact that all of this gave them such intense joy. And that they were proud of their actions.

One of the recordings from the 7th, from that first atrocity video, was a recording of one of the terrorists who had got into the kibbutz of Mefalsim, a community of just over a thousand people in the south of Israel. In the midst of the attack the terrorist made a phone call back to his family in Gaza. The excitement in his voice was obvious. "Hi Dad," the three-minute call begins. "Open my WhatsApp now and you will see all those killed. Look how many I killed with my own hands! Your son killed Jews!" The father replies, "May God protect you." The son is exultant. "Dad, I'm talking to you from a Jewish woman's phone. I killed her and I killed her husband. I killed ten with my own hands." He goes on and on repeating himself. Boasting. "Dad I killed ten! Ten with my own hands! Put Mum on."

"Oh my son. God bless you," say the parents. Their son keeps making the same boasts to his mother. "I wish I was with you," she replies. "Mom, your son is a hero," he boasts. "Kill, kill, kill." Next the man's brother comes on the line and the young man brags to him too. "I killed ten. I swear!" "Hold your head up father. Hold your head up." One of the men on the other end says, "Come back, come back." "What do you mean, come back?" replies the son. "There is no going back. It is either death or victory. Open the WhatsApp. See the dead. Open it. Open WhatsApp on my phone and see the dead. How I killed them with my own hands."

In the days after the 7th, many people tried to make sense of facts such as these. What—if anything—could explain such hate? And what could any man or woman do against it? As I thought about this my mind went back to a late friend of mine named George Weidenfeld.

George was a Viennese Jew who was born in 1919. He died in 2016 having lived to a fine old age. He had fled the Nazis, escaping Austria after the Anschluss, or German annexation, of the country in 1938. He came to England, meeting among others the great author and Hapsburg-admirer Joseph Roth in Paris along the way. George was a repository of stories about those times, but after outliving the Nazi regime he spent much of the rest of his long life trying to understand it. As a publisher he often controversially agreed to publish books by and about Nazis—including the memoirs of Albert Speer. But as the historian Andrew Roberts has also remembered, toward the end of his life George often reflected on the fact that in his view, "There are people who are worse anti-Semites than the Nazis."

It was an extraordinary claim to make, in some ways. But as George used to explain, while Hamas, al-Qaeda, Islamic Jihad, and others had so far not managed to be as genocidal as the Nazis, there was no doubt that they would be if they could. Still, there was something about their actions and their motivations that made them distinct. George would be the last person to ever downplay the culpability of the Nazis who had killed so many of his friends and family. But he noted, as many historians have, that as evil as they were in general, the Nazis attempted to cover over the worst of their crimes.

Consider what the head of the SS, Heinrich Himmler, said in his speech to his most senior lieutenants in October 1943 as he detailed what the Nazis sought to achieve with the Holocaust: "We can talk about it among ourselves, yet we will never speak of it in public. . . . I am referring to the evacuation of the Jews, the extermination of the Jewish people. . . . It is," he said, "a page of glory in our history that has never been written and is never to be written." Himmler and his SS were among the most evil people in human history, yet even they had sought to cover over their crimes. Here, in 2023, in the form of Hamas, were people who were boasting of their crimes, were proud of their crimes, and indeed wanted to broadcast their crimes for all the world to see.[1]

What is the world to do against such groups of death—such cults of death?

For many people in the West, the answer seems to be to ignore it or to wish it away. Mass-casualty terrorist attacks have happened in many Western cities in recent years, from New York, Washington, DC, and the fields of Pennsylvania to London, Manchester, Paris, Nice, Berlin, and Stockholm, among others. Yet the response on most of these occasions was inadequate. Apart from the immediate aftermath of 9/11, the tendency was to look away or to pretend the problem away.

After twenty-two people—most of whom were young girls— were blown up by a suicide bomber at an Ariana Grande concert at Britain's Manchester Arena in 2017, the response, pushed onto the public by the media and others, was to sing an Oasis song—"Don't Look Back in Anger." As though, after twenty-two young people have their bodies blown to smithereens by a bomb packed with nails and ball bearings, the important thing was just not to be angry. But why? If the murder of young women for the crime of being at a concert shouldn't make you angry, then what should? Perhaps the British, like other people, just didn't know what to do about it.

I also wondered why the citizens of Israel seemed so unique among victims. Why they seemed to be the only people on earth who, when savagely attacked, either didn't gain the world's sympathy or gained it only for a matter of hours—if that.

I thought about this a lot in the months ahead. I got to Israel as soon as I could and immediately went to the sites of the massacres. In the months that followed I spent many long days with survivors, relatives of those who had been killed, and the families of the people taken hostage. I also went into Gaza myself, including through the part of the border fence that the terrorists had broken through that day. I saw up close Israel's campaign to defeat Hamas and return the hostages back to their homes.

Few armies in history have had to fight a war in such a concentrated, built-up, and booby-trapped area, in which the other side has deliberately placed its military infrastructure within and amid civilian buildings—including mosques, schools, homes, and hospitals. None has had to fight against an opposition whose leadership (as intercepted messages from the leader of Hamas in Gaza have made clear) sees the loss of their own civilians as desirable because of the advantages it can bring them in the war for international public opinion. Because in this era war is not just waged on the battlefield, but in the efforts to delegitimize a conflict abroad, turning victims into culprits and culprits into victims. It seems to me that the right of Israel to fight and win such a war is vital not just for the sake of that country, but so Britain, America, and every other Western country will be able to fight such a war if—or when—the time comes.

I decided, in short, not just to work out what had happened, but to become a witness. In the past many evils have been permitted because people have allowed them to go on or covered them up. I was determined not to let that happen.

And so I followed the facts wherever they led me. In the morgues of Tel Aviv I visited the pathologists as they were trying to identify the bodies of the dead, and saw for myself the terrible destruction wrought by Hamas. I spoke with political and military leaders to try to work out what had happened that day, what had failed, and what lessons could be learned. And in the maximum-security prisons of Israel I came face-to-face with the Hamas terrorists who had carried out the massacres that day and stared into the eyes of men I recognized from the atrocity footage.

All of this was of great importance to me as somebody who cares about the one thriving democracy in the Middle East and the only Jewish state in the world. But it matters to me also because I believe that what Israel stared into that day is a reality we might all stare into again at some point soon—and that some of us have already glimpsed.

Many people in the West today are not comfortable talking in terms like *good* or *evil*. In our increasingly secular societies, many people seem to think that such words are part of the past—too reductive an idea for our far more subtle and understanding times. We are even used to the notion that criminals in our society who do terrible things must have done them for some reason. That there must be some explanation for them, surely? One reason why real-crime documentaries and books are so popular is that we imagine that we might be able to discover the source of someone's behavior. As if even a mass murderer can in some way be explained.

But it seems to me that it is we who are missing something. Evil does exist as a force in the world. Indeed, it is the only explanation for why certain people do certain things. On October 7, 2023, many Israelis stared into the face of pure evil—1,200 of them in the last moments of their lives. People begged; people pleaded and in some cases cried for mercy. But they were murdered anyway.

At the same time it seems clear to me that such a force as "good" also exists in the world. As I would soon discover, it was displayed by a bewildering number of people on that same day. The fight between good and evil may seem too Manichean for some. Yet it is they—in their search for endless subtlety and limitless understanding—who are actually missing out on one of the greatest divides of all.

Perhaps the only force in the world even greater than evil itself is the great, collected, concentrated evil that is war.

Again, today in most of the West we think we are beyond war—that it is something that belongs in our past but has little relevance to our present. Before World War I many Europeans and Americans thought the same thing. If we have gotten accustomed to living in peace—and taking it as the norm—the people of Israel have not been able to enjoy such a luxury. It is something that has been consistently forced upon them. But the lessons they have learned and are learning are ones that everybody else in the West could do with learning too.

The gulf between peace and war is probably the most stark divide that any person and any society can face.

It is very hard to explain to someone who has not seen it just what that divide means. Leo Tolstoy gave it a good go in *War and Peace* when he describes two armies lining up on the field of battle:

> There was no one between the squadron and the enemy, and there lay between them, separating them, that same terrible line of the unknown and of fear, like the line separating the living from the dead. All the men sensed that line, and the question of whether they would or would not cross that line, and how they would cross it, troubled them.[2]

But that is a description of armies about to clash. When the realm of war comes into someone's daily life it is another level of terror. There is a novel by Ian McEwan in which a child is abducted from a supermarket, and when the parent realizes what has happened he first thinks there must have been a mistake. Then, when he realizes that his child is missing, he starts to shout for help. The first reaction of other people shopping is alarm that a man is behaving like this. Then suddenly—as though a layer of glass surrounding them has suddenly shattered—everybody enters the realm that the man is in. A child is missing. And everybody in the vicinity is now in this new, transformed reality. In Israel on the 7th, dozens of children were stolen and murdered, yet a world that seemed incapable of knowing right from wrong decided that the missing and murdered children were at best an encumbrance.

That shattered reality is the one that the people of Israel were thrown into by the events of October 7. But it is a reality that people in every democracy currently at peace might be thrown into again one day. Possibly soon. The story of the suffering and the heroism of October 7 and its aftermath is one that spells not just the divide between good and evil, peace and war, but between democracies and death cults.

ON DEMOCRACIES
AND DEATH CULTS

CHAPTER 1

WHAT HAPPENED

On January 31, 1979, a flight took off from Charles de Gaulle Airport in Paris. Its destination was Tehran, where it would land the following day. The plane was carrying the Ayatollah Khomeini, a fanatical Shiite leader who had been living in exile from his native Iran for over fourteen years. His return heralded the end of the reign of the Shah (Mohammad Reza Pahlavi), the overthrow of the Shah's government, and the turning point of the Islamic Revolution in Iran. Khomeini and his supporters swiftly seized power, took fifty-two American citizens and diplomats hostage at the American embassy in Tehran, and proceeded to kill their domestic political opponents. This included the communists and trade unionists who had struggled with the Islamists to overthrow the Shah.

Despite this, many Western intellectuals and journalists celebrated the flight of Khomeini from Paris. Among them was Michel Foucault, the left-wing French philosopher, who saw Khomeini as bringing a spiritual revolution to Iran that would finally do away with the Western sins of capitalism and materialism. Richard Falk, professor emeritus at Princeton, greeted the Iranian Revolution by reassuring readers of the *New York Times* that the depiction of Ayatollah Khomeini "as fanatical . . . and the bearer of crude prejudices seems certainly and happily false." In a subsequent piece for *Foreign Policy* ("Khomeini's Promise"), he added that "Khomeini's

Islamic republic can be expected to have a doctrine of social justice at its core; from all indications it will be flexible in interpreting the Koran."[3]

It was soon proved that nothing could have been further from the truth. From 1979 to the present day, the revolutionary Islamic government in Tehran has subjugated the Iranian people, condemned women to second-class status, imprisoned and tortured Iranian students, and instituted public hangings for people accused of "crimes" like homosexuality. The hope that, given time, a "moderate" Iranian revolutionary leader would emerge proved a false hope. And while the new government in Iran railed against the West for the sins of "colonialism" and much more, the regime spent its decades in power taking over not just Iran but the wider Middle East.

In the 1980s it fought a bloody war against Saddam Hussein's Iraq, which killed around half a million people. After the overthrow of Saddam Hussein in 2003, the Iranian theocracy moved in to colonize and dominate postwar Iraq. It was the same playbook that the regime had followed in the 1980s in Lebanon. As that country had fallen into civil war, the Iranians used their proxy armies, notably Hezbollah, to dominate first Shiite communities and then the whole country. They eventually took over the security and government in much of Beirut and colonized vast swaths of the country with their forces. Similarly, after the Syrian civil war began in 2011, Tehran's armies, including Hezbollah, moved in to prop up and dominate the government of Bashar al-Assad in Syria. And when civil war broke out in Yemen in 2014, the mullahs backed and armed the Houthi-led militias as they took over that country.

While decrying Western imperialism, the Iran of the ayatollahs became one of the biggest imperial powers of the age. At every military parade in Tehran, and at Friday prayers across the country, the regime called for "Death to America," calling America "the Great Satan" and Israel "the Little Satan." While accusing Israel of being a colonialist outpost of America, Tehran was busy setting up colonialist outposts everywhere. At a "World Without Zionism" conference

held in Tehran in October 2005, President Mahmoud Ahmadinejad
of Iran reiterated a famous phrase of the late Ayatollah Khomeini.
The "Jerusalem-occupying regime," he said, "must be erased from
the page of time." For years Western academics and politicians de-
bated whether Iranian leaders meant what they said.

***

It is hard to describe the tranquility of the kibbutzim of southern
Israel. These communities, of which there are still several hundred,
originated before the foundation of the State of Israel. They were
originally based around collective farming, and in this way among
others they speak to the socialist ethos that dominated much of the
nation's early life. The idea was that these communities would be
effectively self-sustaining and self-governing. There would be cooperation not just on supply of food but also on the education of the
children of the community and the security and well-being of the
community. Few have more than a thousand or so members, and
though the standard of living is not luxurious, the idea is that nobody in the community wants for anything.

Many of the communities have communal dining areas, and communal play areas for the children. It is hard to think of a more idyllic
or safe place for a child to grow up in. Members of the communities
often talk about how their children can run around playing till relatively late in the evening because, since everybody in the community
knows each other, they all know where the children are and that
they will be safe.

Yet many of the kibbutz in the south have details that suggest
that all is not completely Edenic. First, the communities tend to have
fences around them and gateposts that are guarded and allow the
slow flow of traffic in and out. Second, most of the communities
have at least one person who is in charge of security. The person who
keeps an eye on the security of the perimeter fence is generally armed
in case of emergencies. The third thing that distinguishes the houses

in these communities in what is otherwise a paradise is that each house has a safe room (or *mamad*) in which the family can shelter in case of emergency.

In the communities that run anywhere near the perimeter of the Gaza border, these safe rooms are a particular necessity. Israel unilaterally withdrew from the Gaza Strip in 2005, handing it over to be run by the Palestinian Authority (PA). The decision, by the government of Ariel Sharon, was one of the most controversial in the country's history. On the one hand there was concern about what an independent Gaza might become. On the other, too many soldiers had spent too many years having to guard Jewish and Palestinian families in the Strip. In highly emotive scenes, many Jews who had lived in Gaza all their lives refused to leave their homes. The Israeli government sent in soldiers from the Israel Defense Forces (IDF) to remove these families and tore them from their houses. The Israeli government knew—and the Palestinian Authority had always made clear—that no Palestinian state could have Jews in it. The one absolutely clear precondition for such a state was that no Jews could exist within its borders.

The withdrawal from Gaza was one of the most difficult decisions in modern Israeli history. The territory (which had previously belonged to Egypt) was captured by Israel during the war of 1967. Although there were strategic reasons to hold on to the territory, it had always been a headache for consecutive Israeli governments. Policing the Strip was costly in lives and treasure. Still, it was thought to be a remarkable change of tone in the early 2000s, when Ariel Sharon—known as being a hard-line right-wing prime minister and military leader—decided to withdraw.

Benjamin Netanyahu left Sharon's government over the decision, and the dispute over whether it was the right thing to do went on long before the handover itself and the painful removal of Israeli families. The Egyptian government made it clear that they had no interest in taking back the territory and wanted no role in governing the million or so Arabs in Gaza.

And so the territory—with most of its infrastructure, including its greenhouses for agricultural work—was handed over to the Fatah-dominated Palestinian Authority, which already had control of much of the West Bank (Judea and Samaria). In 2006, under pressure from the United States administration of George W. Bush, among others, the PA were pushed into holding legislative elections in Gaza. The Iranian-backed forces of Hamas beat Fatah convincingly, and in the aftermath Hamas solidified its grip on power by murdering Fatah officials in Gaza. Scores of Palestinians were executed in the streets, thrown off tall buildings, shot in the back, and in some cases had their bodies dragged through the streets of Gaza, tied by rope to the backs of motorbikes driven by exultant Hamas militants

From that day on, there has not been another election in Gaza, though as Hamas's control was made absolute there was one distinct development. Rockets had been fired into Israel from Gaza since 2001, but from the moment Hamas seized full control of the territory these attacks increased significantly. Smuggling the weapons in through the Egypt-controlled southern border between Egypt and Gaza, Hamas was soon able to stockpile thousands of rockets in Gaza. Soon major Israeli cities like Ashdod were able to be hit by Gazan rocket fire, and eventually—in 2008—Israel launched its first operation into Gaza since the withdrawal. Operation Cast Lead was explicitly launched by Israel in order to stop the firing of rockets from Gaza into Israel.

That war stopped after two months, but Iran continued to provide Hamas with rockets and the attacks soon resumed. In 2012 and again in 2014, Israel fought wars with Hamas and other terrorist groups inside Gaza in order to stop Hamas, Islamic Jihad, and other groups from firing rockets into Israel. By this time thousands of rockets had been fired at major cities. More frequently the relatively inexpensive Katyusha and similar rockets were fired the few miles from Gaza into neighboring cities like Sderot and communities like Nir Oz and Kfar Aza.

It was for this reason that every house in these communities and most buildings in the neighboring towns had safe rooms built into them. These rooms were typically located at the rear of these simple buildings. Besides strong walls they tended to have an air vent that could be opened and a steel door to shut behind the family when they entered. The doors could be shut but they could not be locked.

***

Three miles from the Gaza border is a kibbutz named Re'im. On the evening of October 6 a long-planned dance party took place, timed to coincide with the Jewish holiday. The party took place in the woodlands and fields near the kibbutz and was planned to be an all-night rave. It was advertised as being a celebration of "friends, love, and infinite freedom."

The Nova party was part of a psychedelic trance festival that started in Brazil. Taking place amid the copses of trees and open expanses of the Negev desert there were stages, an area with a bar serving food, and away from the dance floors a camping area for tents to be set up amid the trees. The event attracted around 3,500 young Israeli and international partygoers. DJs played throughout the night and the highlight of the party came in the early hours of the morning as the sun was coming up and many of the partygoers were coming up with it. Unsurprisingly for such an event, many of the young partygoers were on a range of psychedelics and other party drugs. Most of these—like LSD and MDMA—were mind- and consciousness-expanding drugs.

The first sign that something was wrong was when the barrage of rockets started to fire overhead from Gaza into Israel. Starting at six thirty in the morning, this coincided almost exactly with the sun coming up over the Negev.

Footage from the phones of partygoers records the exact moment things began—in stages—to go very badly wrong. Some noticed the rockets going overhead. Others were alerted when the warning sirens started to go off. But the music continued. And the party wasn't over until it was shut off and one of the organizers tried to send out a message to the partygoers.

In almost any other country the rockets would have been enough to let people know that it was time to go. But it took the music going off and a shout to all the partygoers, "Guys, we have red alert. Red alert." Still, this was not unusual. What happened next was.

In the distance paragliders appeared in the sky. They were being operated by Hamas terrorists who had managed to fly into Israel from Gaza. These were fitted with high-powered guns. By this time many festivalgoers had started to run. At the entrance to the festival Hamas trucks filled with heavily armed terrorists drove in. Then the shots began to ring out.

The defenseless Nova partygoers were one of the first masses of people that the terrorists managed to drive into that morning. Whether or not they had any advance knowledge of the party, the target could not have been better for them. The party's security guards were overwhelmed early on and the partygoers were un-armed, without even a knife to defend themselves as jeep-loads of Hamas terrorists drove across the site.

Desperate partygoers tried to get to their cars and flee the scene. But very quickly the main road out became blocked. The young peo-ple who tried to drive out of the entrance they had driven in through now drove straight into a Hamas ambush on the main road. As the first cars full of young people trying to escape were killed, and their cars stalled, the cars behind them got clogged up in turn, making the people in these cars sitting ducks for the terrorists. As the gun-fire rang out everywhere, there were only two options for the young festivalgoers: run, or hide.

Many ran, in any direction they could see. Hundreds of people were soon tearing across the open fields that surrounded the festival site. They were easy targets for the terrorists who picked them off with rifles or machine-gunned them in the fields as they ran. Others tried to find places to hide where the now-musicless festival had been going on. From the terrorists' own videos and the camera footage of some of the victims it is clear what happened next.

Some people hid in the plastic portable toilets set up at the Nova festival site. When things were otherwise eerily quiet, the terrorists walked along the rows of these lavatories one by one, firing multiple shots through each closed door to make sure anyone inside was killed. Elsewhere some of the partygoers tried to hide among the trees. They were picked off one by one. It didn't matter if someone hid in a tent or tried to hide up a tree. The results were the same. Some tried to hide in the bar area, hoping they would be out of sight of the terrorists. Footage from one of the first responders who got to the site later—an Israeli reservist—makes it clear how this worked out. "Is anyone alive?" he shouted out again and again. Nobody was.

The testimony of survivors would come out over time. But the assault on the Nova party would be one of the worst massacres of that morning. It took a while for the final figures to come out. But by the next month the Israeli authorities announced that 364 of the Nova partygoers and security staff had been murdered on the morning of the 7th. Another forty were abducted and taken into Gaza.

***

Hamas knew what they were doing in not just killing but also kidnapping Israeli civilians. Part of the social contract in Israeli society—and the Israeli military in particular—is that no person should be left behind. A core tenet of the state is that if one Israeli is caught, then the government and people will do anything they can, at any price, to get the hostage back. When they are initiated into the army or heading off on dangerous missions, soldiers are told that "if you fall into enemy hands or if anything goes wrong, the State of Israel will do all in its power to bring you back home."[4] To take even one Israeli hostage is to have an inestimable advantage over the country. To take hundreds of hostages is to have a strategic advantage over Israel that is incalculable.

Yet even this attack on the weakest possible target—young people dancing at a music festival—was something that seemed not to get the world's sympathies. Within hours of the news getting out, journalists and social media accounts around the world suggested that the young people at the Nova festival were in some way legitimate targets. They were said to have been dancing in the proximity of a "concentration camp." Or they were said to be citizens of an "apartheid" or "racist" state. All these claims, and more, were not just inaccurate or inappropriate but also demonstrably untrue.

In 1948, the year of Israel's independence, the non-Jewish population of Israel was 156,000. By 1970 the non-Jewish population of Israel (mainly Arab Muslims, Arab Christians, and Druze) had almost tripled. By 2000 it had reached 1,413,900. By 2015 the non-Jewish population was 2,078,000. In 2024, amid Israel's supposed genocidal war, the non-Jewish population of Israel was 2,653,000. In other words, from 1948 to 2024 the non-Jewish population of Israel had grown almost exactly seventeen-fold.[5] While the government in Tehran and the Palestinian Authority in Ramallah consistently claimed that the Israelis were "ethnically cleansing" Jerusalem of non-Jews, the same pattern emerged. In 1948 the Muslim population of Jerusalem was 40,000 people. By 2022 the Muslim population of Jerusalem had grown by over nine times, to 371,400.[6] Some genocide. Some ethnic cleansing.

But still there seemed to be a notion abroad that there was something seismically wrong with Israel. Something that made Israelis uniquely undeserving of the world's compassion or understanding. One further basis for this was the claim—which had been pumped around the world with special speed since the UN conference in Durban, South Africa, in 2001—that Israel and the Israeli public lived under an apartheid regime. That just as black and white South Africans had lived under separate laws, and under different rights, in the era of apartheid, so in modern-day Israel did Jews and non-Jews somehow live in a state of similar segregation. If Israelis lived in an apartheid system then perhaps even Israelis at a dance party could be seen as colonialist aggressors and any attack, even on them, as "resistance" to this injustice.

Again, the claim is based on pure misrepresentation. The State of Israel has equal rights for everyone in the country. The Arab and Druze population of Israel makes up around 20 percent of the country's population and they have equal health care, housing, and voting rights as anyone else. Even the most cursory look around Israel—even a walk around any Israeli city—would reveal a population that is bewildering in its racial and religious diversity. There are Ethiopian Jews and Israeli Arabs, Arab Christians and Ashkenazi Jews. There are Jews whose ancestors fled Europe, Jews who have been indigenous to the land for generations, and Jews who fled from Arab lands before or after the creation of the State of Israel. These people fled from pogroms and massacres sometimes predating 1948, sometimes coming after it.

In 1941 a Nazi-inspired pogrom broke out in Baghdad, Iraq. The Farhud (Arabic for "violent dispossession") massacre targeted Iraqi Jews who had been in the country since the time of the Babylonian empire. Some six hundred Jews were massacred by Iraqi Muslims carrying knives, swords, and guns. A red hand (hamsa) sign was painted on Jewish homes to direct the crowds there. As one survivor told the BBC seven decades later, the crowd shouted "Allah" and "Cutal al yehud" ("Slaughter the Jews"). Hiding in a palm tree, the young Jewish boy watched the crowd set upon the house of his mother's best friend. They set the house on fire and were "shouting from joy." In their hands, in jubilation, they were carrying something that looked "like a slab of meat in their hands." It took a moment for the nine-year-old boy to realize what it was. "Then I found out, it was a woman's breast they were carrying—they cut her breast off and tortured her before they killed her, my mother's best friend, Sabicha."[7]

It was not the emerging Jewish state that proved unable to tolerate Arabs, but the Arab and Muslim world that proved itself unable to tolerate Jews. If any form of "apartheid" existed in the region before or after the creation of the State of Israel, it was in those Arab Muslim countries that treated their Jewish populations as second-class citizens, constantly taxed and treated as inferior to their Muslim neighbors and living in endless fear of persecution and violence.

By contrast, the Arabs of Israel have done exceptionally well in the past eight decades. Consider reporting by the left-wing Israeli newspaper *Haaretz* in 2021. "New data issued by the Health Ministry in a 2020 report on health care personnel show that the Arabs and Druze in Israel, who make up about 20 percent of the country's population, constitute almost half (46 percent) of recipients of medical licenses; half of the new nurses, male and female (50 percent, as compared with just 9 percent in 2000); and more than half the dentists (53 percent) and pharmacists (57 percent)."[8] No black South African under apartheid was allowed any legislative or political role. Yet Khaled Kabub (an Arab Muslim) is a current Israeli Supreme Court justice, and not the first. The nation's national soccer team includes players of all backgrounds. In November 2024, when Israel played Belgium, Dia Saba, an Arab Muslim, assisted the sole goal of the match, scored for Israel by Yarden Shua—a Jew. Arab Muslim parties sit in the country's parliament (Knesset), where they have the same voting rights as everyone else. And in 2021 the United Arab List, under its leader Mansour Abbas, formed part of the Naftali Bennett–Yair Lapid coalition government. Yet such facts kept getting buried in a world that seemed to want to see Israel as having some original sin. A sin that made them uniquely undeserving of sympathy.

Some months after the Nova festival massacre, the *Guardian* newspaper ran a report on sexual violence on the morning of the attack. The paper described how one woman who was raped was "shredded to pieces" and another "stabbed repeatedly in the back while she was being raped." One young woman who attended the festival recounted in the paper how she had been shot in the back and was hiding among the vegetation just off route 232 when a large group of Hamas terrorists arrived. As she lay there she saw them rape and kill at least five young women. "They laid a woman down and I understood that he is raping her," she attested. "They passed her on to another person and he cuts her breast, he throws it on the road and they are playing with it."[9]

***

What happened that morning came as a shock not just to Israel but to the world. There was something so completely unexpected about it because—in part—Israel had for years displayed an aura of invincibility. Even its greatest opponents—perhaps especially its greatest opponents in the Middle East and farther afield—believed that the Israelis were capable of almost supernatural displays of self-defense and force projection.

In 2010 there were a number of shark attacks by the Egyptian sea resort of Sharm el-Sheikh. There was a risk that these attacks could further hurt the tourism industry in Egypt, which was already suffering a downturn. But local journalists and politicians knew who to blame. A number of them—including the governor of the region, Mohammad Abdul Fadhil Shousha—suggested that it was possible Israel's Mossad agency had placed the shark in the sea in order to damage the Egyptian tourism industry.[10] Similar "Jewish-controlled animals" scandals regularly erupted in the region. In 2013 a kestrel was found in the eastern Turkish province of Elazig. The bird was accused of having an Israeli monitoring footband and so was condemned on suspicion of being an Israeli spy. It was taken in for examination, including X-rays, before being freed.[11] Similar accusations have been made against eagles, bee-eater birds, and dolphins. While this might seem comical to an outsider, it is not so outlandish to anyone who understands the mindset of the region.

I was in Egypt around that time and was struck repeatedly by the extreme claims that could be made about Israel and the Jews even in a country that had a peace deal with Israel and where relations were relatively normal. On a train trip from Cairo to Alexandria one day, I searched the bookshops to see what the locals were offered for reading material. The book selections were always the same. There were copies of *Mein Kampf*, copies of *The Protocols of the Learned Elders of Zion*, and a range of other conspiracy tracts focusing on Israel and the Jews. If you wanted a mystery novel to read on the train, there were slim pickings in English or Arabic. But if you wanted a pile of anti-Semitic reading material for the journey your needs could always be met. Whenever I have traveled in the Arab and Muslim worlds I have always been struck by this obsession with Israel and the Jews.

It is a combination of superiority and inferiority complexes, and it helps the sufferer in every way. If the Jews are successful at defending themselves or innovating or growing their society, they can be portrayed as all-powerful. And that provides an easy excuse for the failures of the societies around them.

Once when in Cairo I spent some days with a friend who was Egyptian born and raised. He worked for a Western company and was very progressive for an Egyptian. With other local friends we would go drinking and nightclubbing. Acting as a driver and host, he one day drove a group of us around. We passed over the 6th October Bridge. And one day he took me to see the newish developments in 6th October City. Eventually I felt I had to ask him: "What is it with all this October 6 stuff?" As if it were the most natural thing in the world he said, "Oh that's to celebrate our victory over the Israelis." I paused and tried to rattle my brain. "What victory over the Israelis?" I asked, knowing that this might be delicate ground. "In 1973," he replied perfectly happily. "But you didn't defeat the Israelis in 1973," I countered as politely as I could. We went back and forth a number of times before he said, "I thought we whipped their ass." "No—I'm afraid they whipped your ass," I eventually told him. "No shit," he replied.

The idea that Egypt and her allies had lost, not won, the Yom Kippur War (or the 6th of October War, as Egyptians call it) came as a genuine surprise to my friend. And his surprise came as a genuine surprise to me. How was it possible, I wondered, that a moderate, even progressive, and successful young Egyptian man could have such an alternative view of the history of what had happened in the decade before he was born? The initial Egyptian surprise attack on October 6, 1973, had been a tactical victory. But the Egyptian crossing of the Suez Canal and brief occupation of part of the Sinai Peninsula was a very short-lived victory. It took only days and then finally a few weeks for the Israelis to push back the Egyptian army in the south as well as the Syrian forces in the north. If the aim of the Arab armies in 1973 had been to surprise Israel and then overwhelm it, the tactic failed. Israel's counteroffensive ended up coming within sixty miles of Cairo. In the Golan Heights in the north, Lieutenant Colonel Avigdor Kahalani led a counterattack against the Syrian tank battalions that at one point led the Syrians to believe they might be about to lose Damascus. These are deep wounds for any proud society to recover from.

Israel's neighbors had first tried to snuff the state out at its moment of birth. In 1947, when the United Nations voted to approve the partition plan creating an Israeli state and a Palestinian state, there were any number of directions in which history might have gone. The Arab states could have accepted their neighbor, with the area recently ruled by the British under League of Nations mandate divided up as the UN had suggested along clear, agreed-upon lines. In 1948, when the State of Israel was created, it was perfectly possible that a Palestinian state could have been formed alongside it. But the Arab states saw the very idea of a slither of the land becoming a Jewish state as an affront. Instead of accepting their neighbor, they decided instead to kill it. The moment in 1948 when Israel was formally re-created and war was immediately waged upon it by all of its neighbors would not be the last time in the state's history when dancing and war followed one after the other.

Of course, the Arab states failed in 1948. The Arabs inside Israel whom the Arab states told to leave, promising that they would soon return to their lands with no Jewish oppressor, were not just let down but abandoned, becoming in the process citizens of Jordan, Lebanon, and other surrounding countries. At the same time, Jews were either expelled or encouraged to leave the Arab countries in which they had lived for centuries. From Yemen, Iran, and Iraq to as far afield as Morocco, the native Jews were pushed out and encouraged by the new Israeli state to make their new home in what had been their historic homeland. Soon fully half of the population of the State of Israel was made up of Sephardic Jews from across the Muslim world who now had only one country in the world that would protect them.

This was one of the most compelling justifications for the idea of Zionism. It was part of the argument that Theodor Herzl recognized in his 1896 work, *The Jewish State*. It was Herzl's belief even then—before the ultimate catastrophe of European Jews—that the only people who could or would protect the Jewish people would be the Jewish people. Although Herzl spent all of his life building up to this argument, and then traveling around Europe proselytizing for it, the realization came to him because of something he saw in person in 1895. That was when Herzl witnessed the public humiliation of Captain Alfred Dreyfus.

In one of the great scandals in French history, the French-Jewish officer Dreyfus was arrested and charged with espionage. The charge would turn out to be false—as many people, including Dreyfus, insisted from the outset. But the claim fit much of the latent anti-Semitic prejudice in the France of that time. On January 5, 1895, Dreyfus was stripped of his rank in a public ceremony in which his buttons and insignia were torn from his uniform and his sword broken. Dreyfus still professed his innocence, but the furious crowd screamed "Judas" and "Death to the Jews." It was this, Herzl would later say, that made him believe that Zionism was the only answer for the Jews. Europe, and by extension the rest of the civilized world, would not protect them and could not be trusted to do so.

*** *** ***

From the moment Israel pushed back the invading armies in 1948, the idea that the Jewish people were not just forced to defend themselves but were capable of defending themselves became central to the story of Israel. And it soon became all but axiomatic among the country's neighbors. There was another attempt to wipe the state out in 1967. And then again in 1973. But after 1973, Israel was not forced to fight another war against annihilation.

It fought a war that started as an effort to stop rocket fire into the Galilee and other parts of northern Israel from Lebanon (1982), a war that soon saw Israeli forces bogged down too far into Lebanon. It fought another war to prevent Hezbollah from doing exactly the same thing in 2006. But the citizens of Israel and most of its neighbors seemed to have come to an agreement that whatever some of their neighbors might think, Israel was here to stay.

Eventually both sides settled into an uneasy cold war. But it was always in danger of hotting up. In 1972, Palestinian terrorists from the Black September group tortured and murdered eleven members of the Israeli Olympic team inside the Olympic Village and at a nearby airfield during the Munich Olympics. The assault could not have been more public. But over the ensuing months and years, in an operation named Operation Wrath of God, Israel's intelligence agency, Mossad, was able to track down and kill almost all of the masterminds of the attack. The idea that the Israelis had an ability to reach anywhere and everywhere to hunt down those who had done its citizens harm became a part of the Israeli national myth, and something that the wider world viewed with admiration even when it was tinged with envy or disgust. Popular films, like Steven Spielberg's *Munich*, contributed to a whole genre in popular culture: Israeli revenge porn.

Israelis were as good at making this as anyone else. Indeed they perfected it. In time the all-reaching hand of Israel became something that Israelis and its enemies believed with competing vigor.

Popular television series like the Israeli-made *Fauda* showed the moral complexity of Israeli counterterrorism operations. While not showing it at its most glossy, they always showed one thing in particular: Israel's extraordinary and ingenious capabilities. Fiction and real life were constantly blended. After the 2005 withdrawal from Gaza, Israelis would often boast about how complete their knowledge of the scene in Gaza was in spite of their withdrawal. For many years the Israelis had been acknowledged masters of "humint" (human intelligence). Whether it was Eli Ben-Hanan's book *Our Man in Damascus: Eli Cohn* (made into many films), which is the story of an Israeli spy inside Syria in the 1960s, or the many rumors of Israeli spies inside Iran trying to slow down the revolutionary Islamic government's nuclear ambitions for decades, the idea that Israel had world-class humint was unargued. As Israel's tech sector grew and its expertise in surveillance was exported around the world, it also gained an unparalleled reputation as a world leader in "sigint" (signals intelligence).

In the years after 2006, whenever I visited the Gaza border, I would always hear some version of the following boast from Israeli military and officials: "You cannot sneeze in Gaza without us knowing." Like much of the rest of the world, and most Israelis, I suppose I believed it.

Perhaps the ultimate example of the Israeli skill of deterrence came in the form of the Iron Dome defense system. This antimissile defense system had been conceived years before the Israeli withdrawal from Gaza. Throughout the 1990s, after the First Lebanon War, as Hezbollah and other militant groups continued to fire rockets into northern Israel, the need for some type of defensive antimissile system became evident. Israel could not invade Lebanon every time rockets were fired into Israel. Or at least people hoped they wouldn't. But equally, the north of the country had to remain livable.

Shortly after Israel handed over Gaza to the Palestinian Authority in 2005, it was dragged into a second war in Lebanon after Hezbollah ramped up its firing of rockets into northern Israel. In 2006 Hezbollah fired thousands of rockets as far into Israel as the city of Haifa. In the historic town of Safed, by the Lebanese border, I spent a day experiencing the rocket fire of Hezbollah firsthand. I sat in the shelters with the hospital's few remaining patients as Hezbollah attempted to repeat its success of the previous day in making direct hits on the medical center.

During that period a quarter of a million Israelis had to leave their homes and many more were forced to spend their days and evenings in bomb shelters. At the same time, thousands of missiles and mortars were being fired regularly into Israel from Gaza. The need for an antimissile system became acute. If Israel's citizens were unable to live in the north of the country and unable to live in the south too, then the country would shrink to an even smaller size.

On a visit to the city of Sderot in the early 2010s, I sat with the town's mayor and some of the population as rockets came over from Gaza. I could see the effect this had on people, and parents told me the effect that this constant fear, air-raid sirens, and running for shelter had, especially on the children. I asked a pretty obvious question: why anyone would live like this?

Not everybody in a relatively poor town like Sderot has a choice. The cost of living in Tel Aviv, as in most international cities these days, was already too high for any but the most affluent in society. Those with fewer resources tended to live outside the major cities and in places where accommodations, among other things, are just cheaper. But there is another reason. The mayor of Sderot told me as we sat there in the shelter, "If we cannot live in Sderot then we cannot live in Ashkelon. And if we cannot live in Ashkelon then we cannot live in Ashdod. And if we cannot live in Ashdod then we cannot live in Tel Aviv or Jerusalem. And so we cannot live."

It was a hard logic. But it was one that Hamas and other jihadist groups in Gaza were also relying on testing. If people were too afraid or traumatized to live in the south of Israel, then eventually they would be too afraid to live in the center. And if Hezbollah squeezed Israel from the other direction—top down—then eventually you would have no Israel. People like the mayor of Sderot and the leadership of Hamas knew the same thing. Except that one side wanted to continue living where they were and the other wanted them gone.

The Iron Dome system finally came into effect in March 2011 after huge investments from America and Israel. It was touted as being the world's most effective antimissile system. It was swiftly put to use, being used to shoot down a rocket fired from Gaza the following month. This was widely touted as a great victory for Israel and the ability of Israel and its allies to defend its civilians.

But there was a glaring imbalance that was evident from the start. Hamas and other jihadist groups, like Islamic Jihad in Gaza, smuggled their rockets and rocket components into Israel through the Egyptian border with Gaza. In terms of keeping the Gazans out of Egypt this border was in some ways even stronger than the security fence that the Israelis had put up around their Gaza border. But the Egyptian side was also far more porous and the Hamas government in Gaza were already using the international aid they received to develop an elaborate tunnel network under the Egyptian border and throughout the Gaza Strip. Many of the rockets that were being fired from Gaza into Israel were Katyushas—a rocket system developed by the former Soviet Union that is easy to move around and the launchers for which can be easily hidden. The rockets fired from Gaza were also very cheap.

It is estimated that a Katyusha rocket costs around $300. In contrast, the cost of a single antimissile rocket fired from the Iron Dome system has been estimated to cost as much as $100,000. Because the Iron Dome would often need to fire two missiles to knock the Katyushas out of the sky, each intercept of a rocket from Gaza could cost up to $200,000, or around six hundred times the cost of the rocket they were intercepting. The Israeli public within firing distance from Gaza may have been able to feel safer with the inception of the Iron Dome, but the math did not work in Israel's favor. Around two hundred rockets and mortars were fired from Gaza into Israel in August 2011 alone.[12] And this was at a time that Israel and Hamas were not in a full-scale war. This became business—or life—as usual.

In 2014, Israel and Hamas went into another medium-sized conflict during which thousands of rockets were fired into Israel from Gaza. Then, in 2017, a new antimissile system came into use. Known as "David's Sling," this system was intended to shoot down more sophisticated weaponry, of the kind that Hezbollah were stockpiling. The conditions under which the 2006 Lebanon War came to a close was a UN resolution (1701) mandating that Hezbollah would no longer be able to build up and store missiles in southern Lebanon. The resolution led to a UN peacekeeping force patrolling the Israel-Lebanon border, but the UN did nothing to prevent the restockpiling of weaponry in southern Lebanon by Hezbollah. By 2023 Hezbollah was estimated to have stockpiled somewhere between 120,000 and 200,000 rockets in southern Lebanon.

After years of rockets and attempts to infiltrate the northern border of Israel, there is still a question as to why Hezbollah did not join in the attacks of October 7. It seems that Hamas did not inform them of their plan because they had no means to communicate with their fellow Iranian proxy without the communications being intercepted and the assault compromised. Hezbollah did start firing rockets at northern Israel shortly after the attacks, but the groups seem not to have coordinated. Nevertheless, from October 8 and throughout the ensuing months Hezbollah fired thousands of rockets at Israel. Hezbollah's arsenal included guided and unguided ballistic missiles (both short and intermediate range) and unguided rockets (short and long range).[13] This was very much not what was meant to happen under Resolution 1701.

Still, the combination of the Iron Dome and David's Sling was meant to be an answer to all of this. In reality it was a patch on the wound rather than an addressing of it. If Canada fired thousands of rockets into America, or France fired a similar barrage for over a decade into Britain, the likelihood is that the public in the country being targeted would not be content when their government simply came up with better and better ways in which to shoot the rockets down. But Israelis got used to it, and to the idea that whatever the enemy threw at them they would be able to find an answer.

In intelligence, military, and antimissile capabilities, Israel could be termed world leaders. Certainly they were believed to be world leaders. Israeli tech and security firms were employed and sold their wares around the world as pioneers in technology and security—including cybersecurity. Crucially, the Israeli public believed that they were world leaders in all these fields.

In late September 2023, the UN General Assembly held a session at their headquarters in New York. Like many other journalists I was invited for the usual set of off-the-record briefings with a range of delegations. At one briefing, high-ranking members of the Israeli delegation presented over breakfast in New York. Among other things we were told that the Israelis had recently killed the top three leaders of the Islamic Jihad terrorist group. These three leaders were replaced and the three terrorists who replaced them were instantly killed too. This was the sort of conversation people expect to hear from Israeli officials as they discuss their operations in their difficult region. But there was something else in the air that morning which was unmistakable, and which in hindsight made me feel sickened. It was the unmistakable, nauseating stench of hubris.

***

One of the communities that the terrorists hit on October 7 was Be'eri. The kibbutz, founded before the creation of the State of Israel, is one of the communities closest to the Gaza border. Like many of the communities in the area, its members were overwhelmingly people who might be best described as "peaceniks." Its one thousand residents were disproportionately made up of people who wanted to live in peace with their Palestinian neighbors and who worked to make that dream possible.

The residents of Be'eri included a seventy-four-year-old Canadian-born peace activist, Vivian Silver. Vivian had spent decades of her life working for peace between Israelis and Palestinians as a cofounder of Women Wage Peace and as a member of the board of directors of the far-left-wing human rights group B'Tselem. Every week she took part in a joint Israel-Gazan initiative in which she would drive

Palestinian children and others in need of highly specialized medical treatment from Gaza to hospitals inside Israel.

On the morning of the 7th, the residents of Be'eri heard the rockets and the sirens. But none expected what happened next. At 6:42 a.m. Hamas breached the Gazan border. You can see Be'eri clearly from there and it takes a matter of minutes to cross the land in between. The last terrorists made it to the kibbutz by 7:20.

In total more than a hundred Hamas terrorists entered the community that morning, one for every nine or ten residents. The terrorists had already overtaken the local army base and as they made their way into the community from two directions, they swiftly overwhelmed the community's thirteen-member security team, killing most of them before they could even get to their weapons. Almost two hours later a small group of Israeli soldiers arrived and tried to help the few armed locals who were holding out. In the meantime, two other groups of people made it into Be'eri. The first were civilians from Gaza who came into Be'eri to loot. The others were young people fleeing from the Nova festival who ran to Be'eri in the belief that they would be safe there. The battle for Be'eri would continue for more than two days.

In the meantime the terrorists of Hamas had almost complete free rein in Be'eri and they used the opportunity to move from house to house. There the same story kept unfolding. They found families sheltering in their safe rooms and either forced their way through the doors and killed the families there or, if they could not get in or could not be bothered to force the handle being held shut on the other side, set fire to the house.

One house was home to the Bachar family. Avida Bachar, fifty, was the manager of Be'eri agriculture. I met him at one of the recovery units in Ramat Gan. He, his wife, and their two children were woken up by the missiles at 6:30 a.m. They went out and saw the hundreds of missiles overhead. The sound seemed different than normal and Avida said to his wife Dana, "I know it takes a few minutes while the army comes." As he continued saying to me, "But the army's not come. No helicopters. No parachuters. No soldiers. Nothing. And we hear the shots go through the kibbutz and go into the neighborhood, the other neighborhood. And I have two children at home. So I told them, 'It not sound the same. Come to the shelter.' We go to the safe room. And suddenly, we hear one [terrorist] want to get inside our house. Because we have a big bell on the door that we bought in Austria. It's like a cow. The Austrian cow. You know, like the ding-dong? Exactly like this. So suddenly, we heard the ding-dong on the door. And we said, 'Okay. Someone wants to get in.'"

Avida told the family to stay quiet. But his daughter and wife desperately wanted to pee. He told them to stay in the shelter and put a towel inside a pot and pee as quietly as possible into that. Suddenly they heard that someone had got into the house. Avida and his fifteen-year-old son, Carmel, tried to hold the handle of the safe room closed on the inside as someone else was trying to turn it open from the outside. "Open the door!" the person on the other side ordered. "No. Go. Go away from here," said Avida. Before he had said the second "Go," a bullet came through the door. Avida was unharmed but his son's hands were covered in blood. Avida tried again to hold the door closed. "Open the door!" the order came again. "All kids. Go!" Avida shouted from the inside and again the person shot through the door, this time hitting Avida in both his legs. He collapsed inside the shelter.

At this point he was on the floor with bullet wounds to both legs and his son was bleeding badly. His thirteen-year-old daughter used her cell phone to write to all the WhatsApp groups in the community and tell them to come to their home. "They burn us. They kill us. Quick. Quick. Come." But nobody came, and soon they learned from the same WhatsApp groups that their neighbors and friends were being burned in their homes too.

Avida told his wife and daughter, Hadar, to take his belt and use it as a tourniquet on his son's arm. That managed to stem some of the bleeding. But then they realized that their house had been set on fire and that clothes and other items from the outside, including the spare tire from the family's car, had been put against the safe room door and set alight. They were going to burn alive in their own home. The smoke that started pouring into the shelter made it impossible to breathe, but Avida already knew from the sounds outside that the people who were fleeing their burning houses were being shot when they ran outside. He told his family that they would not go out and that maybe they would die in the shelter.

He told them to take the pee-covered towels, now also covered with blood, and breathe through them. Then they heard the safe room window being smashed open. Three grenades were thrown inside the shelter through the opening. Two of the grenades went into the sofa of the safe room, which absorbed much of the blast. They thought they had survived but then a gun was pointed through the window and someone fired two shots inside. Fifteen-year-old Carmel was shot in the chest.

His mother died first. "I can't breathe," she said. It was a combination of the grenade blast and the smoke inhalation. Her daughter cleaned the black around her mouth. Avida told his daughter, "Mommy, she's okay. She not feel nothing now. She's good. Believe me, she's good." They laid her on the floor.

At around 4 p.m. Avida's son, Carmel, started to take increasingly short breaths and told his father and sister he didn't think he was going to survive. He said one last thing to his father. Avida recalled, "He told me, 'Dad, when you bury me, please bury me with my surfboard.' He was a surfer. He was a sailor. He liked the sea. And I told him, 'Carmel, don't even say it.'" After a few minutes of shorter and shorter breaths, he stopped, and died.

Avida and his daughter Hadar managed to stay alive in the shelter until eight in the evening, when Hadar finally heard a soldier speaking Hebrew. They helped them out of the shelter and to the hospital. By the time Avida and I met in the hospital, the community of Be'eri had already buried eighty-six of its members, with many more still to be identified and buried. An additional thirty-two people were kidnapped from the community: thirty members and two survivors of Nova who had fled from the music festival in the belief that they would be safe in Be'eri.

Aside from the horror, two things were especially striking about Avida's testimony. The first was the shock he continued to feel about that first promise he had given to his wife and children. The promise, like so many parents that morning, was that the IDF would be there in minutes. Instead nobody found them for almost fourteen hours. The second thing that was most striking was the shift in his own worldview after the terrorists destroyed his community. Avida had, by his own admission, always been a man of the left. He had believed in the idea of peace. But now he felt differently. "The enemy has changed," he said. Even between two enemies "there is a contract: what you can do and what I can do. And the contract was broken. Something changed." As he saw it, there was nothing Israel could do about Egypt or Lebanon. But the country could choose if they wanted to live beside Gaza. Because the residents of Gaza had changed. "The young people burn us, the others shoot us, and the old ones kidnapped us." He could see no way in which Israel could live beside Hamas-run Gaza. "We need potatoes. We need peanuts. We need orchards. And we need avocadoes. Until the sea. All the way."

It is hard to say how many people from the community would feel that way now, or would say what Avida did—even in the aftermath of what happened to the community in Be'eri. But as the story came out—of the number of people from this small place who had been killed, injured, or kidnapped—some of the most telling testimonies were from the people who could no longer speak.

In the immediate aftermath of the attack it was assumed that the peace campaigner Vivian Silver was one of the residents who had been kidnapped and taken into Gaza. The various peace groups that she had worked with all these years lobbied the Red Cross and others to request that their friend and colleague—a friend and colleague to the Palestinian people—be returned to them. Soon her name and photograph were made into one of the hostage posters that were swiftly put together by friends, families, and volunteers. But over a month after the massacre Silver's fate became clear. Her home had been completely burned out on October 7 by the terrorists, and it would turn out that she had been burned alive with it. There was so little left of her that it took five weeks just to find enough DNA evidence that the house in which she had lived and in which she had dreamed of peace was also the house in which she was murdered.

***

In the weeks and months after the October 7 attacks I spoke with many therapists and mental health professionals who were working with survivors, the wounded, relatives of the dead, and those who had found themselves amid the hell of that morning. To a man and woman they had some version of the following observation: that it was too early, even months later, to talk about post-traumatic stress disorder (PTSD), because the survivors were still in the trauma. In fact it was more accurate to say that the whole nation was still in a trauma. Critics like Naomi Klein would subsequently not even permit the Israeli people to have such trauma. Writing in the *Guardian*, Klein would later argue that Israelis had performed a "dangerous weaponization" of their grief and trauma and had done so to justify "imperial aggression and grotesque rights violations."[14] Meaning that Israelis could not even be traumatized without being accused of being traumatized for their own evil purposes.

But what was that trauma? Obviously it was the scale of the attack, its brutality and the sheer surprise. But there was something deeper as well. And it came across in phrases like that which Avida had said to his wife and children in their safe room in Be'eri: a line that fathers and mothers assured their children of across the country that day. From parents trying to advise their children calling them from the Nova party to the families in shelters across the land: "Don't worry. The IDF will be here in minutes." And they weren't.

That would be a security failing in any country. But in Israel there was another level to it. Since its creation, Israelis believed that the State of Israel was the only place in the world in which Jews would be safe, and that even if they were unsafe it was Jews who were looking after Jews, and Jews who would fight for them as Jews. The horrors that the world had allowed to happen in the twentieth century and in centuries before would never happen again. Not in Israel. Not there.

The question of who would protect the Jews was the question that Theodor Herzl had pondered and which led him to the inevitability of Zionism. It was the question that every Jew in the diaspora had to consider before the creation of Israel. And it was a question which Jews in the diaspora kept thinking about long after the creation of Israel. Events in the years before October 7 had kept the debate alive. In the past fifteen years alone America and Europe had seen a spate of attacks on Jewish sites. Not Israeli sites, or "Zionist" sites, but Jewish sites.

In 2009, an eighty-eight-year-old white supremacist carried out a fatal shooting at the United States Holocaust Memorial Museum in Washington, DC. In March 2012, a thirty-year-old rabbi, his sons, ages three and six, and an eight-year-old girl were all killed by a twenty-three-year-old Frenchman of Algerian origin at a Jewish school in Toulouse, France. In 2014, a seventy-three-year-old neo-Nazi opened fire at a Jewish community center and a Jewish retirement home near Kansas City, Missouri. In May 2014, the Jewish Museum in Brussels, Belgium, was attacked by a twenty-nine-year-old Frenchman of Algerian origin. Four people were killed.

After each of these attacks, politicians in the respective countries talked about how important it was to protect their Jewish communities. And each time, the police presence at Jewish sites was stepped up. Jewish children attending Jewish schools in cities like London got used to going each morning through prison camp–style security just to get to lessons. Jewish areas in cities like Paris had armed police patrolling around them, and in the historic Jewish ghetto in Venice, Italian police stood guard at all hours over the remaining community. A community that had once been locked inside the ghetto each night now had to be protected from people outside of it.

In January 2015, jihadists carried out a number of major attacks in France. At the offices of the satirical magazine *Charlie Hebdo* they gunned down and slaughtered the editorial staff and contributors, among others, for the crime of "blasphemy." Shortly afterward another jihadist walked into a kosher supermarket in Paris and killed four Jews.

In the wave of national mourning and self-questioning that engulfed France at that time, the question of whether or not France was a safe country for its Jewish population returned. On that occasion, Benjamin Netanyahu headed to France for a show of solidarity. But he made an intervention that comforted some French Jews and worried others. Before leaving Israel he stated, "To all the Jews of France, all the Jews of Europe, I would like to say that Israel is not just the place in whose direction you pray, the state of Israel is your home." Many Jews in Europe were critical of this intervention, fearing—among other things—that it would stir up fresh accusations of dual loyalty against European Jews. But many other people voted with their feet, and in the wake of the 2015 attack, as with other attacks on Jews in the diaspora, thousands more French Jews chose to leave France, make Aliya, that is, to make Israel their home.

There is an old line that Jews everywhere in the world know: wherever they are in the world they should keep a bag packed in case they had to leave. The expulsions of Jews from England in the thirteenth century and from Spain in the fifteenth century left a long memory. The forced flight of Jews from across the rest of the Middle East in and after 1948 created another one. For decades the conversation around Friday-night dinner tables across the diaspora regularly turned to this question, often to the tedium of the younger generation, who thought that their parents were simply paranoid. The conversation from Sephardic Jews who had once lived with Muslim neighbors and been expelled from their countries was especially easy for young Jews in the West to dismiss. These were different times. The situation today is not the same.

From the moment the State of Israel was created there was one certainty above all: as embattled as Israel might be, and as hated as it often seemed to be from every side, at least this was a place where Jews could be safe and protect themselves.

And then October 7 happened, and a doubt spread among Jews in Israel and around the world. *What if we aren't safe in Israel either?*

***

In 2006, less than a year after Israel's full withdrawal from Gaza, a group of Israeli soldiers were patrolling along the border. A group of terrorists from Hamas surprised them, emerging from tunnels they had already managed to build beneath the border. In the resulting attack two soldiers were killed and another four were wounded. Another soldier, nineteen-year-old Gilad Shalit, was stolen and taken into Gaza. He would be held there in captivity for the next five years.

Throughout that time there were Israeli efforts to rescue him and many efforts to bring his situation to international notice. But the release was only eventually secured through a negotiated prisoner release. The deal was announced by Prime Minister Benjamin Netanyahu in October 2011 and was a subject of immediate celebration and controversy inside Israel. The prisoner exchanges took place in two phases, in October and December of that year. In total, 1,027 Palestinian prisoners were released from Israeli jails in exchange for the release of one Israeli—Shalit.

While many people saw this as a happy resolution to the problem, almost nobody except Hamas thought it was a good deal. The nineteen-year-old Shalit was doing nothing wrong as he was serving on the Gaza border. By contrast, those released from Israeli prisons included bomb makers and people who had carried out unprovoked knife- and gun-rampages against Israeli civilians. They included people who had been involved in suicide bombings against Israeli civilian targets, from the recruiters to those who made and smuggled the suicide vests. The prisoners released in this more than 1,000-for-1 deal included a man named Yahya Sinwar.

Born in 1962 in Khan Younis, when Gaza was still ruled by the government of Egypt, Sinwar was recruited into Hamas by the group's founder, Sheikh Ahmed Yassin. He soon rose to become one of the heads of the group's internal security unit, tasked—among other things—with finding and punishing Palestinians accused of "collaboration" with Israel. In 1988, one year after the outbreak of the First Intifada, Sinwar was arrested and imprisoned for the murder of four Palestinians he had believed were informers. He told his Israeli interrogators that he had killed them himself, strangling one with his bare hands and suffocating another with a kaffiyeh. Sinwar reportedly admitted to these crimes without any remorse and in fact boasted that he regarded these killings as a religious duty.

He continued his work from inside the Israeli prison in which he was held. Sinwar was believed to have been the person who ordered the beheading of two Palestinian prisoners whose heads and body parts were thrown out of their prison cells with the instruction to the Israeli guards to "take the dog's head."

Sinwar was serving four life sentences, but he used the opportunity of his time in the Beersheba prison in the Negev to study Hebrew and the practices of Israeli intelligence. One of the few Israelis who had semiregular contact with him while he was serving his sentence was Dr. Yuval Bitton—a dentist who worked in the prison in which Sinwar was serving his multiple life sentences. The two men reportedly built up "a wary mutual respect." It was Bitton who, one day in 2004, noticed that there was something wrong with Sinwar. The inmate had one day failed to recognize Bitton. He also started falling over when he stood up from his prayer rituals. Complaining of a pain in the back of his neck, Bitton recognized that it was likely that Sinwar had some kind of problem on the brain.

He arranged for Sinwar to be rushed to Israel's Soroka Medical Center, where doctors carried out an emergency operation to remove a well-developed brain tumor that would have killed Sinwar had it not been found. A few days after the operation, Bitton visited Sinwar in the hospital. Sinwar thanked the Jewish doctor for helping to save his life.

Bitton was under no illusions about who Sinwar was. From hours of speaking with him he was adamant that the motivating factor for Sinwar's extreme ideology "wasn't political, it was religious." On more than one occasion Sinwar said to him, about Israel, "Now you're strong, you have two hundred atomic warheads. But we'll see, maybe in another ten to twenty years you'll weaken, and I'll attack."

Sinwar was the highest-level prisoner to be handed over by the Israelis in the 2011 prisoner release. After his return to Gaza, Sinwar immediately called for the kidnapping of more Israelis in order to release all the other Palestinians serving multiple life sentences in Israeli jails. He would later say that for Palestinians serving prison sentences in Israeli jails, "capturing an Israeli soldier is the best news in the universe, because he knows that a glimmer of hope has been opened for him."[15]

Sinwar also swiftly resumed his position in Hamas. He continued to try to find ways to attack Israel and to punish those Palestinians in Gaza whom he could accuse of cooperation with the Israelis and other activities of which he disapproved. In 2016 he was involved in the torture and murder of Hamas's Mahmoud Ishtiwi, whom Sinwar accused of homosexuality and cooperation with the Israelis. Then, on October 7, 2023, he finally achieved the operation he had dreamed about for all those years. He named the attacks of that day the "Al-Aqsa Flood" operation. He believed Israel was weak and so, as promised, he attacked.

Among the residents of Nir Oz that morning was a thirty-eight-year-old farmer named Tamir Adar. When the rockets went off, he left his wife and children in the safe room of their house in order to try to help the community's small security team with what he already realized was an incursion. Nothing more was heard from him and the family, and the community of Nir Oz believed he was one of the members who had been kidnapped. His grandmother, eighty-five-year-old Holocaust survivor Yaffa Adar, was also kidnapped from her home that day.

Tamir Adar was the nephew of Dr. Bitton, who had saved Yahya Sinwar's life two decades earlier.

***

Immediately after the 7th the families of the kidnapped started to get in touch with each other. Soon they were lent a building in Tel Aviv where they could gather, meet, and coordinate. The Hostage Families Forum became a crucial lifeline for the families and for anyone who wanted to hear their stories.

I spent many days in that center, over many weeks and eventually months. The scenes were terrible. Not all of the families of the kidnapped wanted to take part in the families forum or the resulting campaign—"Bring Them Home"—that emerged from it. A few families believed that their relatives were already dead or at least stood no chance of surviving in Hamas-run Gaza. Others had the firm belief—sometimes stated as much in advance by their relatives—that the price of previous hostage exchanges had been too high and that the price of returning their loved ones should not be paid at some later date by other families.

But most of the families found the hostage center a lifeline during those months. At the beginning they came for news. Then to organize. As the days and then weeks dragged on, it became a place just to meet up with others who were in the same black hole—in the life on hold that they lived in while their children or other relatives were underground in Gaza.

Of course, there was always the waiting for news too. Rumors and theories swirled around fast in those days. Many of the people whose family members had been abducted had been able to piece together what happened because of phone technology or footage taken by their relatives or by their relatives' kidnappers. Others clung to bits of information from other people in the kibbutz or the party—a sighting, an account, a rumor.

At the family center one day I met one of the family members of Tamir Adar, the nephew of the doctor who saved Sinwar's life. Adva is the cousin of Tamir and the granddaughter of eighty-five-year-old Yaffa, who was kidnapped from her own house. Her grandmother had texted her early in the morning to say that there were terrorists in her kibbutz and that she could hear shooting and shouting and gun battles in the yard. "She almost couldn't walk, so we were scared that she wouldn't be able to get to the shelter."

Yaffa had heart failure, high blood pressure, and many other conditions. She couldn't get to the bathroom alone and had a special bed and chair at home and needed a lot of medication. "Around eight a.m. she stopped responding. And we tried to call. We tried to text. But we couldn't reach her anymore." Other family members in the kibbutz were messaging her, telling her about "the horrifying things that are happening. Only at 5:00 p.m., when the IDF started taking people from their houses in the kibbutz, and they put them in one place, and my grandmother wasn't there," did they fear the worst. Someone asked them to check Yaffa's house. They found it completely broken. Yaffa was nowhere to be found. "That night, we saw a video that was posted on the social media of the Hamas kidnapping her," said Yaffa. "She was on a golf cart with four armed terrorists around her being paraded in the streets of Gaza as people were celebrating and clapping their hands and acting like kidnapping an eighty-five-year-old woman makes sense."

I wondered, what did Adva think when she saw that? "That I'm dreaming," she replied. "It's not possible. How can you enter an eighty-five-year-old woman's house and steal her? She had no way to protect herself or to harm them. It's not like she could fight back. They still decided to take her from her bed. I couldn't imagine that it's possible—that it's the reality. I don't think I can still get it by now. We are thirty-eight days after, and I'm still not sure that we're living this nightmare."

In the case of Tamir, far less was known. Adva had heard from the family that at around 8 a.m. that day, after putting his family in the safe room and going off to try to fight the terrorists, he told his family, "Even if I come back, don't open the door."

All morning the family heard terrorists coming in and out of their house. Tamir's family spent all day waiting for news about him. The terrorists tried to force the door to the safe room where Tamir's wife and seven-year-old son and three-year-old daughter were hiding. Tamir's wife managed to hold the door. The terrorists didn't shoot through the door and didn't set fire to the house. "In my aunt's house and in my grandfather's house they set the house on fire," Adva explains. "They had no other choice but hide or run from the house."

But there was no news on Tamir. The instruction to his family to stay in the safe room was the last information they had. "At least with my grandmother, we know she was taken alive," said Adva. "But there's no video. No sign of life from him. We don't know if he's injured. If he's alive. What's his status right now. The only information we have is that the IDF are assuming that he's kidnapped also."

Did the children, including Tamir's seven-year-old son, understand what had happened? "He gets everything. He knows that his father is kidnapped, and he also lost a lot of friends from the kibbutz." And the younger child? "She understands, but less. She knows her father is missing, but she's still in an age that she can't process all the information. But they are very traumatized.

"Tamir really loved his community. He loved his family. And I know he would do everything to protect them. He was a simple guy. He was a farmer. He worked in the fields of the kibbutz growing potatoes, driving the tractor. He had nothing to do with this war or with this life."

In January 2024, Tamir's body was found in Gaza. It turned out that he had been killed while trying to defend Nir Oz. His dead body had been dragged into Gaza, where it had been held with dozens of other Israeli corpses as a tool for negotiations.

***

Each day at the hostage center there were different faces and some people who were there all the time. They walked around, or sat with each other with the same leaden, terrible weight and the same inextinguishable pain on their faces. One man who became one of the most familiar faces is Malki Shem Tov. The look of pain and exhaustion in his features was overwhelming. Every day he wore a T-shirt with his son's face on it, to remind anyone he met of his son and where he was. Malki's twenty-one-year-old son, Omer, was at the Nova festival on October 7.

"Omer is a party guy," his father says, with a memory of a smile. "He has a lot of friends. And he is very social." Omer's parents knew that he was going to a music festival, but all he told his parents ahead of that evening was "I'm going to the south." He went to many parties, "so I'm not really asking which one. But I didn't know how close it was to the border."

It was only at 6:30 a.m. that Malki realized exactly where his son was. As soon as Malki heard the bomb sirens he called his son to make sure he knew about the alerts and was sheltering. They were in touch from 6:30 until around 9:00 a.m., with father and son calling each other constantly. "From time to time, he sounded much more panicked. Much more hysterical." He and the friends he was with "ran away. They split. All the friends split. He tried to find place to hide." In the phone calls Omer began to sound more and more hysterical. "He told us that he sees they're shooting at them, they're running, they're trying to find place to hide. He told me, 'I see dying people all over.' He told me, 'Dad, I love you.' This is something that killed me. Why would he say that? We are at home. We don't understand yet the situation because we are used to all these bombs."

In the last phone call that morning, Omer told his father that he had found a car with another friend and that four of them were together in the vehicle. "We asked him to send live location. He sent a live location. We saw on the phone at the beginning that the point was not moving. And then suddenly, I saw the point is going through the border with Gaza. I am trying to call him. I wanted to tell him, 'Listen, turn. You are going the wrong way.' He never answered. Then the next stop was behind the border. I know the border. I know the huge wall. I know how smart and clever all the system is over there. And I denied it." He couldn't believe that his son was in Gaza? "I denied it. I totally denied it. I said it's probably that the GPS is wrong or something. And then I said, no, it's not logic. And then I drove to the south. After one or two hours we called other friends and tried to understand who saw who. And then I decided to drive to the area." Before he could get to the site of the party he was stopped by the police and army soldiers who had cordoned off the area. For the first time he met up with the desperate family members of other young people who had been at the party. They were already congregating, trying to get through or at least to get news.

They were told that their children might be at the hospital in Beersheva, where some of the wounded were already being taken. Then, after many hours at Beersheva, Malki got a call from a friend. "About eight p.m. a friend called me, and he told me there is a video that Hamas published where Omer is handcuffed in a pickup or something with another friend. Both of them, they were tied and alive." He starts to break down. "It's like a huge, black curtain comes on your body. I don't know how to express this. I don't know even . . . to say what was the feeling." He saw the video and drove straight back home to his wife and family. By the time he got there they had already seen the video.

They all had the same instinct. "Okay, this is the situation. It's terrible. It's something that nobody teaches you how to be ready for, this kind of situation. But now, let's do everything to bring Omer and all the hostages back." The next day the families of other hostages started to gather in their home and the movement began from there. After three days they had 1,500 volunteers helping them. By the time we first met they had 15,000 volunteers. They were professionals in every field. All civilians. "We do everything in order to bring them back home. And we are civilians. We are not government. We are apolitical. We are civilians that care about the families. That care about the hostages."

I wondered how Malki and Omer's mother managed to even get up in the morning. I had already met hostage families who told me that the parents of some of the hostages couldn't even leave their houses or their rooms since their child was kidnapped. One had been sitting in their darkened house since getting the news. How did Malki do it? "We wake up. It's not easy. It's difficult to start the morning. But we know that the energy come from the volunteers. And the energy comes when we see Omer and all the others. We need to wake up with full energy in order to bring them back. We are strong. Very optimistic. And we trust in God. They will come back."

What would he say to his son if he could get a message to him? His face crumpled. "Omer, I miss you. And I want very much to hug you."

***

For a country to lose hundreds of its civilians in this way is almost unheard-of. In 1979, when the Shah was overthrown in Iran and the Ayatollah Khomeini's revolutionary Islamic movement came to power, supporters of the ayatollah stormed the American embassy. They held more than fifty Americans hostage for over a year. It was a cause of such shame and rage for the American public that it was one of the factors that caused them to throw out the president on whose watch this had happened—Jimmy Carter—and replace him with Ronald Reagan, who promptly ensured the release of the hostages.

Shortly after Saddam Hussein's invasion of Kuwait in 1990, the Iraqi Baathist regime took hundreds of American, British, and other foreign nationals hostage and used them as a bargaining tool in the belief that it would help them to prolong their war and be permitted the annexation they had begun. On these occasions and many more, the fury of the international community and the recognition that this was an utterly illegitimate act—especially in an unprovoked war—were unanimous.

More recently, in 2014, three hundred Chibok girls were stolen from their school in northern Nigeria. The whole world took part in a campaign to try to ensure their return. The Islamic terrorists of Boko Haram ended up facing not just the somewhat haphazard response of the Nigerian military, but an international campaign to draw attention to their situation and to get them back. Prominent figures in the worlds of politics and celebrity, including Michelle Obama, had themselves photographed with signs bearing the by-then-viral hashtag "Bring Back Our Girls." It didn't do very much good in actually bringing back the girls. Indeed, some of them are still hostages to this day—in some cases married off to their captors. But the world cared and it wanted to show it cared. And it wanted to do something.

When 250 Israeli hostages were taken on October 7, 2023, the world's response was muted. Perhaps it took time for the world to realize the scale of what had happened, or perhaps it labored under the belief that the situation between Israel and Hamas was simply "complex." But there was no campaign like that for the Chibok schoolgirls. Aside from Jewish celebrities and influencers there was no organized campaign to pressure Hamas to release the hostages. Even the fact that people from a range of nationalities had been abducted on the 7th drew a strangely muted response.

The abductees included American, British, French, and German citizens. Yet in each of these countries there was minimal political, diplomatic, or social pressure for the release of the kidnapped.

The one place where there inevitably was a huge and immediate campaign was inside Israel.

***

Wearing his motorbike gear, Moran Aloni was another familiar face at the Hostage Families Forum. His sisters, Danielle and Sharon; his brother-in-law, David; plus three of his nieces (twins Emma and Yuli [three] and Emilia [five]) were all kidnapped on the 7th. His younger sister Sharon lived in Nir Oz and his older sister Danielle had joined the family to celebrate Shabbat.

From his home in Rehovot, Moran woke up like many families to the sound of the alarms. He immediately contacted his family in Nir Oz. By text they told him they didn't know what was going on, that terrorists had entered the kibbutz but they were all in the safe room. They could hear gunshots and screaming. At about 9 a.m. one of his sisters messaged him that there were terrorists in the house and that they couldn't lock the safe room. For the next hour and a half there was silence. It was "the longest one hour and a half in my life," he said.

Around 11 a.m. he got another message from his sister telling him that the terrorists were burning their house and that smoke was coming under the safe room door. She told Moran that she didn't think they were going to make it. "Send me some locations," he told them. "I can speak with army, police, whoever." After another twenty minutes she sent two messages. "Help." "We're dying." "That was the last contact we had with them."

Later in the day one of the other people in Nir Oz who had survived visited the family's house. "The house was completely burned down. The safe room, everything." But they didn't see any bodies and didn't see any bloodstains. "So it gave us the idea that they might be kidnapped." It wasn't until a week later that the Israeli authorities confirmed that Moran's family had been kidnapped. For three weeks that was all he knew. "And then, about a week and a half ago, Hamas released a video where my sister was the one speaking. It wasn't easy, but at least I know that my older sister is alive," he said.

"She's obviously not doing well. She looked very thin, and she looked different than the sister I know, obviously." From day to day he and the rest of the family had no idea of what would happen. "We're not sure if we'll see them now walking through the border, or if three officers will come to the house saying 'They're gone.' That's where we're at now. That's where we are now."

As he told me about his family, he was clearly still in deep shock. He described what beautiful people his sisters are, and how smart and funny the children are. "Emilia is so sensitive," he said. "She won't go anywhere without her mom." He described how well life in Nir Oz suited them. "Until my sister got married to David and moved to Nir Oz, she was a very stressed person," he said. "Since she was there she actually became more relaxed. Although they live with missiles almost every day, they say 'Yeah, okay, we have missiles, but we have the safe room, and it's a very good place to raise kids.'

"It's a very beautiful place," he recalled, before correcting himself. "It *was* a very beautiful place." The "absurd" thing about the community, he said, was that "these people were the most peaceful people that there are. They wanted to live in peace with their neighbors. Some people are afraid to live there. But they weren't. They trusted this kind of thing won't happen ever." He said that he hurt all the time thinking about how his relatives must be trying to protect the children. "Even now I'm finding myself hurting when I even think about a situation [where] I'm unable to protect them." And when he thinks about his nieces, he said, "It looks like the world forgot that they are kids in the same hands of the people that murdered so many kids and women and civilians and the elderly. That's not an army versus an army. It's not war between countries. We're all grown-ups. We understand war. We understand that war has a price. This is humanity against evil. There's no other way to say this. What happened there . . . I don't know when, and if we even saw it in the history of humankind. In this dimensions. With zero purpose. Why would you kill a baby? Why would you see a baby, ten months old, one year old, two years old, and shoot him?"

"If we don't stop this here, it will continue to the rest of the world. Now. In a year. Ten years. Fifty years. And that's, I think, what I want to say to the world. We need to stop it here. We need to explain there's no justification. They should be released now. There's no justification for them to be there now." He mentions the Red Cross, who have just made a demand to the Israelis that they be allowed to visit Palestinian prisoners in Israel. But with them and other international bodies like the United Nations, Moran cannot understand why his family seems not to be of any importance.

"Why the silence?" he asks. "Why are they silent? It makes me feel that there's something very wrong in the world today."

***

The first thing people notice when a war is waged on a civilian population is the human casualties. The second is the extraordinary heroism that often comes from such horrors.

Sometimes the people who step forward are people who have a history of heroism. Often they are people who did not know what they had inside them until they were suddenly put through circumstances they should never have seen.

In country after country I have marveled at this. In Ukraine, a year before October 7, I was with the Ukrainian armed forces as they retook territory from the invading Russians. In Mykolaiv and Kherson, Ukrainian soldiers demonstrated the extraordinary feats that people are capable of when they are defending their country and their people.

But it is the unlikely heroes who stand out. People who did not know what they had in them. At one frontline post so secret that I was not allowed to report where it was, I met Ukrainian reservists who had been there for some eight months. One was a beautiful young woman who had given birth to her first child just before the war began. When she was called up she handed over her child to her mother and went straight to her positions on the front lines. She had hardly seen her baby since. "There is no rotation," she said matter-of-factly. But she was doing her duty by her country and knew that she was fighting not just for her country but for her child.

In Israel on October 7, almost every part of the state failed. The intelligence services failed. The military failed. The politicians failed. But the ordinary people of the country were still there and many rose to the occasion when they realized that the safety of their country was not in the hands of other people but was solely down to them.

Over the months I came across many examples of heroes who had excelled that day. Sometimes in the hospitals and recovery units, but also in the streets. Some had already become legends in their own country because of what they had done that morning. One of them is Nimrod Palmach.

Nimrod, thirty-eight, is a father of two who was separated from his children's mother, Liron, but just two weeks earlier had become engaged again, to Miriam. On the morning of the 7th he was staying for the holiday weekend in a small community in the center of Israel and did not hear the sirens at 6:30 a.m. As he watched the sunrise and birds singing, he had no idea what was already underway.

Nimrod had initially spent five years in a special forces unit for his army service and was now a major in the reserves, overseeing a unit of search-and-rescue specialists. Just before 7 a.m. he checked his phone as a matter of habit only to see multiple calls from his commander telling him that he was needed at their base in Jerusalem. Nimrod raced out of the house, still in his bare feet, and drove toward Jerusalem. That's when he began to see videos of armed Hamas terrorists driving around inside Israel. "Sir, it looks like we are needed south," he said to his commander, who insisted they follow their orders to defend Jerusalem. Nimrod arrived at his base and told his commander he intended to drive south. "Defying an order in a war situation carries serious consequences," his commander warned him.

Nevertheless, Nimrod left the base and started driving toward the area around Gaza in his family car with only a handgun and nine rounds of ammunition. On the way, his ex-wife, Liron, called him, screaming hysterically.

"Where are you, Nimrod? Where is the IDF?" Her new boyfriend, Nir, was from Kibbutz Nir Oz and was trapped at that very moment in his safe room along with his two little girls. Hamas were in his house, shooting at the door to the safe room. Liron pleaded with him to go and save her partner and his daughters.

"I'm already on my way, just send me a pin of his house, I'll get to them." Now he was a man with a clear destination.

He told me that as he drove south he knew that he was going to die that day. He stopped by the roadside at Netivot and left a message on his phone for his children, telling them how much he loved them. He knew that later in the day his phone would be found on his body, and the authorities could pass the video on to his children.

On the way south he picked up his colleague Kiril. Together they managed to get through or around a number of police and army checkpoints that had already been set up along the main roads. But at a checkpoint near Shuva, he was told he would not be allowed to go any farther. At that moment an older man arrived in a pickup truck, wearing the shirt of a colonel. He was en route to Kibbutz Be'eri to save his niece. Together the three trained soldiers broke through the military barrier as civilians, armed only with three pistols.

The sight that met their eyes was a scene out of hell—burned-out cars and charred bodies littered the route. As they arrived at the junction to Kibbutz Alumim, just a mile or so into the Gaza envelope, they encountered heavy semiautomatic fire. As Nimrod ran for cover, he saw the scattered bodies of young people everywhere. He wondered why they were dressed in party clothes on a Sabbath morning in the countryside. He did not know about the Nova festival.

"It was only when I got there and saw the devastation that I realized how bad it was," he said. Near the side of the road he found the body of a young woman with her tights and underwear down, and blood on her backside. "It was obvious from the scene that they were raping the women," he said. Out of some instinct, Nimrod pulled up the girl's pants and tights to give her some decency in death.

Nimrod made a number of calls and sent messages from his cell phone, saying, "If you have a gun come here now. You'll save lives." As he lay there taking cover he saw a machine gun that had been discarded in a ditch near a dead IDF soldier. He crawled and grabbed the weapon. Soon after, a unit of Israeli soldiers appeared on the scene. Now armed, he started to fight alongside them. For the next fifteen hours Nimrod fought without a break, engaging scores of Hamas terrorists.

That morning, fighting around the Alumim junction, he helped kill over thirty terrorists. The soldiers he was with found a detailed map of the kibbutz on the body of one of the terrorists. Nimrod was shocked to see detailed instructions that included how many kibbutz members they were allowed to kill, in what manner, who they were permitted to rape, what to do with an IDF soldier's body, and more. They had come well prepared.

Once the Alumim junction was secure, Nimrod moved to Kibbutz Be'eri. He got there in the afternoon. From the first part of the morning until around 7:30 in the evening everyone he saw was dead. He never made it to Kibbutz Nir Oz, but thankfully Nir and his two little girls made it out alive.

"I saw Auschwitz before my eyes," he told me. "So many dead bodies, many were mutilated." He looked disillusioned as he spoke. "Our army was caught by surprise that day. I now know what happens to the Jewish people when they are without an army, even for half a day. Women were raped, kids were killed in their cars, families burned, some with body parts, some without. The damage to buildings was like a tornado had passed through." Nimrod was clear about what it meant for him now. "That day I promised I would be a combat soldier for the rest of my life. I also promised myself that I would tell the story for those that cannot."

***

In one of the hospitals in Tel Aviv I went to visit another one of the people who had shown extraordinary courage on the 7th. Harel is a thirty-four-year-old police officer from Ashkelon. He is married with three kids. For the past seven years he has served as a police officer in Sderot. His head is wrapped with bandages. His arm has an elaborate metal device holding it together after many surgeries.

What was the morning like? I asked him. "Hell," he replied simply. As he was turning up for his shift the rockets started to fire overhead. He got to the station and tried to understand what was happening. Before the 7th "everything was quiet" with Gaza, he said. Then he heard shooting in the street. "Then I understand there's a terrorist in Sderot city." As he heard more and more shooting he realized that far more than one terrorist had gotten into their city.

Harel and his fellow police officers ran to the roof, understanding that if they stayed on the ground floor they would all die. The terrorists were already coming into the building as they were running to the roof. "Then an RPG went through the building and up to the roof. We knew that they would come and waited for them." Two terrorists came up and there was a lot of shooting. "We had Glocks and one M16 rifle. They had Kalashnikovs and grenades and the full kit." The policemen were vastly outnumbered and outgunned. There were seven of them on the roof. "Another four terrorists came up. We killed them as well. They threw a grenade, and Shoshanah, a policewoman, was the first one injured. She threw the grenade back at them." All the time he was telling me this Harel was rolling back and forth in his wheelchair. He could not stop trying to move. As his mind took him back to the morning he said again and again, "Crazy."

One of the other policemen saw a lot of terrorists in the parking lot, so he got the only M16 rifle and shot them. Afterward the bodies of some forty-four terrorists would be found in the vicinity of the police station, out of around sixty to seventy who came into Sderot that day. A major battle happened there. By the time I made it to the police station to see the remains of the fight there was little of it left but rubble. For Harel and his colleagues it was the longest of days. "It started at six thirty or seven, and the fight was until four a.m. the next morning from the police station," he said. At around 3 p.m. on the 7th, Harel was shot by a Hamas sniper. He lay there bleeding. It is unclear to him how long it was. What happened after he was shot was like a terrible dream.

"I have shrapnel in my body," he said, signaling downward. "And my head. I was bleeding for four hours on the roof before they got to me. I swear. While I was bleeding, a terrorist came up and was about to shoot me. My friends shot the terrorist. I was conscious. I was bleeding. I saw the whole scene. I was playing dead. I saw the terrorist coming up. Like the movies." At some point Yamam, an Israeli special forces soldier, came and joined the firefight and finally managed to evacuate Harel and his surviving colleagues.

His own body was wrecked by the gunfire and blasts. Signaling to his hand he said, "A bullet went in and out of my arm, and then it affected the nerves in my hand." How many colleagues did he lose that day? "A lot," he replied, sadly. Eight, ten. "We were working together for many years. We were best friends. Very sad. Not easy. I think it is not real. I still think I am dreaming.

"Crazy," he adds again. "Crazy."

***

Some units of the IDF did make it south on the morning of the 7th. The elite unit Duvdevan made it south and fought with extraordinary bravery at the junctions and kibbutzim. They lost some of their best men, like Captain Ben Bronstein, twenty-four, while they were fighting there.

It was soldiers like him and ordinary people who just used their own initiative on the 7th who would be most celebrated from every corner of Israeli society. In any sane world people would notice them all and what this says about the country they are living in.

Tariq is a Muslim Arab Israeli. He is a doctor and a volunteer with the United Hatzalah. Whenever an accident like a car crash or any other incident happens in Israel, he, like the seven thousand other trained volunteers, will get an alert. If they are in the vicinity of the problem they will go straight to the scene to provide first aid and any other assistance. The scheme has been so successful that it has now got chapters across the US. Governor Kathy Hochul of New York is among those who have also looked into replicating its success.

Tariq is also somewhat overqualified for the role. He is a doctor of medicine at the Barzilai Medical Center in Ashkelon, about twelve miles from the border with Gaza. We met on a roadside not far from where his morning on the 7th ended. He got out of his car and hobbled over to me on crutches.

He described the morning of October 7 as perfectly normal. He was going to his usual shift at the medical center. But as he was on his way his wife called to tell him that a large number of rockets were coming from Gaza into his village. He stopped and put on his protective vest and the Hatzalah first-responder kit that he carries with him all the time. Without realizing it Tariq was driving straight into the middle of a war zone.

He came to the intersection in Sderot and thought it was strangely silent. The first thing he noticed was a number of crashed cars. At first he thought it was a normal accident. He could see someone who had clearly been injured in the head. He saw that the person was dead. Then he heard someone call to him, urging him to come over to them. He thought it was something to do with IDF soldiers who needed help. No sooner had he gone toward them than from about one hundred feet out he was shot in the chest. "My protective vest saved me," he explained. He started to realize what had happened. "I started to say to my God to save me." Then he realized that the people he thought were IDF were in fact Hamas. There were around twelve of them and they came over to him on the ground where he was lying. They started to take his protective vest and his telephone off him, took the keys to his car, and then tied him up in the middle of the intersection.

He was there for three hours. "They shot everyone coming in the way. These cars. They shoot everyone," he said. The Hamas terrorists asked him, "What is your name? Where are you from?" Tariq told them, "I am Arab. I am Muslim." He told them his name. "I tell them something from the Quran. Everything. They didn't care about that, and they continued to kill people and to be sure they killed."

I asked him about his statement "I'm an Arab, I'm a Muslim." Did it have any effect on them? "No," he said firmly. They saw him as a hostage. They wanted to use him. They believed that the IDF could not kill them from the air if they had Tariq there as "a human shield." The terrorists used the time that they bought to kill other people. As Tariq says again, "They didn't care if I am a Muslim."

When the IDF did arrive, after many hours, the terrorists questioned what they should do with him. In the end they shot him in his right knee. It was actually a Hatzalah ambulance that ended up rescuing him and taking him to Soroka Medical Center. He is still recovering.

Had he ever seen anything like that day? "No—I didn't see anything like that day." How many people did he think he saw being shot while he was tied up and being used? "Sixteen, seventeen, something like that. They were people of all ages. But they just shot and killed anyone who was driving in a car. Every car coming this way, they'd shoot the person in the passenger seat and the driver."

There was a question I couldn't avoid asking Tariq. Were you born in Israel? "Yeah. I'm born in Israel."

And Hamas. They say they're acting in the name of their faith. What does he say to that?

"We are born in Israel, and we will all the time be Israeli. I am here for my country. That's all."

***

These are just some of the extraordinary heroes who were created that day. But still the question lingered of just where the IDF and other security forces had been. Every conversation in Israel after the morning came back to this question. How could there have been such a catastrophic intelligence failure followed by such a catastrophic military command failure?

When the war is over there will be a commission of inquiry much like what took place after the 1973 Yom Kippur War, which was the last time, under the leadership of Golda Meir, that such a surprise attack had occurred. Most Israelis expect any forthcoming inquiry to have similar outcomes. On that occasion Meir took much of the reputational hit for what had happened on her watch. After the 7th, top political figures as well as the high command in the army and security services were widely expected to do the same. But despite such an inquiry being currently stalled, some conclusions can already be drawn.

The first is that the security consensus in Israel had for many years been unified around what became known as the "conception." This "conception" held, among other things, that while Hamas was undoubtedly an apocalyptic Islamist movement, its leadership had fallen into a familiar pattern of terrorist movements that ended up in government. That is, eventually the trappings of power and the enjoyment of the benefits it brings supersede the dreams of the movement's youth. From the Soviet Union, among other precedents, we commonly see revolutionaries end up simply enjoying being corrupt.

By 2023, Hamas had enjoyed billions of dollars of funding in international aid from the United States, United Kingdom, European Union, and other international entities—largely doled out by the UN to its various wings like the UN Relief and Works Agency (UNRWA). By the time of the October 7 attacks it had been estimated that the group's leadership alone had accumulated personal wealth of around $11 billion. Ismail Haniyeh, head of the so-called political wing of Hamas (a distinction without a difference from the military wing), had for years been living in a luxury apartment in Qatar. By the time of the October 7 attacks his personal wealth was estimated at roughly $4 billion.

Other leaders similarly enriched themselves, with their children and wider families enjoying the greatest luxuries imaginable. All while they kept the citizens of Gaza in a degree of poverty that gained the attention of the world.

There was a belief—incorrect though it proved—that almost two decades into their governance of Gaza, the leadership of Hamas were happy with their personal lot, however much they had immiserated their people. The thinking went that they just wanted to be corrupt and to enjoy the fruits of their corruption. Crucially there was a belief that the leaders would not be willing to do anything that might jeopardize the luxury lifestyles they and their families enjoyed.

Among a number of other things this "conception" failed to take into account was one of the most cardinal lessons: while it is true that some fanatics can moderate due to the worldly luxuries placed before them, others are simply fanatics. And while some fanatics may be able to be bought off, others simply mean what they say, and the leadership of Hamas were among those types that meant it.

Their actions aside, it was never hard to judge Hamas's leadership and its aspirations by their words. In 2012, the deputy speaker of the Hamas parliament said in a sermon, "Oh Allah, destroy the Jews and their supporters. Oh Allah, destroy the Americans and their supporters. Oh Allah, count them one by one, and kill them all, without leaving a single one." In 2019, senior Hamas official Fathi Hamad said, "You have Jews everywhere and we must attack every Jew on the globe by way of slaughter and killing." In April 2023, six months before the October 7 attacks, senior Hamas official Sheikh Hamad al-Regeb said, "Bring annihilation upon the Jews. Paralyze them, destroy their entity." And perhaps most importantly there was the leader of Hamas in Gaza, Yahya Sinwar.

In 2018 he gave an address to the citizens of Gaza in which he said, "We'll take down the border [with Israel] and tear out their hearts from their bodies." The Israeli leaders who believed in their own "conception" would not be the first group of people who failed to take an enemy at their word. But in all of these cases the Hamas leadership said it because they meant it, because they wanted to act on it and were planning to do so.

For many months after the 7th I spoke to every Israeli political leader I could, from left to right. I spoke with people who were in government on the 7th, people who had long been out of government, and those who longed to be in government. I spoke with military chiefs and intelligence experts. And each time I started by asking the question I heard from survivor after survivor. How did it happen? How did the country with one of the world's best military and intelligence apparatuses get surprised by this enemy? And where were the soldiers? What had gone wrong that day? Eventually I got to ask this to the nation's top military and political leaders and worked out the answer. But for now the most important thing to me was to work out what had happened, how the day that soon became known as "Black Saturday" had ever occurred.

CHAPTER 2

WHAT I SAW

What is the scene of a massacre like? People often describe it as "indescribable." But that is not true. It just reeks of death. You can feel the death. You can see the death. Worst of all, you can smell the death.

The Russian Jewish writer Vasily Grossman (1905–1964) was a reporter as well as a novelist. And as a journalist he covered everything. He was there in the battle for Stalingrad and was the first journalist to tread into the Nazi death camp of Treblinka. Treblinka was not a concentration camp. It was a death camp. The plan was to annihilate everyone immediately or almost immediately after arrival.

In July 1944, entering with the Russian army, even Grossman, who had seen everything, was shocked. He saw the scene that the Nazis had tried to cover over and only partially succeeded in doing so. And he was one of the first to work out what happened there. Among the many haunting details of his account is his description of the remnants of lives that still covered the ground. The gold and valuables of the Jewish dead or soon-to-be-dead were carefully collected from their bodies. Even the most pathetic piece of a life, valueless though it might seem, could be taken if it seemed of use to the murderers. Grossman describes how papers, including personal documents, were still lying on the ground.

He writes, "An amazing thing was that the swine utilised everything, even paper and fabric—anything which could be useful to anyone, was important and useful to these swine. Only the most precious thing in the world, a human life, was trampled by their boots."[16]

Nir Oz was also the site of a terrible massacre, on a different scale from Treblinka, but like Treblinka it is hard to know how to walk on this land.

It was a relatively poor community, but it was also a beautiful one. Around four hundred people lived there on the morning of October 7. Among a small community where everyone knows each other, and knows what is happening in the house next door, over a quarter of the population disappeared in a few hours, either slaughtered or taken into Gaza. Fully a quarter of the kibbutz was gone at a stroke.

While the blood was still wet, Ron Bahat showed me through the ruins of his community. Ron is a fifty-seven-year-old man, a husband and grandfather.

On the 7th he was preparing to celebrate the holiday with his family, including his wife, two of his daughters, and his dog. They heard the sirens at 6:30 a.m. and recognized the red alarm that went off. Shortly afterward, Ron got information that there were terrorists in his kibbutz. He knew that he would not just have to get his family into their safe room but also find a way to lock it. He went out, took some rope, and tried to tie the handle from the inside. He and his family would be in the safe room for almost ten hours. During all that time they could hear people running all around them, being shot, heard people trying to break into their house, smashing the window of the safe room and trying to kill everyone he knew. As he heard the shooting behind the house he had one overwhelming, terrible feeling—the realization that everyone outside their house that morning wanted to kill them. That the people flooding through their community "came here to murder us."

Ron and his family heard the noise all day. It was terrible. All day long, as he and his family were sheltering, they could hear people entering the houses of their neighbors and slaughtering or kidnapping whomever they could find. As we walked around the charred remains of their community, he said perhaps "every second house" was affected. He took me into what had been the homes of the people who were his neighbors. In almost every case we ended up standing in what had been the "safe rooms." As the evidence on the floors, walls, and doors showed, in house after house these were the places where Ron's neighbors' stories ended—with people desperately trying to hold their door handles closed. On one side that morning were the Hamas terrorists. On the other were people, sometimes alone, trying desperately to keep them out.

We stood in one of these rooms. What had happened here? It was one of his neighbors who "couldn't hold the door." The community found blood on the floor. The army found their bodies on the ground outside the kibbutz.

We went to the house of Ron's eighty-two-year-old mother. That morning she was with her sister and Ron's two cousins. They managed to hold the door. As he said matter-of-factly, "If you couldn't hold the door, you're not with us."

The next house had belonged to seventy-four-year-old Bracha Levinson. The child of Holocaust survivors, she was alone in the house when the terrorists came in. We stood in the safe room where she had hidden. She had no chance to hold the door. The terrorists took her phone off her and recorded her killing. They then used her phone to post a video on her Facebook page of her lying in a pool of her own blood with her killers standing over her. All her family and friends saw it. The terrorists then set fire to the home. It took a month to identify her charred remains.

On and on it went. The house of the Katzir family—where seventy-nine-year-old Rami was found dead inside, his wife, Hanna, kidnapped into Gaza. The house of Adina and Said Moshe, whose safe room door once again had shots fired through it. Inside, the walls were all covered in gunshots. Ron found the body of Said on the floor. His seventy-two-year-old wife was kidnapped into Gaza.

The house of the Shalev family was burned beyond all recognition and still reeked of smoke. The wife had been on a tour of Egypt, so David (also the son of Holocaust survivors) was alone at home with his son Tal, who had come to visit his father and so was there when the terrorists came in. "We find the remains here," Ron said, with a terrible weariness. "Both of them. Father and son." The roof had collapsed and as we clambered among the debris Ron signaled where they found one of the bodies outside, the other in the safe room.

House after house—every one had a story. The Munder family had four members kidnapped. Roi, a massive Liverpool football fan, was found murdered here. The Mozes family's two small daughters were taken hostage. Of all the houses in the community there were perhaps four where the terrorists didn't enter at all. They took a moped from outside one but didn't go inside. Or took something from the shed but didn't enter. Everywhere else it was variations of the same story. People killed, people missing, and people who the community hoped had been taken hostage. There were houses with blast marks where grenades had been thrown in. Houses into which an RPG had been fired. Houses where a charge had been placed on the safe room door to blow it open. And then the room itself riddled with bullet holes. I ask what the trail of blood in one of the houses is. "Ada Sagi," Ron said. They wounded her and then dragged her out. "You can see all the signs on the wall that she tried to hold herself." Her blood-covered handprints and nail and finger marks were visible all along the walls. "You can see that she tried to hold herself to prevent them from taking her." Ada was seventy-five years old.

The Cunio family were all kidnapped. In the ruins of their house Ron explained that the mother and father were taken hostage along with their twin girls, age three. Sharon, the mother, had her sister staying for the holidays. She was kidnapped too along with her five-year-old daughter. These were the relatives of Moran Aloni. There were also a couple in their eighties who survived because they had managed to pile books against the safe room door. But the list was remorseless: Some people were shot where they were, the bullet and blood marks still showing the story of their final moments. Some people had already been buried. Others had not been identified yet. Some people had been taken into Gaza alive along with the bodies of some who were known to have been murdered. Marks along the walls of the houses showed people desperately clinging on as they were taken from their homes. Other marks showed where someone bled out or was burned alive on the floor.

Then there were all the incongruous sights. Outside one house was a collection of cooking pans in a pile. They had been collected by the looters who came in from Gaza after the terrorists had done their work. One of the looters clearly wanted this set of pans but forgot them on the way out. In another house there were the charred remains of a burned-out piano, with what had been the instrument's soundboard lying burned against a wall.

Eventually we came to the house of Ron's sister, Renana. Ron opened what remained of the door and showed me inside. On the morning of the 7th his sister's two sons, Yigal, twelve, and Or, sixteen, were alone in the house. When the attack began, Ron was in touch with them by phone. He tried to show them how to tighten the handle of the safe room door with a winding sheet and hold it from a place that wouldn't put them in the path of bullets being fired through the door. Ron showed them how the method might work and urged them to hold on. "Unfortunately, they couldn't," he said, simply. The two young boys—one not even a teenager—inside their mother's house didn't stand a chance against the fully grown terrorists on the other side of the door. You could see huge force had been used on the door. Ron's nephews had fought hard. But they were taken hostage. Ron doesn't know how long the boys managed to hold out but he knows they fought. "You can see that there was a fight—no doubt," he said.

Otherwise it is the same terrible litany. The house of Yossi and Stella, where the husband was shot in front of his wife and his dead body dragged outside. The house of Johnny, thirty-six, and his wife, Tamar, thirty-five, where the terrorists came in and killed them both along with their three children (five-year-old twin daughters and a two-year-old son). "They killed all of them?" "All of them." The house where Sasha Troufanov, twenty-eight, was staying with his girl-friend to visit his parents. Sasha worked for Amazon in the US and was kidnapped into Gaza. "He came for a vacation," Ron said sadly.

This was a place that was almost idyllic in its openness. "Nobody locked their door," Ron explained. As we walked among the burned buildings it seemed as if a horrible game of chance had played out.

The community at Nir Oz had a student village with a building where people from the nearby college could stay. Most of them weren't in the kibbutz on the morning of October 7, which was fortunate because the terrorists went door-to-door through the student living quarters. One lone student, also called Ron, was staying in the accommodation. He hid under his bed for twelve hours. At one point the terrorists entered his room to take a rest, refilled the magazines in their guns, and sat on the bed under which he was hiding. The student underneath "couldn't breathe even" throughout this time. But he was safe. The older Ron said, "So he's lucky." Other people were not.

Many residents of Nir Oz allowed other people to use their homes if they were away. One of the members of the kibbutz was away for the 7th and someone else said they had some friends from England coming and could they use the house? Daniel Darlington, thirty-four, originally from Manchester, England, was not meant to be in Nir Oz on the day of the attack. But on his visit he decided that he loved the community so much, and regarded it as such a haven ("this little piece of heaven"), that although he was meant to leave for Tel Aviv on the 6th he would stay another night. Daniel was killed. His peace-activist father was taken hostage.

Despite the charred debris, and the ruin and the blood everywhere, it was worth trying to remember what a tranquil and peace-loving community this was until this Armageddon.

Everywhere things had been left just as they were on that morning: clothes strewn around, full dishwashers waiting to be emptied.

Some of the houses had peace stickers on what remained of their homes. I asked Ron what one of them meant—a sticker that sat at the bloodied doorway of this burned-out house. "It means live and let live and if you are not happy have a good day." A moment later a rocket landed and we went inside for cover.

On the perimeters of the community you can clearly see the Gaza Strip. It is less than a mile away. Just 1.6 kilometers. And at the edge of the village, near what had been the fence, was the house of Amitai Ben Zvi, eighty. He had lived here happily, and from the balcony of his house you could clearly see Gaza. Here in his house the community found him shot dead on his sofa.

Amitai had liked to sit on his balcony. Ron and I walked up to it. "Amitai used to say that he had the best balcony." From here you could see the locals' attempt to start a vineyard. And then the gap in the fence. "They blew this gate and entered," Ron said, pointing. "That was their main entrance in and out,"—one of the entrances through which the terrorists came and through which the hostages were taken out.

On one side of the community was an area of the kibbutz in which a group of Thai workers had lived. Their quarters all had separate rooms and communal facilities for the foreign workers to live in as they helped the community's members with work in the fields and more. There were eighteen Thai workers here on the morning of the 7th. Walking through their living areas it was clear that the terrorists that morning had gone room to room and shot into a number of them. Every room and its contents had been completely demolished.

The terrorists had ransacked through their belongings. Passports with the photo page open were lying on the floors. The terrorists took whatever they could, including cell phones and the small amounts of money the workers had. "There's no purpose," said one of the forensic experts, trying to make sense of what happened there. "It's without purpose. They're not the rich people. They're not, you know. It's pure insanity." Then, again, we saw marks on the floor where the terrorists had grabbed a badly wounded person and dragged them outside.

At the end of the Thai workers quarter were two bomb shelters. It was clear that on the morning of the 7th the Hamas terrorists had decided to centralize most of the eighteen Thai people into one of these shelters. "Something very terrible happened here," one of the experts said. A forensic expert was still taking photos of the scene. "I have to warn you. This scene is very, very graphic. It's very graphic. It's very tough. But the world needs to see."

The short passageway inside was covered in bloodied handprints. And then the tiny interior of the bomb shelter into which these human souls were packed. It was dark inside so I turned on my phone light. There were bullet shell casings on the floor and the belt of an old Soviet PK machine gun. There were bullet holes in the walls, on the floor, in the ceiling, and in the air-conditioning—and blood absolutely everywhere. The floor was covered in it, the walls were all smeared with it, and the ceiling was sprayed with it. The blood splatter over the ceiling and air-conditioning suggested that some of the victims were finished off with machetes. The walls were covered with the smear marks from blood-covered hands of people trying to save themselves. At least eleven people were killed in that tiny, dark room.

As we walked out of this scene of horror we came to a piece of land where there was no blood, no burned-out cars or houses, only a reminder of the peace that had been here before. "Nir Oz was one of the nicest kibbutzim in Israel," said Ron, wistfully. "It's a green bubble in this area with all those beautiful trees and grass. A lot of love and cultivation had gone into this place for decades."

It makes it even harder to understand who would want to attack such a place. And how the community was left completely helpless for hours. Ron thinks that Nir Oz was alone from six thirty a.m. to almost two p.m." Then at around 2 p.m. the army came in. "I'm not sure that they shoot one bullet," said Ron. "The terrorists already left."

Ron was born here and had spent most of his life living here. I asked him if he ever thought something like this could happen here.

"No," he replied. "I never thought about it. You know. We were thinking that maybe people would come, but nobody thinks on those murderers, killers. You know, when we saw ISIS and Daesh, everyone's thinking it's far, it's nothing here. Now it's clear that those people, those Hamas people are worse than Daesh. Worse than ISIS."

As he said this I was looking over at Gaza. *How could anyone live here after what happened?* I wondered. "I think it will be a challenge," he said. "It's clear that not everyone will come. I have some terrible experience here. Some wounds that will never heal. But yes, the kibbutz will come back." But still, how could anyone live so close to Gaza, knowing what we know now?

"First of all, it's home. And you don't leave home. I'm not saying it will be easy. I'm confident and hope that the army will do what it needs to do now. Get rid of Hamas. Get rid of those killers, murderers. And hopefully, we'll be able to live one day in peace here."

I left Ron and headed back out toward the security gates of Nir Oz, the gates that failed to secure the community on that morning. On the way I bump into one of the pathology teams still raking over the scene of this crime. They are literally sifting through the ashes of the community to look for the remains of the last few people whose fate is unknown. People who may have been taken hostage or whose bodies may have been so badly destroyed in the fires that there will be almost nothing left. They have been doing this for days. One of their number, Yoel, explains what they are looking for. "Teeth, a piece of flesh, bones—anything that we can take DNA from and understand—friend or foe." Because there is the possibility that some of the terrorists who were fired back at could have died in these places too.

But yes, he said, they were still finding things. The previous day they found bones and teeth. "We don't know yet who they belong to. It's sent to a special lab where they try to understand who it belongs to. And we also find personal belongings: a necklace, a piece of a diary, a half-burnt child's book. A lot of personal belongings." It's difficult work. "Yes," he said. "But it's all part of the job. And we're honored to do what we can to help the families get some closure to where their loved ones are."

***

In the weeks following the massacre at the Nova party, many of the survivors sought out the company of others who had been there. Some had known each other before the party. Many were newly bonded by what they had been through and seen together. As the weeks went on, a space was offered to them in the historic town of Caesarea. There they were able to gather in the days and evenings. They took the opportunity to talk, play music, and sometimes even dance again.

As the weeks went on the need for some kind of care for these young people became increasingly obvious. At any time there are stories that the press in any liberal country can barely cover—not because they are ordered not to cover them, but because to reveal certain things (particularly in wartime) could be so terrible for public morale. When it came to the survivors of the Nova party, there was one story in particular that the Israeli media barely mentioned: in the aftermath of the party a number of the young people who had survived had been sectioned into mental institutions. A number had killed themselves. Others had tried to kill themselves in the hospitals.

There was one particular reason why again the media did not like to discuss this. Obviously many of the young people at the Nova party had been on drugs. Obviously most of those drugs are illegal in Israel. But nobody wanted to be seen to be either condoning their use or blaming the victims for having been on them.

Health care professionals and therapists I spoke with circled this question often. In time, they said, studies would be made of the drugs that people were on, the effects they had on them, and the way in which some drugs may have helped people to survive while others clearly hampered their chances of survival.

A number of those who survived had been on cocaine, which is a stimulant. Some of them were among those who ran many miles to escape the terrorists. A number of survivors told me that they could not believe how far and how fast they had run. Looking at maps afterward, they were amazed at their stamina. Of course, some of this was what kicks in for anyone in a "fight-or-flight" situation, where the body is flooded with adrenaline and cortisol. Still, the people on cocaine may have had an advantage.

Perhaps the worst drugs to have been on when the massacre began were consciousness-expanding drugs, which involve a psychedelic "trip" and can make people feel at peace with the world. These drugs include LSD, MDMA, and psilocybin mushrooms. People who had taken them would have almost no ability to comprehend the situation they found themselves in. People who had literally prepared themselves to be at one with the best aspects of the universe instead found themselves face-to-face with the worst things anyone could see. Who can comprehend the confusion and terror that many of the young people on one or other of these drugs felt in their final moments?

For those who survived, who had been on some of these drugs and had seen the worst of the horrors of that morning, the combination of factors would already be too much. One of the truths about trauma is that anyone who has been through a dangerous situation is in an infinitely better position if they were in some way anticipating the situation or expecting to go into harm's way. But anyone who comes across such a thing completely unexpectedly is far more likely to suffer long-term trauma from the event. To come across the worst sights imaginable—of friends being murdered in front of you—at the exact moment when your mind and body are least expecting it, is something very few people could live through. I asked one professional about what had happened to some of the young people who had been sectioned in the hospitals from the party. "Their minds just collapsed," she explained. The mixture of openness and horror, tranquility and terror was too much for the brain.

A few weeks after the massacre I spent a night at the reunion center in Caesarea. There were memorial stands and walls of candles commemorating their friends who had been murdered. There were murals of the missing. There was also an inside dance floor and a stage for musicians to perform on. Early in the evening there was no entertainment, but as the night wore on and more of the survivors came in, something like the ghost of a party restarted.

Around the perimeter were a range of activities. They included craftwork. It may be a part of the festival scene and part of recuperation to focus on achieving small goals. Elsewhere there were healing activities for the survivors. There was an area for massage, one for yoga, and one for physiotherapy.

Among the assortment of people who gathered there I got some sense of the range of victims who had been affected. For instance there was a fifty-eight-year-old man named Eran who was briefly standing on his own outside. He turned out to be the father of a beautiful twenty-six-year-old girl, Oriya. She had gone to the Nova party with friends.

On that morning Eran was woken by calls from Oriya and one of his other daughters. Oriya was calling in desperation and terror. At first Eran could not believe what he was hearing. Amid telling him how much she loved him, she managed to relate how she had managed to escape from the gunmen at the Nova festival and had managed to get into a car with her friends Sharon and Shahar—a brother and sister. They managed to drive a few miles from the party, toward the kibbutz of Mefalsim. It seemed that they thought they would be safe there and desperately tried to get in. They had no way of knowing there was a massacre going on inside Mefalsim too.

More than an hour after the terrorist attack had begun, the car Oriya was in was shot at by terrorists. It flipped over and after that the sequence of events became opaque. Eran was on the phone to his daughter for as long as he could be. He told her to leave the place where they were but she said that the police had told her to stay. There was confusion, not least because it would turn out that the terrorists who shot at the car Oriya and her friends were in were wearing Israeli police uniforms. They had taken them off murdered policemen. So it seems likely that the people who told Oriya to stay in place were actually terrorists.

At some point Sharon cried out to her brother in panic. Shahar was shot as he tried to get back into the car to help her. Eran could hear all this on the phone.

One of the last communications he got from his daughter was a photo of her friend lying dead in her hands. He showed it to me. It was as if his daughter had been trying to prove to him that all this was real. And as if she still hoped that he would know what to do when you are in the middle of a firefight with a friend lying shot in your lap.

Eran didn't know what happened to his daughter in the last minutes of her life. While the frantic search of the massacre sites was going on in the days afterward he held out a hope. "I hoped she'd been captured," he told me. But three days after her death, Oriya's boyfriend found her body. She was lying under a tree about one hundred yards from where the car was found. It seemed that she had walked to the tree and died underneath it from blood loss. As her father again showed me the photo of Oriya's bloodied friend in her lap, he said, "Girls do not listen to their fathers till the last minute." Tears streamed down his face.

Like a lot of people, Eran was still in the process of trying to work out what had happened not just to his daughter but to his country. He himself fought in the First Lebanon War and his father fought in 1973. In 1973 he didn't see his father for a hundred days. Then Eran was back in the present. "How did they catch us sleeping?" he asked. "They slaughtered our beautiful flowers."

***

It may seem strange, and in many ways it is, that people should hold on to images that most people would hope to forget. I came across it a lot in those days. People in the most ordinary circumstances suddenly produced images on their phones of absolute horror. I had versions of this before. In northern Nigeria, community leaders in remote villages sometimes produced a binder of images to show me. Image after image on page after page of bodies lying dead in the fields. Men, women, and children shot or macheted, the images of their bodies now incongruously placed in an office-style ring binder to show to a visitor. These bodies were evidence and the only way the communities could prove to anyone from the outside world that what they said had happened had in fact happened.

But in the age of the smartphone and at this moment in Israel, this incongruity was stepped up a notch. While I was at the Israeli parliament one day some relatives of people killed on the 7th approached me. They were there to lobby politicians. But as they told me what had happened to their relatives, two of them, both women, pulled out their phones and showed me the images of their dead family members lying in pools of blood. They wept as they showed them to me, looked at them again, and put their phones away.

Of course, it is an attempt to keep hold of the evidence—to be able to keep reminding anyone who wants to listen that what happened had happened. But I noticed another thing here too: these images— even the ones of horror—were precious to them.

One of the clearest examples of this came from a young man who had attended the Nova party and whom I met at the reunion. He was slightly alone there, but to anyone who would listen he told the story of what happened to him that morning, and did so in slow, excruciating detail. He had gone to the party alone but met up with friends there. He said that he didn't like going to parties in a car with friends, because he liked to be able to leave whenever he wanted to and not have to wait till others were ready. It was an advantage that morning.

He described how when the shooting started, he managed to get to the place where his car was parked. He hid in the driver's seat, hardly daring to move, let alone start the engine. At this point with me he produced his phone and began showing me and walking me through video he had taken on his phone camera. He had sunk down in the front seat but recorded the images ahead of him and to the side. You could hear his breathing as he watched figures in the distance going from car to car. These were unarmed Gazan civilians, in civilian clothing, not Hamas terrorists, he explained. They were part of the large number of people who flooded into Israel after the terrorists had broken through the border. They were women and men and they were looting the cars that had been left at the festival parking site. When they found someone alive in one of the cars they alerted the terrorists, who then came and killed them.

You could feel the young man's attentiveness even now as he rewatched what he had seen that morning. Close by his car, to its right, was another car and between the two vehicles a young man was hiding. He was an attractive-looking twentysomething and he was peering over the hood at the people who were moving between the cars. The young man showing me this explained that he had tried to persuade this young man to get into his car. But the other man just couldn't do it. He couldn't make himself take the risk of opening the passenger door and being heard by the terrorists or coming to the attention of their helpers.

Eventually the looters came too close and the young man with the car drove off. He explained that as he did so the attention of all the people scavenging among the cars turned to him and then to the young man he had tried to persuade to get into his car moments earlier. As he drove off he could see the crowd descending on the crouching young man. In his rearview mirror he saw them lynch him.

The main exit was already clogged with shot-up cars and bodies but he knew that there was another route out of the festival. At some point he managed to pick up another young partygoer who lay across the back seat as he tried to get out. He described in excruciating detail the terror in this young man's voice. Maybe he was on drugs or maybe he was just screaming in terror. But when the driver tried to work out how to get out of the area, the young man in the back kept screaming advice at him. Eventually the young driver could take it no more. He told him that he had to be able to think. The young man leapt out of the car. The man at the reunion had no idea what happened to him. But in his car he managed to get out through an exit that was not blocked, and despite being fired at a lot, he managed to escape.

As he relayed this story he kept cradling his phone, bringing up the videos or the images of the morning whenever they were relevant. I noticed that even on the second telling of his story he looked at the images with a kind of wonder, as if he was still trying to work out what he had seen, or needed evidence that it was real. It was as though he had to keep looking at them, or as if he might next time better understand something about it. He was obviously in a deep trauma, but for the time being there was no way out of it. I doubt he would ever forget the young man who didn't get in his car or stop wondering about the one who got out. There was no way to bring closure to any part of his story.

Instead, as the reunion went on around him he just stood there, holding his phone and preparing to give anyone else who asked the same second-by-second, detailed account of what he had been through and what he had seen.

***

Even in the religious petri dish that is the Middle East, the Druze are a remarkable people. Today the community totals less than a million people, spread out between Israel, Lebanon, and Syria. Though they speak Arabic and have many Arab customs, their religion is unique. It bears similarities with Islam and Christianity but is generally regarded as a breakaway from Shia Islam. Druze communities in Israel are relatively independent (the religion opposes intermarriage and it is not possible for an outsider to convert in). And although they make up only slightly more than 1 percent of the Israeli population, many Druze serve in the IDF. A number of prominent Druze have reached cabinet level.

It happened to be a Druze family who had one of the food-catering contracts for the Nova party. Two of the men, brothers in their thirties, persuaded a cousin of theirs to stay and help them out at the party. The cousin lives in New York and was back visiting family in Israel when his cousins told him they needed an extra pair of hands to cater the Nova party on October 6 and 7. He postponed his flight back to New York and stayed to help out.

Raif (thirty-nine), Amar (thirty-three), and Rada (thirty-three) are huge, strong, bearded men. But when we met it was clear that they were still living that morning. It was moving that they felt compelled to come to the Nova reunion and be with others from that day.

It is impossible to know how many lives the three men saved. But when they found themselves in the midst of the horror, they had a few advantages. Crucially they all spoke and understood Arabic, so when the terrorists broke into the party that morning they were more able than most of the partygoers to understand what they were saying when they overheard them.

Like everyone else, they remembered the moment at just after 6:30 a.m. when the first rockets flew overhead. By 8 a.m. they were at their car and were being shot at by the terrorists who had come in. They got out of their car and ran for cover. With around thirty other people they managed to run to a patch of forest. As they ran, Raif saw people being shot and falling down all around him. "This is the strongest country in the world," he told me. "And I felt naked." He spent some hours among the trees before he decided, with half of the group, to make a run for an Israeli tank they could see in the distance.

In total he was there for eight hours. He remembered the first soldiers arriving between 11:30 a.m. and 12 noon. But he stayed hiding behind the tank until 5 p.m. That is the bare timeline, but like his relatives he saw things in that time that no one should see. All the time he was hiding he could hear the Hamas terrorists and the Gazan citizens. He saw and heard the Gazan Palestinians who were with Hamas encouraging the young Israelis to come out of hiding. But when anyone did, Raif saw what happened. At around 10:30 a.m.

he saw the Hamas terrorists find a young partygoer. They set upon him with hammers and other tools. After killing him he overheard them debating whether they should put him on the truck and take the body to Gaza.

Amar was in the bar area that morning and came across another young partygoer whose head had been caved in with hammers. He described how he wet the lips of the young man as he lay dying. But it was after he had joined his brother in the forest that he had the clearest sight of the terrorists. At one point as he was taking cover some Gazans asked him if he spoke Arabic. "Come to us, come to us," they said in Arabic. He crawled back to the group and told them it wasn't safe. As soon as he left, Hamas fired a rocket-propelled grenade into the group. Many of the group were killed. His cousin was thrown many feet by the blast. He estimates that of the seventy young people who were in the forest, perhaps eight came out.

Rada too could hear the terrorists speak from where he was hiding. They were perhaps a hundred feet from him. As he was watching he saw them debate what to do with a nineteen-year-old girl. "Should we kidnap her or kill her?" he heard them debate in Arabic in front of her. They decided to kidnap her. Then one of the terrorists came over with a gun and decided to shoot her in the head. Rada remembered her voice clearly. "Don't kill me. Don't kill me," she cried. He saw the terrorist shoot her in the head as she was still shouting. She was still shouting when only half her face remained.

From about sixty feet away he saw them shoot another young girl in the stomach. Rada is a powerful man but as he described all this he had a terrible distant stare. When he described the scene at the tank, huddling behind it with the partygoers he had persuaded to run there with him, he began to break down. He felt certain that he was going to die there and said he kept thinking that he was too young to go. As people were trying to hide behind the tank, another RPG was fired at them. He was blown many feet in the air. As he was flying through the air, he said, he saw everything in his life flash before him, from himself as a baby being held in the hands of his mother to his own young daughter being cradled in his hands. Tears began to stream down his face as he related how he found himself on the desert floor, miraculously still breathing. He ended up hiding in the space beside a young woman who kept saying, "I have kids. I don't want to die." He lied to her and kept telling her that he had spoken to the police and that they were coming and would be there at any moment.

As it was, their group spent hours there, never knowing if the police or army were going to show up. He too had phone footage of them as they were hiding, as well as from later in the day when the army arrived and transported them to a nearby gas station. There they saw some of the Hamas terrorists they had seen earlier in the day, this time detained and bound up by the Israeli army.

There was one last, terrible question I still felt I had to ask them. There had already been multiple reports of rape and sexual violence being perpetrated at the Nova massacre—against men and women. Multiple witnesses as well as first responders confirmed that some of the dead and those who survived had been raped and gang-raped by the terrorists that morning. But equally—and predictably—there were already attempts to deny that any such thing had occurred. Many of the people in the West who had spent recent years saying "Believe all women" did not believe the women who said they had been violated in the Negev that morning. Since the Druze men had seen more than most that morning, I said I was sorry to have to ask this, but that the world was currently seeing real-time denial about this question. Among all the violence they saw that morning, did any of them actually see anyone being raped?

There was a pause and then one of the family said, "No, I only saw them shoot a girl in the genitals."

***

It is a statement of the obvious, of course, but it still needs to be said that all wars have at least two sides. That does not mean, as many Western journalists seem to think, that those sides are morally equal—any more than they will be militarily equal.

One side starts a war and the other responds, though who started it can also be disputed. But it is somewhere in the melee of the response phase that many reporters and others become lost. If they cover the punch, they must also cover the counterpunch. And if the counterpunch is seen as being in some way excessive or even carrying horrors of its own, then it is perfectly possible to get lost yourself.

Something that has dogged Israel in each of its recent conflicts is the idea of "proportionality" and "disproportionality." It is a curious concept that has gained prominence almost solely in wars involving Israel. For years, whenever Israel had responded to an assault on its people, the world's media has fallen into a debate on "proportionality." By contrast, it is rare to hear a discussion of whether the Ukrainian response to Russian aggression is "proportionate" or not. Or whether the Western and Kurdish assault on ISIS strongholds like Mosul, Iraq, was "proportionate" or not.

As it happens, there is no law of war that says you can start a war and then complain when you begin to lose. And there are no wars in human history in which the response to aggression can be exactly calibrated as equal to the initial aggression.

Early in the aftermath of October 7, a number of media outlets started to ask the traditional question of whether Israel's response to the attacks was going to be, or was already, "disproportionate." As I explained to a number of them early in this process, the very idea is absurd. If an enemy breaks into your country, murders your citizens, rapes women at a music festival, and carries hundreds of your citizens into captivity what is the "proportionate" response? Would Israel be permitted to call it quits if it killed precisely the same number of men, women, and children as Hamas had killed that day? Or raped precisely the same number of women? Or kidnapped precisely the same number of innocent civilians from their homes and then held them in underground tunnels? Of course not. In fact, the world would rightly condemn any such move.

There are laws of war. And there is a rightful concern with arbitrary or excessive use of force. But the aim of a war can never be to simply even the scores or respond in kind. The aim of any war is to achieve a strategic, and preferably also moral, victory. Also, one must deter the enemy or any future enemy from trying to achieve their aims in a similar way.

For any country as small as Israel, the necessity of deterrence is absolute. Israel could not fight a war of parity with any of its enemies or neighbors. Iran, for instance, is a country of 88 million people, which is almost ten times the population of Israel. There is no way that in a conflict between Israel and Iran—which trains, sponsors, and funds Hamas—either country could accept the same number of casualties. So Israel has to fight a different kind of war, while under perhaps the closest level of observation on earth.

**

The great Prussian general Carl von Clausewitz (1780–1831) is still studied today because of his posthumously published work, *On War*. It contains an insight into what was once widely seen as one of the key rules of war: that to defeat an enemy, that enemy should be struck at its "center of gravity." For Clausewitz, that center existed where the largest mass of the enemy was concentrated. To hit them there and defeat them in their position of greatest strength was the surest way to achieve victory.

Clausewitz's thinking was based on his study not just of historical battles but of the Napoleonic Wars. He had fought in those wars himself, most famously as part of the unit that prevented reinforcements from reaching Napoleon at the Battle of Waterloo. Whether it was true in his own time, his analysis was soon dated. Modern warfare makes it clear that the best way to defeat an enemy is to knock them off their center of gravity. A cage fighter does not knock over his opponent by simply running at their core strength. In fact that would be the least effective way to bring them to the mat. The best way to force an opponent to the floor is to knock them somewhere they do not expect it—at one of their outer flanks. To knock an enemy off balance it is in fact best to hit them where they are at their weakest.

The presumption that Yahya Sinwar expressed in prison to his Israeli doctor was that Israel was strong because, among other things, it is believed to have a substantial nuclear arsenal. It was the presumption of Sinwar and his backers in Tehran that to hit the Israelis in one of their centers of gravity would mean not just certain failure but also immediately bring about the attackers' own defeat. For example, a strike by Iran or its terror proxies on the Dimona nuclear plant in the Negev would almost certainly be the precursor to the complete destruction of the attacker. The same would be expected of any attack on the headquarters of the IDF or any of the other conventional targets that a conventional army might seek to strike.

But Hamas and Iran are more intelligent than that, and on October 7, 2023, they chose to hit Israel exactly where it did not expect it: a peaceful community of civilians, of dancers at a music party. It is a very long way from hitting an enemy at their center of strategic gravity. But the targets were well chosen, in their eyes. Again, these were places where the Israelis were not expecting to be attacked and for a time it seemed they did not know how to respond when it did happen.

Most terrorist groups do not distinguish between civilians and combatants. Or they regard all the citizens of a country they oppose to be one and the same. The professed logic of Hamas is that since Israel has military conscription for most young Israelis—both men and women—any military-aged Israeli is a legitimate target, whether they are in uniform or not, that the elderly could have served in the army, and that any young Israeli—even a baby—could grow up to be in the military. By this logic absolutely every Israeli is a legitimate target and there is no such thing as innocent and guilty, combatant and noncombatant.

Still, in order to achieve their aims, Hamas certainly attacked some conventional targets on the 7th. Some weeks after the attacks I visited the Erez crossing. This is the northernmost crossing between Israel and the Gaza Strip and was the main thoroughfare between the two. Before October 7, thousands of Palestinians used to pass through this crossing every day, as did trucks going in both directions, carrying goods and supplies. The crossing was the place where Gazans with permits to work inside Israel would cross each day. And it was where Palestinians in search of any medical help they could not get inside Gaza would cross over. The crossing consisted of a large checkpoint with fences and barriers that were raised to allow people and vehicles through.

On the morning of the 7th, Hamas entered Israel from around sixty different places on the border. But taking over the Erez crossing was one of their greatest victories. Videos uploaded by the Qassam Brigades on their own Telegram channels that day showed that the terrorists made a significant breach at the crossing with an explosive device. They then swiftly overwhelmed the soldiers based there in a gun battle. Even weeks later the buildings at the crossing were still covered in shattered glass and other evidence of intensive fighting. Many rooms bore the blast marks across the walls, floors, and ceilings that showed hand grenades had been thrown into them. The soldiers at the crossing were overwhelmed and hundreds of terrorists in hundreds of vehicles poured through with enough weaponry for what one soldier would describe as "a long stay" inside Israel.

For Hamas this was a major coup. Most of the Israeli soldiers and civilian security personnel on duty that morning were killed in the fight, while others were seized on camera and taken captive into Gaza.

Farther south along the border an even worse massacre took place.

The Nahal Oz base was a small observation base near the border and equidistant between Kibbutz Be'eri and Kfar Aza. Unit 414 of the Israeli Border Defense Corps was stationed there. Less than a kilometer from the Gaza border, the unit was almost all female. They were trained in reconnaissance, not combat, and they were unarmed.

In advance of the October 7 attack, Unit 414 was reported to have sent multiple warnings to their superiors about unusual activities at the fence. For some months they reported that Hamas seemed to be preparing to attack the border. These unusual movements went back as far as May 2023. One member of the unit who had served at Nahal Oz but was not there on the 7th said, "It felt like something out of the ordinary was about to happen." She reported that members of the unit had observed training deep inside Gaza "very much like a military routine, rolling over, shooting." Closer to the fence, right before the 7th, she said that she had noticed "ten pickup trucks, three hundred meters away. It was unusual to see those. They stopped at every Hamas post, looking at our cameras, at the fence, at the gates, pointing." This soldier, twenty-year-old Roni Lifshitz, would blame higher-ups in the IDF for ignoring the warnings from her unit.

After the 7th many Israelis speculated about why the warnings from Unit 414 were ignored. Several members of the military told me that the simple explanation was that the warnings of activity close to the fence had just been nothing unique. Such events happened all the time, and when the intelligence from 414 was fed back it was perhaps dismissed as excitable feedback on something that was routine. Lifshitz had another interpretation. "No one really listened to us, mainly because I am not an officer. Because I am just a simple twenty-year-old who knows nothing."[17]

When the border infiltrations began on the morning of the 7th, the Nahal Oz base and nearby kibbutz were two of the first targets to become overwhelmed. A number of the spotters on the base saw the attackers coming but they were swiftly overtaken by hundreds of terrorists. According to one female corporal who survived the attack, on entering the base the terrorists swiftly shot all the security camera screens so nobody could see anything. Then there was no electricity and everything went dark.

Four soldiers from the IDF's Golani Brigade who were posted to defend the base held off as many terrorists as they could, but the latter swarmed through it and then set it on fire. A small number of the young, unarmed female soldiers managed to escape from the blaze through a bathroom window.

There is video footage from inside the base on the morning of the massacre. A collection of young women, some screaming and clearly terrified, are in various states of undress as the male terrorists enter the room. In another video from that morning, young Israeli women in their pajamas, covered in blood, are being tied up by Hamas terrorists wearing military combat gear and carrying rifles. "You dogs, we will step on you," one of the men says to them. One girl, her face streaming with blood, tries to bargain with the terrorists. "I have friends in Palestine," she says to them. "We will kill you all," one of the Hamas men says. Later the same girls can be seen leaning against the wall as their captors pray to Mecca. At various points in the footage the young women are streaming with blood lower down, the result of rape, bullets to their lower bodies, or knife cuts to their tendons to keep them from running away. In one exchange a male terrorist points to the handcuffed girls and says, "Here are the girls that can be impregnated. Here are the Zionists." One of the Hamas terrorists then says coaxingly to one of the terrified young women lined up against the wall, "You are so beautiful."

Sixty-six young soldiers, mainly women, were slaughtered at the base that morning, including fifteen observers. Another seven observers were taken hostage. A final piece of footage taken by Hamas shows a number of the girls limping, their hands still tied, clearly badly wounded, being bundled into a Hamas truck to be taken into Gaza.

⁎

In the immediate aftermath of October 7, the world's media went straight into focusing on what the Israeli retaliation was going to be. It seemed to be almost universally assumed that it would be swift and vengeful. In fact, though, the most notable thing was the pause. It was almost as though Israel had been winded and needed a moment to get back on its feet. Two people in special forces later told me that in the immediate aftermath of the 7th, there was a plan for an operation to go into Gaza by sea and head straight to the Shifa Hospital compound in the center of the Strip. There was intelligence that a majority of the hostages had been taken to the hospital and were being held there. The plan was for the IDF to do an amphibious landing on the shores of Gaza and for the IDF to fight their way street by street to the hospital compound. In the end this was one of a number of plans that were considered, prepared for, and then abandoned. There would have been too many casualties on all sides and too little likelihood of operational success. CCTV footage subsequently found inside the Shifa compound showed a number of the hostages being taken there on the 7th. But it seems possible that they were dispersed swiftly across the Gaza Strip through Hamas's tunnel network and deliberately not kept in a single location.

In fact, while the Israeli Air Force began carrying out targeted strikes against Hamas positions inside Gaza within a week of the 7th, major ground operations did not begin until the 27th. Shortly after they had begun I sat down in Tel Aviv with a retired IDF general who had been involved in the "conception" and in planning for such an eventuality in Gaza. I asked him why it had taken the IDF such a long time to go in. Would it not have been better to go in immediately and to try to chase after the Hamas terrorists right away?

He was adamant that this would have been wrong. He was one of the architects of the plan that was currently unfolding. He said that if they had gone in straightaway they would not have known exactly where they were going and they would have lost many soldiers. The fighting would have been chaotic. He insisted that the IDF needed the weeks after the 7th to get its plan in order, train for the specifics of the operation, and ensure that the response was as clinical and precise as possible.

In the days that followed I went into Gaza to see for myself what this response looked like.

***

One of the biggest breaches of the border fence on the 7th was at a point in the fence near Kibbutz Be'eri. This was where footage that went around the world that morning showed a bulldozer tearing down the wire and security fencing, allowing hundreds of Hamas terrorists and Palestinian civilians to flood through. As well as heading straight for Be'eri, this is where the terrorists also flooded a short way south to Re'im and the site of the Nova party, a short way north to the observation base at Nahal Oz, and much more.

A month after the massacre, in the second week of Israeli ground operations in Gaza, I went through that fence myself. By this point the IDF had considerable hold over the northernmost part of the Strip.

The Israelis had two stated objectives: to free the hostages and to destroy Hamas. Inside Gaza there was now a third objective, which was to separate out the civilian population from the combatants of Hamas, Islamic Jihad, and other terrorist groups. It was already clear that this third objective could be as difficult as the first two. Hamas was reported to be stopping people in the north from leaving their homes, making sure that their fighters who wore civilian clothing and operated from civilian buildings continued to blend in among the civilian population as much as possible. Out of uniform an enemy combatant and a civilian are difficult—sometimes impossible—to tell apart. But that was how Sinwar and Hamas wanted it. They wanted as much confusion as possible.

Added to this is Hamas's well-documented and long-running practice of using civilian infrastructure for military purposes. Although this is against the Geneva Conventions, Hamas has long used civilian homes, mosques, schools, and hospitals (among much else) as sites to store weaponry, create entrances to the underground tunnel network, and—it was already believed—hold Israeli hostages.

To go through the terrorist-made opening into Gaza during those early days of the fighting, you had to pass the fruits of Hamas's labors. On the journey to the meet-up point I went past the woods outside Re'im where the Nova party had taken place. It was already a makeshift shrine, with candles and photographs of the dead and missing and huge burn and explosives marks on the roads all around. Once I was in the IDF's military vehicles, embedded with one of their units, we began to make our slow progress through the fence. On the way we passed the burned-out shells of houses that were all that was left of the community of Be'eri. As the sound of artillery and other munitions exploded all around, there seemed an eerie stillness.

The moment we passed through the fence, there was a palpable rise of tension in the convoy. That divide between the zone of relative peace and the zone of war—the largest leap of all—had been crossed. And while there were rockets being fired from Gaza into Israel throughout this period, at least in Israel at this point you could take your chances. In the zone of war anything can happen and everybody has to be prepared at all times for everything.

Israeli warplanes were flying over the north of the Strip and occasionally the sound of a ground strike could be heard, with the vast plumes of smoke rising up. Tank shells and antitank munitions sounded regularly, as did sudden outbursts of heavy machine-gun fire and other artillery being exchanged by the two sides.

We came upon a Palestinian village that had also borne the brunt of war. Most of the buildings were bombed out, with evidence that a heavy standoff had already taken place here. The usual detritus of war fluttered everywhere—shell casings, everyday utensils, and personal belongings. Then there were the houses that now presented as though in a cross section. Their blown-out walls showing an obscene X-ray of people's lives during wartime. The bedrooms and kitchens of the residents could be seen as though their homes had been carved right through. The piles of people's belongings on the ground revealed not just the evidence of a great fight, but the search for something.

The IDF had just discovered another tunnel entrance in the village. It was right behind a couple of houses, and it seemed astonishing that the IDF were still discovering such tunnel entrances even here, so close to the Israeli side of the border. It had already been carefully opened up. Just a couple of days earlier more young Israeli soldiers had been killed while opening a tunnel entrance only to find it had been booby-trapped by Hamas.

On this occasion the tunnel had already been checked for explosives and for people. As well as being places from which Hamas fighters could at any moment pop up and attack their enemies, they were also known to be the most likely places where Hamas would hide the hostages. Cameras were lowered, and excavations made. Eventually it was decided that this tunnel entrance could be blown up so that no more use could be made of it.

After showing me the tunnel and the ways Hamas had gone about hiding it, a number of detonation experts carefully winched a large amount of dynamite down through the tunnel's entrance. Everybody retreated behind a nearby farm building and then one of the soldiers turned the switch. As we crouched to the ground, the explosion shook everything under our feet. In such a moment you may think of who was farther along these tunnel entrances, what they might have heard, what they thought of the sound, and who they were.

At this point in the conflict the Israelis had set up a border of their own, between the north and south of the Gaza Strip. They had messaged the civilian population of the north—by text messages and leaflet-drops from planes—telling the civilian population there to make their way south. The route south was along the main thoroughfare in the center of Gaza—Salaheddin Street. This passage was already a focal point of the world's media. What had been set up was being termed a "humanitarian corridor." I was among the first outside observers to get to the center of the Gaza Strip and see it for myself.

We crawled along the dirt roads of Gaza to get there and saw the results of the war everywhere. Most buildings were either bombed out or severely damaged and there were no people visible until we got to Salaheddin Street. All the time there was a fear of snipers everywhere, and for any reporter, as for any soldier, this is always the worst fear. With munitions and rockets you can take a relatively relaxed approach. After all, you have as much chance of being hit by a mortar or missile as anyone else. But snipers always induce a special dread. In Ukraine a year earlier, the group I was with was targeted by a sniper from across a Dnipro River bridge, and as one colleague there said, the problem with a sniper is that it feels personal. Largely because it is.

We finally came to the place that the world was talking about. The whole length of Salaheddin Street was a stream of human misery. Men, women, and children of all ages were lining up patiently to move through the Israeli military checkpoint that had been set up to sift for Hamas terrorists and find any Israeli hostages being smuggled south. It was a pitiful sight, and a reminder of the utterly avoidable devastation that Hamas had brought on the people of Gaza.

Every day thousands of Gazans were now moving this way. Twenty-five thousand had done so the day before. Fifty thousand the day before that. And it was not an easy task for the Gazans to simply follow the instructions of the IDF. Just a day earlier, video had emerged from up the highway where the road was strewn with the bodies of Gazan civilians shot by Hamas for trying to make their way south. Hamas had actually been gunning down the Gazan civilians, even as they accused the Israelis of wishing to do the same. Roadways like this one were already covered in bodies.

But here were the living, shuffling forward to relative safety. The process was an incredibly delicate one and every movement had to be carefully watched. The Israeli soldiers at the checkpoint were clearly on the lookout for young men of military age—the people most likely to be Hamas fighters. Some of the people who fit this demographic were taken aside for a further inspection. From a distance the men were told to lift their clothes to show that they were not wearing a suicide vest or other explosive device, or were not smuggling weaponry south. The soldiers at the checkpoint all knew that if one mistake was made, a suicide bomber could kill them and their unit as well as any surrounding civilians.

Of course, the soldiers were also looking for the hostages. This was only weeks after the hostages—including forty Israeli children—had been kidnapped. Over a megaphone the soldiers called out messages in Arabic and in Hebrew. The messages in Arabic advised the people to raise their hands if they understood the message being relayed and, if so, to move slowly toward the checkpoint. Some of the Palestinians waved white flags as they went.

But the occasional messages in Hebrew were the ones that stood out. These told the crowd to make themselves known if they were Israeli. They also said that if there were any Israeli children in the crowds who understood Hebrew, they should jump out now and make themselves known. Having spent the day before with the parents of the kidnapped children, I suppose I was as hopeful as anyone that one of the children I saw in the crowd might make themselves known. No one did. The convoy of Palestinians just moved steadily forward while Israeli troops crouched in formation everywhere, guns pointed at the bombed-out buildings surrounding us.

I can't have been the only person on Salaheddin Street that day thinking the same thing. While all of this was going on above the surface, everywhere beneath our feet were the hundreds of miles of tunnels that Hamas had spent all its years in government building. A network longer than the London Underground. Perhaps the children were not making themselves known at this checkpoint in the middle of the Gaza Strip because they had already been taken south. Perhaps they were not available for the Israelis to find overground because, like Sinwar himself, they had already made the long journey south beneath our feet. The world's attention was also on the Shifa Hospital compound, just south of where we were standing. Hamas claimed that the compound was just a hospital. The Israelis insisted that it was a well-known Hamas command headquarters and a likely storage site for the Israeli hostages as well as for Hamas weapons stockpiles. The world's media was obsessing about the compound, debating the wrongs of Israel operating there. The light was failing and that day's mission had already conspicuously failed—other than in allowing the safe passage of Gazans from north to south.

As we started to think of getting back into the vehicles and heading the other way through the fence to Be'eri, I spoke to a senior IDF commander and decided to do some very British small talk. There was no point asking him what he did. I knew that. I wondered about asking him if he came here often, but in the end asked him simply if he had been here before. "Yes," he replied. "When were you last here?" I asked. "In 2005," he said, with a look of infinite weariness. "When I had to pull family friends from their houses. Now eighteen years later, here I am—back again."

CHAPTER 3

HOW THE WORLD TURNED

History gets rewritten all the time. But it gets rewritten especially fast in wartime. Within a couple of months of the war starting there was a narrative that went something like this: Israel had the world's sympathy and support in the immediate aftermath of the 7th, but had squandered it by prosecuting its war against Hamas in Gaza. In fact, it isn't true that the world's sympathy lasted hours or even minutes. It certainly didn't outlive the day. By the evening of 7th a great crowd of anti-Israel protesters had gathered outside the Israeli embassy in London, among other places, to celebrate the massacres of the day. They waved flags and lit flares while shouting the same war cry and victory cry as the terrorists, "Allahu Akbar!"

The Times Square rally against Israel took place on October 8, while Hamas terrorists were still murdering their way through the south of Israel and the battles were still going on. That same day there was a protest in Manchester, England, at which one of the co-founders of Palestine Action told the crowd, "When we hear the resistance, the Al-Aqsa Flood, we must turn that flood into a tsunami of the whole world."[18]

The following day, October 9, thousands of anti-Israel protesters gathered outside the Israeli embassy in the Kensington section of London to celebrate the attacks, carry out acts of criminal damage on the area, and attack Israel in their own way. Many of the attendees carried signs saying "End the Occupation." Chants included "Intifada, Revolution." Other celebratory crowds gathered outside the prime minister's house at 10 Downing Street, again lighting flares, chanting "Allahu Akbar," and carrying signs praising the massacres. Just one of these read "Decolonization is not a metaphor." In these early celebrations the vast majority of the participants were British Muslims, with the men dressed in terrorist chic and many of the women in burkas and other face coverings.

The first big march against Israel in London took place on October 15, this time with thousands of people in attendance. At this and smaller protests the previous day, whenever the crowd spotted anyone they identified—rightly or wrongly—as Israeli, they chased them. The British police stood by idly during almost all of this, allowing the mob to police the streets themselves, with the Metropolitan Police as some sort of bystander. By October 21, central London was just one of the British cities that came to a standstill as over 100,000 anti-Israel protesters gathered in the capital. That demonstration included the group Hizb ut-Tahrir, an Islamist group that is banned in a number of Muslim and European countries. One of their members in the United Kingdom, Luqman Muqeem, had already declared that the Hamas attacks of October 7 "made us all very, very happy" and had shared a message on social media about "killing the Jews."

At the October 21 rally the group's members held a huge banner reading "Muslim Armies! Rescue the people of Palestine." One of the speakers in London shouted out, "What is the solution to liberate people in the concentration camp called Palestine?" In reply the crowd shouted, "Jihad, jihad, jihad!"[19] Other marchers waved the flags of Islamic Jihad and other terror organizations. Some wore depictions of hang gliders, of the same type as those that had descended on the Nova party. Two young Muslim girls spotted with these—

presumably celebratory—emblems were eventually found and appeared before a Muslim judge who let them go without charges.

Although there was a police presence, throughout all these marches it was perfectly clear who ran the streets. The protesters intimidated not just local shopowners and any locals—especially any Jews—who they thought were in their way. They also tried to intimidate the police, who admitted privately that there was little they could do because they were so vastly outnumbered. As protesters clambered freely over the buildings of Whitehall, covering monuments in terrorist flags and letting off flares and fireworks, the police tried to stop them from assaulting certain monuments. The Cenotaph—Britain's national monument to the fallen of the two world wars—was repeatedly assailed by the protesters, as was the statue of Winston Churchill in Parliament Square and the statues to the airmen of World War II.

It was clear that the British police had either lost control or did not care to take control of the capital. Aware that not all of this was a good look for their organization, the Metropolitan Police issued a number of statements about the failure of their officers to arrest people who were clearly going against the 2006 Terrorism Act, by not just glorifying terrorism but by inciting terrorism on the streets of Britain.

One of these police statements responded to the chants of "Jihad" that had rung throughout the capital. Perhaps the most craven was one that opened with the following claim: "The word jihad has a number of meanings but we know the public will most commonly associate it with terrorism." They went on, "We have specialist counterterrorism officers here in the operations room who have particular knowledge in this area." They went on to claim that the members of the London Metropolitan police's crack Quran-interpretation unit had "assessed" video of some people calling for jihad but "have not identified any offences arising from the specific clip."

Not all Western capitals went the same way as the UK. With one of the largest Muslim populations in Europe, the French government realized early the potential for unrest on their streets. President Emmanuel Macron announced a ban on public protests—something the French president has within his rights to do, and which his predecessors have done many times for a range of protests. And while there were some initial protests, the French police moved to shut them down. As a result, while the center of London was shut down week after week by marches that even the country's own home secretary described as "hate marches," the streets of Paris remained largely tranquil, with shops and restaurants able to go about their business.

In the year that followed October 7, I saw protests in a bewildering array of cities. I saw crowds protesting against Israel in snow-covered Toronto and icy Vancouver, in Sydney and Melbourne, in Johannesburg and Cape Town. Everywhere the same thought came to my mind: *What has it got to do with you?* Why does this one conflict matter so much? Of all the conflicts going on around the world, from Syria to Myanmar, from Sudan to Ukraine, why was this the one that it seemed people from around the world had chosen to immerse themselves in, to throw themselves into, and not against the invaders but against the victim?

In city after city across the West, Jewish communities and others put up posters of the kidnapped Israelis. And in city after city, they were torn down. In almost no place outside of Israel did these posters stay up. Cities in which a poster of a missing dog would be left up with reverence seemed to have a colossal problem with allowing posters of missing Israelis to be put up in the same way. In East London, among many other places, people—often young women—jubilantly and exultantly ripped away at the posters. In Dublin, members of the Bibas family, among other hostage families, went on a visit to the Irish government to plead for the plight of their family members. At the age of just eight months, Kfir Bibas was the youngest hostage stolen into Gaza by Hamas on October 7. One of his family members described getting out onto the streets of Dublin for their visit and seeing a poster of his by then one-year-old relative. The poster had been ripped through, as if there was anything that a one-year-old could have done to make himself a culprit or undeserving of sympathy. But this was the way of the protests outside of Israel. While Israelis protested daily for the return of the hostages, Western populations seemed to consider even recognizing the plight of these people as an affront—a terrible provocation that must be repelled.

Why did this happen? Why did the world's sympathy seem to be not with the victims of the massacres but with the perpetrators? Why had the whole world seemingly got this conflict so completely upside down?

***

Most curious of all—and perhaps more extreme than anywhere else—was the response in the US, where there were street protests against Israel from the moment that October 7 happened. Like Britain, Sweden, Australia, and Canada, these protests sprang up on the streets of major cities. But one of the most curious things about the response in America was that the focal point for the anti-Israel protests turned out to be not among Islamist rabble-rousers on the streets, but at nearly every elite educational institution in the country. If the protests in Britain seemed to be taking place from the bottom up, those in America seemed to be coming from the top down, and not least at its most expensive, elite, and historic schools.

On October 7 itself a number of prominent professors at the most storied American universities gave their immediate takes on X. As the massacre was going on and news of civilians being murdered was already out, Yale University professor Zareena Grewal issued a tweet saying, "Settlers are not civilians. This is not hard." In another post she wrote: "My heart is in my throat. Prayers for Palestinians. Israel is a murderous, genocidal settler state and Palestinians have every right to resist through armed struggle, solidarity #FreePalestine."[20]

Taking to the same platform on the day of the 7th, Albany Law School professor Nina Farnia wrote, "Long live the Palestinian resistance & people of Gaza, tearing down the walls of colonialism and apartheid. As the Biden admin builds more walls at US borders, the people of the world are rising up and tearing walls down. The Palestinians are a beacon to us all."[21]

Shortly after this, Professor Danny Shaw of City University of New York posted his view: "These Zi^nists are straight Babylon swine. We need to protest their neighborhoods. Where is your humanity? Why are you racist arrogant bullies? You think you are better than others? Zionism is beyond a mental illness; it's genocidal disease. #Israel #Gaza #Gaza_Genocide."[22] Cornell University history professor Russell Rickford was filmed at an anti-Israel rally praising Hamas's massacre and telling the crowd, "It was exhilarating. It was exhilarating, it was energizing. And if they weren't exhilarated by this challenge to the monopoly of violence, the shifting of the violence of power, then they would not be human. I was exhilarated."[23]

Also on the day itself, a range of student groups at Harvard University who seemed to be under the impression that the world expected them to have a foreign policy and were awaiting their pronouncement, issued a joint statement: "We, the undersigned student organizations, hold the Israeli regime entirely responsible for all unfolding violence."[24]

On October 12, just five days after the massacre, there was a "martyr vigil" at Georgetown University. Attendees carried signs saying not just "Free Palestine" and "Solidarity Forever" but also "Glory to Our Martyrs."[25] On October 24, at George Washington University, the words "Glory to Our Martyrs" and "Divestment from Zionist Genocide Now" and "Free Palestine from the River to the Sea" were projected onto one of the university libraries.[26] All this and much more set the pattern for what would happen in the months ahead.

Soon tent encampments started going up on American campuses. The tactics everywhere looked strikingly similar and inexplicably coordinated. In each campus the same tents and tactics were on display. As replica protests sprang up at campuses in the UK and Canada, there was speculation about what level of coordination was going on, and who was paying for these often significant-sized protests. By the following July, US director of national intelligence Avril Haines released a statement in which she gave her assessment that the Iranian government, which was the prime backer, financier, and trainer of Hamas, was also "providing financial support to protesters."[27] Iranian agents had already been caught in 2022 attempting to assassinate former secretary of state Mike Pompeo and former national security advisor John Bolton. On American soil. But this seemed to be an intervention in American society at least as brazen as these acts, and markedly more successful.

It was striking from the outset that the same misunderstanding seemed to have broken out. This misunderstanding centered on the idea that the university in question was somehow involved in the purported Israeli "genocide" that was taking place. It was a claim that was almost never explained. In what way were these campuses "investing" in or "supporting" genocide? In the search for someone to blame for the funding of a foreign war, an Ivy League campus in another country seems like a surprising place to start. And while the claim was never explained, the delusion that America's universities were somehow part of Israel's war machine emerged almost everywhere. Perhaps some of the students—and certainly those who were directing them—knew that their institution was not in any way involved in supporting Israel's war against Hamas. But they wanted to protest the war and so pretending their university was somehow central to the conflict gave them something close to home at which they could direct their rage.

One of the campuses that went the furthest down this route was Columbia University in New York. At protests on the campus that went on for an entire academic year, protesters were filmed calling for jihad and issuing open calls for violence. Among the calls for terrorism screamed at Columbia in 2023–24 were "Al-Qassam you make us proud! Take another soldier out!" "We say justice, you say how? Burn Tel Aviv to the ground!" "Hamas we love you. We support your rockets too!" "Red, black, green, and white, we support

Hamas' fight!" "It is right to rebel, Al-Qassam, give them hell!" and "It is right to rebel, Hamas give them hell!"[28]

Protesters were also filmed vowing to repeat the terrorist attacks of October 7. One speaker used the platform of Columbia's protest movement to promise more massacres. Of October 7 he screamed that it "[w]ill happen not 1 more time, not 5 more times, not 10 more times, not 100 more times, not 1,000 more times, but 10,000 times!"[29]

In order to try to work out what was happening, students from the Columbia student newspaper did a set of interviews with people involved in the protests. Among others they interviewed people who were at the first tent "encampment." The accounts of these students and their opinions were fascinating. For instance, Liam, a junior who had joined the first encampment at its earliest stages, related that "[f]or me, joining was a bit of an impulsive decision. I was like, *I just need to do it.* I take out $50,000 in student loans every single year, and it sucks. I have to work 20 hours a week to pay off the interest. I hate sitting here knowing I'm working my ass off only so my money can go to supporting genocide."

Others seemed to think that not attending classes and instead sitting outside their classrooms in a tent was what Columbia student life was all about. One senior student identified only as "K" said, "I had learned so much about the precedent of organizing at Columbia and understanding that we have this massive history of protests and that there are all these eyes on us. I have so much privilege being here. I'm from a first-gen, low-income background. So I knew that if there was ever going to be an escalation, it was something I wanted to be a part of." The central claim of many of these protesters was not just that Israel was a terrorist state that needed to be dismantled, but also that activism of the kind these students were involved in could actually make it happen. They had been trained to believe that the highest form of student life is protest and they were trying to live up to the examples that had been set.

At the start of the Columbia protest camp, student K said that he had worried it might be a mistake to be a part of it because the encampment might not be sufficiently well organized. In hindsight he said that this fear had been unfounded. "We racked up so many food donations it was ridiculous. We started organizing all the food stuff because it was slowly coming in a bunch of carts." These included soy milk. "I was like, 'At least they have alternative milk.'" But not everything in the camp was so rosy. K related that in the early days, the lavatory facilities were not as full of promise as the selection of alternative milks. In the early days the camp was meant to have a camping toilet but K complained that it wasn't even a bucket. It was more "a bucket with no bottom, and it had a little lip thing and these little black trash bags that you put on there. You would do your thing, and there were poo gels to make it smell better. And then you would close up the bag and throw it in the bigger bag of everyone's shit." Still, it seems that K and other protesters thought that this was a rich and rewarding way to profit from their experience as $50,000-a-year students at Columbia.

Whether or not the students were missing much by skipping classes was a lively debate. Steven, another junior who had joined the encampment, said, "I missed a lecture on Wednesday about literature and cultures of struggle in South Africa." Two students who had made the class told him afterward, "You didn't miss anything."[30]

From snapshots like this it was unclear whether there was more encouragement of protest and radicalization among the tents on the university's South Lawn or in the teaching activities inside Columbia's classrooms. As people who had been on faculty told me during the period in which the encampment was going on, for many years the faculty had expressed a number of views to students as points of truth. These included (as K had said) the idea that the highest expression of higher education in America is to be found in creating "activists"—people who will know that when their time comes they can have their own 1968 moment, or perhaps something even grander. Second, there was the idea, apparently baked into the curriculum across every discipline, that America itself was a colonialist, racist, and apartheid state in its past—and potentially in its present—but that anyone who wanted to identify a state guilty of all of these crimes and more could find its most egregious exemplar in the State of Israel.

It is true that there were some students—and one solitary Jewish professor at Columbia—who deeply objected to all this. The slogan "From the river to the sea" was omnipresent but it was also a subject of considerable debate as to whether it broke some speech boundaries. In some ways that debate was academic because it turned out that one of the other favorite slogans of the encampment—"Globalize the intifada"—was absolutely fine as well.

There was occasional debate about what these slogans meant. But to anyone who was Jewish, or anyone who had any knowledge of recent Jewish history, the slogans could not have been clearer.

Intifada is not a neutral term, any more than "Sieg heil" is a phrase that simply means "Hail victory." Since the 1980s, Palestinian leaders and clerics have twice called for an "intifada" against the Jewish state. The First Intifada (1987–93) and the Second Intifada (2000–2005) were among the bloodiest periods in Israel's history. During those periods Israelis could not board a bus without wondering whether a Palestinian terrorist was going to detonate a suicide vest and turn the vehicle into a charnel house. Terrorist attacks against innocent civilians happened on a weekly, sometimes daily, basis for years. They often targeted people of the same age as those who spent the aftermath of October 7 calling for just such a thing.

For example, on June 1, 2001, during a beautiful summer evening in Tel Aviv, scores of young Israelis were milling around the city's beachfront, many of them lining up to get into a nightclub exactly like that which students from Columbia and Harvard might go to on the weekend. The Dolphinarium was packed that evening. A Hamas terrorist detonated a bomb right beside a group of young women in line for the club. It killed twenty-one of them. Sixteen of them were teenagers. The youngest, who was also in the area, was fourteen-year-old Maria Tagilchev. Eyewitnesses described the limbs of the young victims lying strewn all across the road. Many of the bodies lay in piles.

Did the protesters at American colleges know this? One of the American student protest leaders, Khymani James (pronouns "he/she/they"), said during the Columbia protests that "Zionists don't deserve to live. . . . I feel very comfortable, very comfortable, calling for those people to die." When people like this called for "intifada" did they have any idea of what they were actually calling for? Perhaps some did, and others just went along for the ride in ignorance. But the reality of what they were calling for was something that had led to the deaths not just of their contemporaries but of their fellow Americans.

On July 31, 2002, during the Second Intifada, students at the Hebrew University of Jerusalem were enjoying a lunchtime break in the crowded cafeteria of the Frank Sinatra International Student Center. A bomb planted by Hamas exploded as they were ordering their coffees and eating their lunch. Survivors streamed out—eighty-five of them seriously wounded—with limbs missing and burns from which they would never recover. Among the nine people lying dead inside the wreckage of the cafeteria were five American students, including Benjamin Blutstein, twenty-five, from Harrisburg, Pennsylvania; Marla Bennett, twenty-four, from San Diego; and David Gritz, twenty-four, from Massachusetts.[31]

While many of the students on American college campuses were calling for "intifada" they were also busily accusing Israel of being an "apartheid state." Perhaps some of them knew that almost a fifth of the population of Israel are Arabs. Perhaps they imagined that these people do not enjoy the same rights as Jews in Israel. But clearly none of them were aware of the name George Khoury. He was a twenty-year-old Arab student who was also at the Hebrew University of Jerusalem. On March 19, 2004, he went out jogging. Members of the Al-Aqsa Martyrs Brigade thought Khoury was a Jew, and so they shot him—first in the stomach, and then in the neck and the head, just to make sure. Khoury's distraught father called the murder "barbaric." "Terrorism," he later said, "is blind."[32]

But perhaps not as blind as people like thirty-three-year-old Jo-hannah King-Slutzky, a Columbia PhD student in English and "com-parative literature." She was one of the protest leaders who said that she and other people in the encampment needed "humanitarian aid" to continue their protest. According to her Columbia web page, the person who did this performative suffering while calling for "inti-fada" spends her academic time researching "theories of the imagi-nation and poetry as interpreted through a Marxian lens in order to update and propose an alternative to historicist ideological critiques of the Romantic imagination."[33] Did she or any of the other protest leaders at Columbia know the names of people many years younger than them who never made it into their twenties or thirties because of the exact same "intifada" that King-Slutzky and friends were call-ing for? While calling for fresh supplies for her encampment, did she or the other protesters know how lucky they were to be able to grow up at all?

***

Of course, it is possible to overstress the free speech debates of stu-dent protesters on American college campuses. Harvard, Columbia, and UCLA are not America. They are not the American street. But they are among America's elite institutions, and to that extent what goes on at such places—not least because all these institutions bene-fit from government grants—does matter. Certainly the effect of the opinions expressed on such campuses tells us something about the generation coming up in America and perhaps across the West.

In December 2023, just two months after the Hamas massacres, a Harvard CAPS/Harris poll asked Americans about their support of Israel. Overall the survey found that 81 percent of respondents backed Israel in its fight against Hamas. The only age demographic in America in which this was not the case was the youngest one. Among eighteen- to twenty-four-year-olds polled, an extraordinary 51 percent said they agreed with the statement that Israel "should be ended and given to Hamas and the Palestinians." Fully 60 percent of people in the same age bracket agreed that the attacks of October 7 were justified. When the questions came closer to home, the poll showed that 53 percent of eighteen- to twenty-four-year-olds believed students should be able to advocate the genocide of the Jews without sanction.[34]

It is bewildering that these opinions come from the exact same generation of students who were brought up to believe that words are violence and that silence is violence. Yet calls for genocide appear to be just about the only thing that is not violent.

If anyone was under any illusions over whether such views were top-down or bottom-up in the American academy, events in the same month as this poll was taken suggested that it was clearly both at once.

In early December 2023, a congressional committee on education and the workforce held a hearing on "Holding Campus Leaders Accountable and Confronting Antisemitism." Among those called in for questioning were the presidents of three colleges that had some of the worst outbreaks of anti-Semitism since October 7—Harvard, MIT, and the University of Pennsylvania. Congress was taking an interest in the activities of these protests, the disruption they were causing, and why college administrators were having such a difficult time working out where free speech ended and incitement to violence began.

At the hearing in Washington, Claudine Gay of Harvard, Liz Magill of UPenn, and Sally Kornbluth of MIT were asked repeatedly whether they thought that racist, anti-Semitic abuse of the kind that had gone on across their campuses was acceptable or not. One of the many strange things about their responses was that they were delivered in pure legalese. Indeed the answers sounded like they were prepared by lawyers ahead of time in order to cover the legal backs of the institutions in question. If the answers given sounded like they were composed by lawyers, it is because they were.

For instance, Representative Elise Stefanik asked the president

of Harvard whether she believed that "hateful speech is contrary
to Harvard's code of conduct or is it allowed at Harvard?" Gay replied, "It is at odds with the value of Harvard, but . . . we embrace
a commitment to free expression even of views that are objection-
able, offensive, hateful." The idea that Claudine Gay actually believed in free expression at Harvard was provably untrue. Four years
earlier, in 2019, she was one of the Harvard faculty who decided
not to renew the contract of Harvard Law School professor Ronald
Sullivan Jr. as a faculty dean. His crime had been to have been one of
the members of the defense team for disgraced movie mogul Harvey
Weinstein. A number of students complained that it was wrong that
someone who acted on such a defense team should be at Harvard.
Instead of using the opportunity to explain the basis of the right to
a defense in US law, Gay was one of those who decided it was easier
to get rid of Sullivan.[35]

It was also perfectly obvious to members of the congressional
committee that no other minority group in America would be expected to put up with the type of incitement that had become the
norm against Jews at American Ivy League campuses. If there had
been even one call for, say, the lynching of black Americans or the
killing of trans people, it could be said with a considerable degree of
certainty that such a student would be detained, carted off campus,
expelled, and most likely hit with criminal charges. Yet when it came
to open calls for genocide against the Jewish people, Gay and her
fellow college heads suddenly became First Amendment absolutists
and more.

Each college president was asked whether calls on their campus
for the genocide of Jews constituted bullying and harassment. Kornbluth of MIT said that calls for "intifada," for instance, would "de-
pend on the context when calling for the elimination of the Jewish
people." Magill was asked if "calling for the genocide of Jews vio-
late[s] Penn's rules or code of conduct" if it leads to "bullying and
harassment." Magill replied, "It is a context-dependent decision."
Magill had a strange smirk on her face while she was saying all this,

as though she believed she was cleverly running rings around the congresswoman or was exasperated to be even asked such questions. When Gay was asked whether calling for the genocide of Jews violates "Harvard's rules of bullying and harassment? Yes or no," she too replied, "It can be, depending on the context." Pressed and pressed, Gay, like the others, continued to insist that all of this depends on context.[36]

As it happened, a friend of mine at MIT called me after these hearings. I remarked that the college presidents' replies all sounded like they had been produced by artificial intelligence, so devoid were they of any human feeling. My friend suggested we try something out and ask ChatGPT the same questions that Elise Stefanik had asked the three Ivy League presidents. The results were enlightening. When we asked ChatGPT whether calling for the genocide of Jews violates Harvard's code of conduct, the app replied, "Advocating for genocide violates Harvard University's policies against hate speech and harassment, which are outlined in their code of conduct. They prioritize creating a safe and inclusive environment for all members of the community." We went on to ask the app, "Are there any contexts in which it is permissible? Yes or no?" ChatGPT replied, "No, advocating for genocide is not permissible in any context at Harvard University or in most ethical frameworks." Finally we asked, "You say 'most' ethical frameworks in which it is permissible?" only for the app to reply, "Advocating for genocide is generally considered unacceptable in nearly all ethical frameworks due to its severe violation of human rights and moral principles."

So there we had it. Artificial though the answers of the college presidents may have sounded, the exercise suggested something rather different, which was not just that artificial intelligence expressed a better knowledge and intelligence than the heads of these three institutions about their own codes of conduct. It also showed that when it came to ethical frameworks and an understanding of them, ChatGPT was distinctly more moral than the presidents of Harvard, UPenn, and MIT.

✻✻✻

Some Jewish students and professors also testified in front of Congress about their own experiences. But this drew even more ire, as though Jewish students who testified to their experience on a US campus were somehow to be treated as traitors and quislings.

One freshman student, Parker De Deker, told Columbia student journalists that he believed that the camping students had the total rights of "sitting there and exercising their rights to free speech and advocating for peace in the Middle East." He was also keen to stress that in his own view, "advocating for peace in the Middle East is not anti-Semitism." He went on, "What is anti-Semitism, though, is the numerous experiences I've been faced with. Wednesday evening, I was walking from my dorm to go to Chabad, a space for Jewish students at Columbia, and someone yells, 'You fucking Jew, you keep on testifying, you fucking Jew.' I had clearly not been in Washington, DC, that day testifying. I was not involved in anything political. I was simply a Jewish student wearing my yarmulke."[37]

But students like him were facing a movement that was not just focused on Jews, but it seemed to be focused on Jews as a means to address every problem in the world.

A lot has been written in recent years about the theory of "intersectionality"—a convoluted word for an even more convoluted idea. That is, that all oppressions in the world are interlocked, and that to unlock one form of oppression is to go some way to unlocking them all. Throughout the months of protest many people noticed that the protesting students at Columbia, Barnard, and dozens of other American campuses all had a similar costume. Keffiyehs, obviously—aping their Palestinian heroes. But added to this form of radical chic there was a widespread wearing of face masks from the era of Covid.

There was a virtue in wearing these masks, of course, which is that if you are joining in calls for terrorism against a minority, it may be wise to cover your face—as the Ku Klux Klan also did. The masks suggested a certain coyness or shame among many of the protesters—as though they had one eye on the global revolution and the other on their future job prospects. But as one of the posters I saw plastered all over Columbia showed, everything can be connected.

The poster seemed innocuous. "Thank you for masking" was the headline. Beneath it the poster stated: "Disability oppression is intertwined with Israel's settler-colonial project in Palestine." You may have thought, like me, when you read that, *Huh?* But the explanation continued. It claimed that Israeli officials had refused to distribute Covid vaccines in the West Bank and the Gaza Strip, which is a flatout lie. The Israeli government handed Covid vaccine distribution over to the Palestinian Authority, partly because it was unclear how many Palestinians would even take a vaccine that was given to them by the Israelis. Still the poster continued, "Covid continues to spread unchecked in Palestine today." And "Covid is still a global struggle." But the crux of the matter was that, as the poster concluded, "Disability justice and anti-imperialism includes wearing a mask beyond the encampment." In other words, when a student wore a Covid face mask they could do so safe in the knowledge that they were not just protecting themselves from being recognized, but were also—in the act of wearing a cloth mask—fighting imperialism in America and the Middle East.

Whether it was Covid protocols or the Middle East, it was clear that the Jews were the focus of any and every problem.

Another Jewish student at Columbia, a senior, Eve, saw a video on her phone of a Columbia student standing beside a group of visibly Jewish students on campus. The protester was holding a sign that read "Al-Qasam's Next Targets" and was pointing it at the Jewish students ("my friends," as Eve put it). She went straight to where she knew the video was being shot. "I thought my friend was going to get punched." But as is often the case, the pro-terrorist students were experimenting with violence and working out the limits of their intimidation tactics. As Eve said, by the time she got there and joined her Jewish friends, "They were screaming at us: 'You fucking inbreds,' 'Uncultured-ass bitches,' and 'All you do is colonize.'" As the Jewish students started to walk off campus, a new person screamed at them, "Go back to Poland!"[38]

***

During these protests a number of interesting things emerged. The first was that a form of revolutionary cosplay appeared to be going on. Students did not require "humanitarian aid," but a large number seemed to enjoy the pretense, as well as the identity that the protests gave them. After the first encampment at Columbia was cleared, a second encampment sprang up. And like the first, it seemed that part of what was on offer was an identity for students who clearly felt they didn't have one but deeply needed one. An undergraduate at the second encampment, Jillian, told a student journalist about the activities available: "We had dabka lessons, which is a Palestinian dance. We had the People's Library for Liberated Learning. There were books in there we could check out. A main takeaway for me was applying the learning I've done in my own classes, where we have talked about transnational movements against imperialism, capitalism, colonization. There was a really strong understanding that all of these struggles were intertwined."[39]

Still it was strange to hear students pick up the slogans and struggles of the most extreme Palestinian groups. For instance, "From the River to the Sea" was one of the most common slogans heard at the encampments and other protests across the West. Many people questioned about this chant didn't seem to know which river they were talking about or what the sea in question might be. But there did seem to be a general awareness that this slogan was a call for the elimination of the Jewish state. After all, if "Palestine" is to be "free from the river to the sea," that means a Palestinian state should exist from the Jordan River to the Mediterranean Sea. That means that the whole of the land of Israel should be occupied by the Palestinians. And since both Hamas and the more moderate Palestinian Authority have insisted from their beginnings right to the present that there must not be one Jew in such a state—that it must be, to borrow a term from history, *Judenrein,* or *cleared of Jews*—then that means the Jews must all either be killed or forcibly evacuated from the land of Israel. None of the student protest leaders or their followers ever put forward any nongenocidal plan for the orderly removal of the Jews of Israel. So it is not a stretch to say that the chant was genocidal.

But two further aspects of the protesters' behavior stood out. The first was the idea that chanting something repeatedly, day in and day out, might achieve something. Many of the protesters shouted themselves hoarse by chanting "From the River to the Sea" and similar slogans. What is interesting about this is that it is the absolute antithesis of what communication in a university is meant to be about. Academic life is meant to be about reasoning, winning arguments with facts and persuasion. What the protesters were doing was the opposite of such communication. At the same time they were demanding that the American and Israeli governments should do what they want, they were communicating their message by a form of intellectual bludgeoning. It was as though to say a thing again and again might, in time, force the people they were trying to persuade to change their minds. That is an odd art of persuasion, for it expects not a change of mind but a demand that another person accept their attitudes. It is like hitting someone over the head repeatedly. But it is not intended to persuade. It is intended to beat another party into submission.

The second aspect of the protests that were interesting was the way in which the protesters aped one aspect of the behavior of Hamas at a lower level of violence. At the campuses where police were deployed, it seemed that the students wanted the police to harm them—or at least harm the student next to them. This was a version of the radicalism employed by the student protesters of the 1960s who believed that if you provoked the police enough, they would reveal the violence of the state, force the government to rip off its mask, and reveal the true fascist face of capitalist democracy. The provocations of faculty and students in 2023–24 had the same tenor, but with a Hamas twist. Just as the strategy of Hamas in Gaza was to push the Israelis into killing innocent civilians in their search for hostages and terrorists, so the American students seemed to want to be hurt for the cameras. The levels of violence were different, to be sure. But the aim was the same: hurt me for the cameras and then the whole world will be able to see what you are really like.

The similarity of these tactics and their usefulness not only brought the student protesters to the attention of members of Congress and other politicians in the West. They also caught the eye of a number of notable foreign leaders.

In May 2024, one of the leaders of Hamas, Khaled Mashal, addressed a conference in Istanbul hosted by the Muslim Brotherhood. The conference was called "Flood of the Free." During his remarks the Hamas leader made sure to thank the "great student flood" that had emerged at American, British, and other Western universities. Mashal also spoke of the multipronged international strategy that he and his colleagues in Hamas were pursuing. In his words there needed to be a "financial flood" to supply the Palestinian people with weapons. He called for an even greater "media flood" to spread the narrative that Hamas endorsed. He called for a "legal flood" involving moves such as those already afoot at the International Criminal Court (ICC) to prosecute Israel's leaders. He reminded his audience that there should also be a flow of blood, specifically a "jihadi flood," from holy war. In the words of Hamas's own leadership, what students on Western campuses were doing was all part of Hamas's plan. A plan that led direct from campus demonstrations in America to jihad on the streets of Israel.[40]

The endorsements kept coming. In May 2024, the supreme leader of the Iranian revolutionary Islamic government, Ayatollah Ali Khamenei, wrote a letter to the students of America. At the opening of his letter the leader of the Islamic Revolution thanked and praised the students protesting on American campuses: "You are now part of the Resistance Front, and you have begun a dignified struggle under the ruthless police pressure of your government that evidently defends the oppressive and brutal Zionist regime." There's more than one irony in this, but in the years since the Islamic Revolution in 1979, Khamenei and his predecessor, Ayatollah Khomeini, have killed, tortured, and imprisoned thousands of Iranian students—especially when they have come out and protested against their own government. In 2009 alone, during the thwarted "Green Revolution," many students came out onto the streets of Iran. The government's Basij security forces shot the student protesters in public. The young Iranian philosophy student Neda Agha-Soltan was shot through the chest by a member of Khamenei's police force; the shooting was caught on camera. After the crackdown the Iranian authorities ordered the digging of mass graves for the bodies of those who were murdered and tortured. Students who were detained in the regime's prisons in the aftermath of these protests attested to having been raped in prison, with batons and bottles.

But the ayatollah wasn't going to allow something like his own track record to get in the way of destabilizing America. In his letter to American students, Khamenei talked about "Zionist" and US government involvement in "state terrorism and ongoing injustice." He said, "I want to assure you that today, the situation is changing. Another fate awaits the sensitive region of West Asia. Many consciences have awakened on a global scale, and the truth is becoming clear. The Resistance Front has also grown stronger and will continue to strengthen while history is also turning a new page." He concluded his salutations with citations from the Quran and said, "I empathise with you, young people, and I respect your steadfastness."[41]

The fact that 2024 saw a record surge in executions inside Iran was left out of Khamenei's letter to American students, as was the fact that his regime publicly executes people convicted of homosexuality by hanging them from cranes. Khamenei was clearly pleased

with the ignorance of America's students and his own ability to fo-
ment dissent in a country he describes as "The Great Satan."

***

One of the most striking things about this is that all of it has happened before. Most Israelis of a certain age have a very clear memory
of the people who joined the Palestine Liberation Organization in its
early years.

The PLO was founded in 1964. Yasser Arafat, who was born in
Egypt, became its chairman five years later. For those people in the
West who chant about Israeli "occupation," the year 1964 ought to
be suggestive. After all, when Arafat and his friends founded their
movement they did so in order to object to "Israeli occupation." Yet
1964 was three years before the Six-Day War of 1967, when Israel
took control of Judea and Samaria (the West Bank) and Gaza. The
Israelis did so in order to prevent another invasion of Israel from
these territories. While the legal status of the West Bank is still disputed, what cannot be disputed is that Israel holding the hills of Judea and Samaria prevents the thin slice of land that is Israel from
being under constant rocket attack from those hills. Go to the hills
of Judea and Samaria at night and you will see the lights of Tel Aviv
blinking clearly in the distance.

In 1964, these territories were not in any sense "occupied." You
might say that they were occupied by Jordan and Egypt, but in no sense
were they occupied by Israel. But Arafat and his friends also called for
the liberation of the "occupied territories" a full three years before the
war of 1967, when Israel responded to its threatened annihilation by
seizing control of the Golan Heights from Syria. Again, if an enemy
army occupied the Golan Heights they would be in rocket range of all
the rest of Israel. The official view of the British Foreign Office, among
others, remains that the Golan Heights are "occupied" and that the
Israeli government should hand this territory over to Assad (or any
leader who succeeded him), as if he did not have enough land in which

to massacre his own people after 2011. But whatever the status of the Golan Heights today, there was no occupation in 1964. The PLO was set up in 1964 because it believed that all of Israel was an occupying force and that nothing but the complete "liberation" of every piece of the land, including Tel Aviv and Haifa, would be sufficient.

But even then, many Western celebrities and intellectuals joined in this movement. The PLO may have been kicked out of Jordan in 1971 after bringing terrorism to that land. And it may have been kicked out of Lebanon in 1982 after bringing terrorism to that country. And it may have finally left Tunisia in 1991 after bringing violence to that place too. But the organization could always rely on a certain type of Westerner to sprinkle some celebrity stardust on their campaign. The gay French author Jean Genet wrote an entire love letter to the Palestinian liberation movement in an obscene 1970 book called *Prisoner of Love*.

In 1977 the British-born, Oscar-winning actress Vanessa Redgrave even made sure to have herself filmed dancing around a campfire with the PLO, waving a Kalashnikov rifle. She could hardly have claimed ignorance about the movement she had joined. This was just five years after the massacre of the Israeli athletes at the Munich Olympics, and just a year after Israeli special forces carried out a raid in Entebbe, Uganda, to rescue hijacked passengers.

In 2023, a month after the October 7 massacre, another actress, Susan Sarandon, addressed an anti-Israel protest near Bryant Park in Manhattan. At that protest the crowds chanted "From the river to the sea," "Israel is a racist state," and "There is only one solution—intifada, revolution." It was a reminder, if such was needed, that there is always a type of Westerner who is desperate to see the land soaked with blood—so long as it is not their own.

***

That early period of Western anti-Zionism is important for many reasons. One is the light it shines on what has happened in much of the West since October 7. But perhaps the best way to understand it is to go back to postwar Germany and the generation that grew up after 1945.

As Paul Berman recounts in his 2005 book, *Power and the Idealists*, the generation that grew up in Germany after World War II had pretty much only one guiding political principle by which to orient themselves. Essentially that was Don't be Nazis. Don't be like our parents' generation. It seems to be similar to the guiding principle that many young American and Western students have today. And as guiding principles go, it isn't a bad one. But as the postwar political left in Germany was to learn, it was also insufficient.[42]

The German left that grew up in the 1950s and '60s assumed that they were going to be able to hold fast to this principle. They were of the left, after all. Many of them were also involved in the nascent green movement. But by the 1970s there were parts of these movements that had taken a distinctly revolutionary turn. Many of the people involved would go on to be significant figures in German politics, not least the future German foreign minister and vice chancellor Joschka Fischer. The most radical went into the notorious Baader-Meinhof Group, who were dedicated to revolutionary communist ideals and "anti-imperialism." Many of their allies fell away as the group descended further into political violence—including kidnappings and bombings.

But the most interesting development was the movement's adoption of the Palestinian cause. In the aftermath of the 1967 and 1973 wars in Israel, something crucial shifted in the international left's attitudes toward the Jewish state. From 1948 until 1967, Israel had broad sympathy and support from the international left. In part this was because of the leftist origins of the state itself including the kibbutznik movement. Time spent working on a kibbutz in Israel was almost a rite of passage for leftists in those days. At that time there was no contradiction in a figure like the British Labour Party leader Harold Wilson being an ardent Zionist and even writing a book (*The Chariot of Israel*, 1981) that expressed those sentiments. Leftists supported Israel for a number of reasons, but one that has often been a baseline of left-wing politics was support for the perceived underdog. From 1948 to 1967, Israel was the plucky underdog in the Middle East. Its neighbors had attempted to wipe it out but the Israelis had seen them off.

Then in 1967, and even more so in 1973, something changed. If Israel had been David up until this moment, a number of its supporters now saw it as having transformed into Goliath. The fact that Israel was still a tiny country with a tiny population in comparison with its neighbors was not the point. It now came to be seen by many as the overdog.

The change came about in part because Israel had won those two wars with relative ease. Also, they had taken ground from the places their enemy had attacked them from (principally Judea and Samaria and the Golan Heights). At the same time the idea grew that the Arabs who lived in Israel were not to be referred to as Arabs, like their brothers and sisters in Egypt, Jordan, or Iraq, but rather as "Palestinians" with a unique and long-recognized identity of their own. With the turning of the Arabs into Palestinians it was now the Palestinians who were the beleaguered minority and the Israelis who were seen as the oppressive majority. So the Palestinians became the new Jews, with the Jews becoming the imperialist, brutish overlords.

Members of the German left took this to its most logical conclusion. Solidarity with the Palestinian cause became a shibboleth on the German left as much as support for the Jews may have been in the 1950s. Palestinian nationalist movements were suddenly anti-imperialist and anticolonialist movements. And it was here that a remarkable turn occurred. Many parts of the New Left made common cause with the various militant Palestinian factions that had already emerged, including the Popular Front for the Liberation of Palestine. Groups like the so-called Revolutionary Cells went into active cooperation with them. Left-wing groups coordinated with the Palestinian terrorists who carried out the massacre of Israeli athletes at the Munich Olympics in 1972. They worked with Ilich Ramírez Sán-chez, aka Carlos the Jackal, who targeted Jews around the world, including prominent businessmen in London. Most notoriously, they were central to one of the worst terrorist events of the 1970s.

June 1976 brought some clarity. That was when the Revolution-ary Cells, saying that they were acting on behalf of imprisoned Palestinian terrorists, hijacked Air France flight 139 as it flew from Athens to Paris. The hijackers ordered the flight to change its route and eventually land in Entebbe, Uganda.

Only after the standoff did the identities of the hijackers become known. Their leader was a man named Wilfried Böse, a well-known figure on the German left, an acquaintance of Fischer, and a prom-inent member of various groups, including Frankfurt's Black Pan-ther solidarity committee. And it was on the hijacked plane, on the tarmac of Entebbe airport, that Böse and his German comrades did something remarkable—or not. They arranged a "selection" of the passengers, dividing them into Jews and non-Jews. The Jews were put on one side of the plane and the non-Jews on the other, with the Jewish passengers slated for execution. Some apologists for the group claimed afterward that the "selection" was "only" of Israelis. But it was not. American Jews and Belgian Jews, among others on the flight, were put to the same side as their fellow Jews.

The German "guards" screamed "Schnell!" at the Jews—hurry up—and told them at gunpoint where to move. At one point a Jew-ish hostage, who was one of a number of Holocaust survivors among the hijacked, showed Böse the number tattooed onto his arm from the Nazi concentration camps. The hostage reportedly told Böse that he had supposed that a new and different generation had grown up in Germany, but now he suspected the Nazis had not gone away after all.

Böse was reportedly indignant, and told the Jewish hostage that he himself was in fact completely different from the Nazis. What his group wanted was not Nazism but worldwide Marxist revolution.[43]

One of the other German hijackers of the plane, Brigitte Kuhlmann, pistol-whipped the passengers and identified a number of non-Israeli Jews and detained them because she spotted their prayer shawls. As the standoff continued the only hostages that Böse and his colleagues would release were the non-Jewish ones.

On that occasion, famously, an Israeli unit carried out a successful raid at the airport and saved the majority of the hostages. The only IDF soldier to fall in the operation was Yonatan Netanyahu, brother of future Israeli prime minister Benjamin Netanyahu.

But the story of Böse, Kuhlmann, and their accomplices is a highly suggestive one. If you had asked any of them during their youth if they ever expected to be carrying out a "selection" of Jews, they would almost certainly have said no. If you had asked them if they ever imagined that their lives would end with them desperately trying to hold on to Jewish hostages, they would almost certainly have said no. But it turned out that "anti-Nazism" was not enough. The German left of that generation showed that somebody's whole political foundations could be based on anti-Nazism, only for them to end up behaving exactly like Nazis.

***

There is one question that must at some point be confronted: Why the Jews?

It seems to be an eternal question. Why have the Jews been singled out and hated by so many people throughout history? Why are they still hated by so many people today?

For anti-Semites the history of anti-Semitism is itself a justification for anti-Semitism. In their rationale the fact that the Jewish people have been so hated and so persecuted so often is proof that there is something wrong with them.

In fact, most forms of anti-Semitism throughout history follow certain patterns. Christian anti-Semitism and Islamic anti-Semitism are very different. Yet both originate in hostility to the Jews for their rejection of the new faith. Yet among all bigotries and prejudices one especially distinctive thing about anti-Semitism is that it is a shapeshifter. As the late rabbi Jonathan Sacks, among many others, pointed out, Jews were once hated because of their religion. Then sometime after the Enlightenment it became hard to hate people because of their religion. At that point the Jews were hated because of their race. Then, after the twentieth century it became unacceptable to hate people because of their race. So, in the twenty-first century, when civilized people cannot hate the Jews for their religion or their race, Jews can be hated for having a state—and for defending it.

That does not simply mean that people will always find a reason. The truth is harder than that.

The reason? Anti-Semitism locks Jews in an unresolvable set of challenges. Gregor von Rezzori captured one aspect of this in his masterful, if luridly titled, novel, *Memoirs of an Anti-Semite*, published in 1979. In his work, von Rezzori, who was born in the Hapsburg Empire just before it fell apart, gives snapshots of the attitudes that existed in those times. In one especially evocative chapter he relates the tale of a young man who ends up having an affair with an older Jewish woman. They go out for dinner and the young man sees some of his friends, who he knows will have noticed who he is with. He becomes embarrassed by his companion. She, meanwhile, is enjoying the experience of being out in society. She subtly changes her manners in order to fit in among the people around her. Instead of charming or comforting the young man, this act of assimilation enrages him. He becomes furious at the grotesque spectacle that he believes she is making. The scene culminates in him hitting her in the face in front of everyone.

The scene neatly encapsulates one of the tragedies of anti-Semitism. The older Jewish woman stands out because she is Jewish. For that reason some people dislike her. Yet when she tries to be like the non-Jewish people around her, she is despised afresh. This is just one of the impossible moves that the anti-Semite condemns the Jews for: integrating and not integrating.

There are a number of other versions of the same impossible conundrum. For example, historically it is the achievement of the Jewish people to be able to be hated for being rich and also for being poor. Much nineteenth-century anti-Semitism was based on the idea that Jews were poor and dirty. This was in part a reflection of the Jews from czarist Russia and Eastern Europe who escaped pogroms and went west with nothing to their name. Yet at exactly the same time in history the Jews were stereotyped for being rich. The Rothschild family, among others, came to be seen by anti-Semites as almost typical Jews. Jews could also be hated for being religious and for being atheistic. This was never more so than after Karl Marx and Leon Trotsky.

Finally, for centuries Jews were hated for being stateless. "Rootless cosmopolitans" was one of the phrases that the extreme right once used in their discussions of Jews. The idea of the Jew as stateless and therefore likely to destabilize any country they were in was a commonplace of anti-Semitism for centuries. Yet from 1948, the Jews once again had a state—reestablished in their ancestral homeland. Today the only acceptable form of anti-Semitism comes in hatred of the Jews for having a state.

Anti-Semitism provides a perpetual conundrum for Jews. But the thing that makes it stand out as a challenge for non-Jews is what it says about a society that indulges in it. Because a final aspect of anti-Semitism that is worth dwelling on is what it in fact means.

There is enough evidence to say that anti-Semitism does not just pose a challenge to Jews. It also presents a surefire way to diagnose the health of the wider society. Among the most perceptive insights on this was written in the last century by Vasily Grossman. In his masterpiece *Life and Fate*, Grossman journeys into the darkest parts of the twentieth century, from Stalingrad to the death camps—even into the minds of Joseph Stalin and Adolf Hitler.

But in the very middle of the novel, the dead center of its nine hundred pages—and at the midnight of the twentieth century—Grossman suddenly takes a step back from his narrative and in fewer than four pages says nearly everything that needs to be said about anti-Semitism.

He starts by making a statement of fact. "Anti-Semitism can take many forms," he says, "from a mocking, contemptuous ill-will to murderous pogroms." It can be met "in the market and in the Presidium of the Academy of Sciences, in the soul of an old man and in the games children play in the yard." It has been equally strong, he says, "in the age of atomic reactors and computers as in the age of oil-lamps." But it is what he says next that takes the passage to another level. Grossman writes, "Anti-Semitism is always a means rather than an end; it is a measure of the contradictions yet to be resolved. It is a mirror for the failings of individuals, social structures and State systems. Tell me what you accuse the Jews of—I'll tell you what you're guilty of."

Grossman gives examples from the era of serfdom, in which even a genius like Fyodor Dostoyevsky could fall pray to this viruslike hatred. Citing more recent instances, Grossman points out that the Nazis accused the Jews of being racist and of having a desire for world domination. Of course in doing so national socialism was simply describing its own features. As Grossman writes: "States look to the imaginary intrigues of World Jewry for explanations of their own failure." This was as true at the dawn of capitalism as it was during the industrial revolution, the atomic age, and the age of revolutions.

Finally, he says, there are three different levels of anti-Semitism. First is the "relatively harmless everyday anti-Semitism." Grossman elaborates.

This merely bears witness to the existence of failures and envious fools. Secondly, there is social anti-Semitism. This can only arise in democratic countries. Its manifestations are in those sections of the press that represent different reactionary groups, in the activities of these groups—for example, boycotts of Jewish labour and Jewish goods—and in their ideology and religion. Thirdly, in totalitarian countries, where society as such no longer exists, there can arise State anti-Semitism. This is a sign that the State is looking for the support of fools, reactionaries and failures, that it is seeking to capitalize on the ignorance of the superstitious and the anger of the hungry.

He concludes, "The first stage of State anti-Semitism is discrimination. . . . The second stage is wholesale destruction."[44]

Seen in Grossman's light, much that seems inexplicable becomes explainable, and is as relevant in our own day as it was in his. The Arab countries that repeatedly invaded Israel and sought to steal the land accuse Israel of stealing land. Muslim countries accuse Israel of "colonialism" yet the whole history of Islam has been a history of colonialism. The only reason the Islamic empire grew was what we would now call "colonialism."

Today the government most responsible for spreading the accusation that Israel is expansionist and colonialist is the revolutionary Islamic government in Iran, which has spent recent years assiduously expanding its colonies. What has Gaza become but a colony of Iran? Or Iraq after Iran moved into the vacuum left by America after the overthrow of Saddam Hussein? Or Yemen? Or Syria, into which Iran had poured Hezbollah and other forces? Iran and its proxies and mouthpieces in the West have spent years accusing Israel of being a colonial, expansionist state while all the time expanding and colonizing everywhere they can reach in the region. Why did the mullahs order Hezbollah to engage in the Syrian civil war except to prop up Syria as a forward base of Iran? And what of Lebanon, which even in 2006 still had a government able to distance itself from the actions of Iran's army Hezbollah. By the time Hamas started its October 2023 war against Israel and Hezbollah joined in, Lebanon had become a virtual colony of Iran—with Hezbollah ruling the country by terror and setting up their weaponry among Lebanese civilians. For years they had set up checkpoints at Beirut Airport to act as passport control and government of that country, whether the people wanted them or not. And there is much evidence that they do not.

Everywhere the same rule holds. Groups like Hamas that delight in their bloodlust accuse the Israelis of being insatiable killers. Palestinian groups and their supporters who encourage their youth to view death through "martyrdom" as the highest form of valor claim that the Jews are bloodthirsty child-killers. People who use rape as a weapon of war accuse the Israelis of insatiably raping prisoners in Israeli jails. President Erdogan's regime in Turkey consistently accuses the Israelis of being "occupiers," while Turkey has been illegally occupying northern Cyprus (part of an EU member state) since 1974.

On and on it goes. Within weeks of October 7, before Israel's war in Gaza had even begun, Queen Rania of Jordan went on-air to claim that the Palestinians in Gaza face "two choices" at the hands of the Israelis: "between expulsion or extermination, between ethnic cleansing and genocide."[45] If Queen Rania is interested in this subject she could have asked her father-in-law, the late king Hussein, about what happened in Black September. That is when her father-in-law ethnically cleansed the PLO from Jordan; casualties were somewhere between the official figures of several thousand dead Palestinians and Arafat's claim that King Hussein massacred as many as twenty-five thousand Palestinians.

And what of the critics of Israel in the West? The people who march down the streets and set up tents on their university campuses accuse the Jews of many things. And here too there is a mirror at work. A poll in 2022 found that British people ages eighteen to twenty-four are the only group in British society who think students should be taught that "Britain was founded on racism and remains structurally racist today." They think that by a 42–25 percentage point margin.[46]

Young Americans agree with their British contemporaries about the ills of their own country. A 2022 Harvard Youth Poll found that almost half of Americans ages eighteen to twenty-nine would vote for a candidate who agrees that pupils in K–12 public schools should be taught that racism "is a fixture of American laws and institutions."[47] They are also demonstrably less patriotic than older Americans. As recently as 2013, 85 percent of Americans ages eighteen to twenty-nine said they were "extremely" or "very" proud to be an American. By 2023, just 18 percent of young Americans agreed with the statement that they were "extremely proud" to be American.[48] Perhaps that's because among Americans ages eighteen to twenty-nine, 44 percent had a positive view of socialism while only 40 percent had a positive view of capitalism.[49] Or because by 2020 only 39 percent of Americans under the age of thirty saw their founding fathers as heroes while an astonishing 31 percent saw them as "villains."[50]

This and much more data suggest that young people in the West have a historically low view of the virtues of their own country. A generation has come up that has been taught that by dint of being born into the West, they have been born into countries built on ethnic cleansing and genocide, founded by people who are settler-colonialist racists, and that their societies perpetuate these evils right to this very day. Perhaps the vast rise in antagonism toward Israel is a manifestation of what psychologists would call "projection."

How does Grossman's law apply to these people then? Perhaps all that is required is a slight twist to his phrase: "Tell me what you accuse the Jews of—I'll tell you what you *believe* you are guilty of."

CHAPTER 4

THE DISCONNECT

At a reunion of the survivors of the Nova party, one partygoer re-layed his experiences to me and then said something startling: "What would you do if this happened in your country?" I immediately thought, though I did not say, *But it has*. It happened in Paris in 2015 when terrorists stormed the Bataclan theater. Rock music fans were packed into the venue to hear the Eagles of Death Metal play to an audience of some 1,500 people. The moment the shooting began was caught on the cell phones of people in the crowd. At first it sounded like something had gone wrong with the sound system. Then the unmistakable sound of Kalashnikov fire alerted concertgoers that they had been taken into that other realm. The band stopped playing and through the noise also came the sound of terrified confusion—of people seeing people shot down in front of them, of people running to hide anywhere they could. One survivor described how the ISIS terrorists circled the young people like vultures, picking people off as they lay on the ground or tried hiding under seats and tables. The terrorists attacked the easy targets first, going to the disabled section and shooting the people in wheelchairs in the back of the head where they sat.

Many people were shot as they tried to get to the exits. One of the terrorists was positioned at an exit precisely in order to pick people off that way. Other concertgoers found a lavatory, then a way to get into the ceiling from it, and hid from the terrorists there. Ninety people were killed in the theater, mainly in the first twenty minutes of the attack. Hundreds more were injured. It was a night that changed Paris. The Bataclan was just one of the terrorists' targets across the city that night.

There was a different scale to the Nova party, but it was the same change in reality that happened in that moment. What was meant to be an evening of fun, friends, and music turned instead into a massacre site, with police taking hours to identify the bodies.

I thought also of the Pulse nightclub shooting in June 2016. That was when Omar Mateen walked into a gay nightclub in Orlando, Florida, and opened fire. Saying that he was acting on behalf of ISIS, he gunned his way through the clubgoers on Latin Night. Forty-nine of the clubbers were killed and fifty-three were injured. As with the Bataclan attack, survivors recalled afterward that they thought it was firecrackers that had been set off. After all, who would go into a nightclub and open fire?

One other attack that immediately came to mind was the Manchester Arena attack in May 2017. On that occasion it was young people attending an Ariana Grande concert who were the target. The suicide bomber was Salman Abedi, the twenty-two-year-old son of Libyan migrants to the UK. Abedi cased the venue carefully, wandering around for some time with his huge rucksack with its explosive device that included nails and ball bearings in order to cause maximum injury. The explosion killed twenty-two people, mainly women. More than a thousand concertgoers were injured, many of them with their lives changed forever.

Again it was that transformation—that meeting between two worlds that should never meet. The realm of dancing and fun and the realm of devastation and war. It cannot make any sense when these two worlds meet, because they are never meant to.

Yet there was something different here, because at no stage did the world turn on the victims of these other atrocities. Survivors of the Manchester bombing did not get pursued by mobs of people supporting ISIS. Survivors of the Bataclan did not find that when they left Paris they were treated not as victims but as guilty parties. Yet that is exactly what happened with those who survived the atrocities of October 7, 2023.

In March 2024, two survivors of the Nova party traveled to the UK to talk about their experiences as victims of terrorism and to raise funds for a nonprofit organization they had cofounded to help other victims. The men, brothers Neria and Daniel Sharabi, had saved the lives of a number of other partygoers on the morning of the 7th. Both reportedly suffer from PTSD. They arrived into the UK through Manchester Airport, arriving in a city that might have been able to share their experiences. But as they went through British customs they were detained by immigration authorities. Asked what they were doing in the UK, the brothers said that they were survivors of the October 7 massacres and were here to share their story.

"The second I said it, he just flipped," said Neria. "From that moment he just started to interrogate us. He told us to sit over there, don't move, we need to interrogate you." Detained for over two hours, they were reportedly humiliated and degraded by the border authorities. Officials shouted at them, "We are the bosses, not you!" When asked why they had chosen to detain the young Israelis, the border officials told them, "We need to make sure you are not going to do here what you are doing in Gaza."

Three months later one of many other manifestations of this trend emerged in New York City when an exhibit that had started in Israel and traveled to various other cities ended up there. It was a re-creation of and memorial to the victims of the Nova festival. I had seen the exhibit in Tel Aviv some months earlier. As well as a re-creation of the dance floor and the woodland camping areas there were also some of the portable toilets and burned-out or shot-up cars. Part re-creation, part shrine—including to the kidnapped— the exhibit was a success. But when it opened in New York it got a different welcome.

New York City mayor Eric Adams attended the exhibition with

the families of some of the victims. But outside the exhibit in lower Manhattan a large protest gathered. The protesters lit flares and smoke canisters, waved the flags of Hamas and Hezbollah, and made genocidal chants. On the way to the protest the masked activists swarmed subway cars demanding that any "Zionists" identify themselves.

One of the people inside the exhibit, Manny Manzuri, stumbled into the protest. His daughters Roya, twenty-two, and Norelle, twenty-five, were among those murdered at the Nova party, along with Norelle's fiancé, Amit Cohen. Manny's daughters had been born in Los Angeles and attended a school in Hollywood before moving to Israel. They were among the partygoers who had sheltered inside a bomb shelter. The Hamas terrorists threw grenades into the shelter, set fire to it, and shot at people inside as well as those running out.

The body of Manny's younger daughter was identified first, and while the family were sitting shiva for her they went on a Zoom call with President Biden and the parents of other children who had been murdered or kidnapped. During the call they received a knock at the door telling them that the body of their other daughter, Norelle, had also been identified. One of the other parents on the call said that Roya and Norelle's mother went back to the computer and said, "I just got the knock on the door that my other daughter is dead." She started screaming and President Biden, among others on the call, reportedly put his head in his hands and started sobbing.

In New York a few months later the girl's father walked straight into the demonstration of people supporting the killing of his daughters. "I cannot find the words how I felt when somebody [is] shouting and supporting the people who murder your daughters," he said. "It was like they killed me again and again and again." The protesters harassed and tried to intimidate people going into the exhibit.

"Intifada, intifada!" was among the chants that the protesters screamed at the people passing into the exhibit. "Fuck the Nova Music Festival," said one of the protest organizers over their sound system to the keffiyeh-wearing crowd. Describing the exhibit as "Zionist propaganda," one of the speakers went on to scream that the Nova festival had been "the place where Zionists decided to rave next to a concentration camp. That's exactly what this music festival was."

Even some anti-Israel activists like Congresswoman Alexandria Ocasio-Cortez condemned this behavior, saying that "the callousness, dehumanization, and targeting of Jews on display at last night's protest outside the Nova Festival exhibit was atrocious antisemitism—plain and simple."[51]

***

It is telling, this claim that Gaza was a concentration camp and that to even live or dance beside it makes a person complicit in a Nazi-like evil. Telling because accusing the Jews of setting up a concentration camp has been a constant claim against the Jewish state. From the moment the Israelis withdrew from Gaza it was claimed that the Strip was a "concentration camp."

The fact is that once Hamas seized full control of Gaza, both of its neighbors—Israel and Egypt—were forced to carefully monitor everything going in and out of the Strip, mainly to stop Hamas and Islamic Jihad from stockpiling weapons that they could then use to attack Israel.

Yet despite the flow of food and provisions into Gaza, the difficulty of stopping Hamas from using any and all trade as well as aid as a means to transport weapons was continuous. There were many disputes about what should and should not be allowed in. Whenever the Israeli authorities worried about building supplies entering the Strip they were told by the international community that these were vital. But the Israelis knew that much of this material would be used by Hamas to build its tunnel network. And it was.

Still, the claim that Gaza was ever in any way a "concentration camp" should have been seen as absurd at face value. In 2005, when

Israel withdrew all Jews from Gaza, the population of the Strip was around 1.3 million. By 2023 it was over 2 million. That would make it the first concentration camp in history in which the population actually grew. There was no population boom in Auschwitz in the 1940s.

So why the claim? There are many things that Gaza under Hamas may have been called. But why a "concentration camp"? It seems it was for the same reason that Israel was accused of being "Nazi-like" in its actions. The aim of Israel's critics for many years seemed to be not just to insult Israel and smear its actions, but to try to use the most powerful terms in Jewish history to wound and hurt the Jewish state. It was not enough that Gaza should be said to be under carefully controlled border checks. Or that one supply or other was being unfairly kept out. People had to accuse Israel of running a "concentration camp" in Gaza.

Once again it was noticeable that a considerable amount of "projection" was going on, as well as a deliberate attempt to wound Jews as deeply as possible with this claim.

Anti-Israel politicians and activists in Europe seemed especially keen to use the concentration-camp smear against Israel. For instance, the movement of far-left French politician Jean-Luc Mélenchon particularly embraced these claims. Two weeks after October 7 there was an anti-Israel protest in Paris. In an X post, Mélenchon wrote "This is France" alongside a picture of the demonstrators. He then alleged that the president of the national assembly, Yaël Braun-Pivet, who happens to be Jewish, was "camping" out in Tel Aviv in order to "encourage a massacre" in Gaza.[52] That is the language of the French far left but it is interesting that it comes from people who agree with the old far right on one aspect of history.

In 2017 Emmanuel Macron gave a speech in which he acknowledged that France had been complicit in the Nazi Holocaust of the Jews. Mélenchon was one of the figures who lambasted Macron for this acknowledgment. He made similar arguments that those on the French far right had long made. Disputing the legitimacy of the Vichy regime, Mélenchon claimed that it was "totally unacceptable" to say that "France, as a people, as a nation, is responsible for this crime."[53] As though 75,000 French Jews had been deported to the concentration camps in the 1940s by some error in no way connected with anyone French.

But Mélenchon was not alone among European politicians in trying this move. Similar efforts were made by politicians in the Netherlands, Italy, and many other countries. The same people who claimed that their own countries had no involvement in the Holocaust or who tried to downplay their own involvement in the concentration camps were strangely eager to accuse the Jews of carrying out just such atrocities in the here and now. It is as though if the Jews can be accused of running concentration camps and carrying out "ethnic cleansing" today, then it is easier to say first, "You see, we all do it," then to move on to say, "But the Jews actually do it more."

**

One of many things that Mélenchon and others seem unable to accept—and with a lack of empathy that should be unusual—is that nothing had to be this way in Gaza. For almost two decades taxpayers in Europe and North America poured money into Gaza through direct aid and through international aid programs.

Since 2009 alone, two years after Hamas took full control of Gaza, the US government sent over $400 million there, mainly through the United States Agency for International Development.[54] Between 2021 and 2024 alone, USAID also sent more than $500 million to the Palestinian authorities in Gaza and the West Bank.[55] After October 7 the Biden administration announced a further $100 million in aid to Gaza and the West Bank.[56] Tens of millions of dollars of additional US funds were sent in the preceding decade through a labyrinthine set of government agencies.

In 2023 alone, the European Union sent over $100 million euros to Gaza, and according to the Associated Press, between 2014 and

2020 UN agencies sent almost $4.5 billion to Gaza, with funding from Qatar alone from 2012 to 2021 totaling $1.3 billion.[57] Most of the UN funding to Gaza went through UNRWA. In 2021, the US was UNRWA's largest contributor, with donations of more than $338 million. Germany was the next-biggest donor, with more than $176 million.[58]

The leaders of the Palestinian Authority in the West Bank used these funds for their own purposes, including building mansions for themselves that a homeowner in the Hamptons might envy. But without exception, the money that went to Gaza ended up in the hands of Hamas. Since 2007 there has been no other government in Gaza, and anything that comes in, from the lowliest food truck to the largest suitcase of cash, goes straight to them. For years the Israelis had warned the US, UN, and others that UNRWA in Gaza was part of Hamas's network and for years the Americans and Europeans continued to throw money at them anyway. Even after up to a dozen UNRWA employees were found to have taken part in the October 7 massacres, support to UNRWA from the British government and others continued. It seemed that these governments didn't care where the money went in Gaza, just so long as they kept sending it.

In fact, by the start of the 2023 war the international community had made every Hamas leader into a billionaire. By then Ismail Haniyeh, Moussa Abu Marzouk, and Khaled Mashal were estimated to have a combined worth of some $11 billion. While claiming that their people were living in a poverty-stricken concentration camp, these leaders lived in luxury hotels and penthouses in Qatar. Haniyeh alone, the leader of the Hamas politburo on October 7, was worth more than $4 billion, while Abu Marzouk and Mashal were worth $3 billion and over $4 billion, respectively.[59]

If these leaders had simply been corrupt, that might have been one thing—and the oldest story imaginable. And it is true that every dollar they stole was money that could have been used to actually improve the lives of Palestinians. Instead of buying weapons, building tunnels for terrorists, and living the high life in Doha they might have actually created the Singapore on the Mediterranean that so many people hoped for when Gaza was handed to the Palestinians in 2005.

Yet while they stole money on an international scale, Gaza until 2023 was not what the Hamas spokespeople abroad said it was. For years the journalist Tom Gross updated an online list of the luxuries and attractions available to people in Gaza. Even in 2010, while Western media talked about a place that constituted one great humanitarian catastrophe, Gaza boasted fancy restaurants, an Olympic-sized swimming pool, and shopping malls. As even the Lonely Planet guidebook noted, at the Roots Club in Gaza you could "dine on steak au poivre and chicken cordon bleu." Hamas very much ran things their own way, for instance on one occasion burning to the ground a UN-run summer camp for Palestinian children, and threatening the UN staff with murder because it was deemed "un-Islamic." But still the living standards in Gaza were high for the region.[60]

In an interview in August 2024 for the YouTube channel Sama-Quds, one of the sons of Hamas leader Ismail Haniyeh even boasted how wonderful Gaza had been. Abd Al-Salam Haniyeh said on camera:

After the 2008–09 [war], the world opened up [to Gaza]. For the first time, a huge thing happened. There were twelve hundred martyrs, and there was destruction. . . . I don't know . . . The world, Al-Jazeera TV, the media, there was an Arab summit, and people were sympathizing. It was a big deal. The convoys to break the siege started. . . . These convoys started, the tunnels began to be active, and whatever. . . . Then there was the Arab Spring and then, in 2013 . . . It was a time of progress, and [in 2012], the emir of Qatar came, and laid the cornerstone for the reconstruction. . . . People who came to Gaza in 2020–21 could not believe that this was Gaza, because it was so beautiful—buildings, the Doha Promenade, the Egypt Promenade, restaurants, and so on and so forth.[61]

So all the time that Hamas's paymasters and mouthpieces in the region and across the West were saying that Gaza was a concentration camp and a humanitarian disaster, Hamas's princelings knew that it was a place that much of the rest of the region would envy. There are no Olympic pools in Yemen; no beautiful, peaceful promenades in Sudan. Yet the Hamas authorities insisted simultaneously that this place was under "siege" and that Gaza was beautiful.

***

If the leadership of Hamas was able to tell two different stories to the world, it was nothing compared to the cognitive dissonance outside the region.

When the Israelis pointed out that UNRWA was teaching young Gazans not to aspire to a better life but instead to see killing the "Zionists" as the highest value in life, the Western taxpayers kept paying them money anyway. When the Israelis pointed out that food and every other provision was being diverted by Hamas for their own means, the Western taxpayers continued to pour their money in still. And when the world was told that the Israelis were somehow starving the booming population of Gaza all the time, the Israelis knew that the people inside Gaza were preparing for something else.

Inside Gaza I visited the tunnels that Hamas had constructed during their eighteen years in power. One was a tunnel that had an opening within walking distance of the Erez crossing. It had been constructed by Sinwar's brother and had become famous, in its own way, because of footage showing Sinwar himself traveling along the tunnel in a military vehicle.

When people think of a tunnel network many think of small scurry-holes. In fact, besides being longer than the entire London Underground, the network was also much more elaborate. In the 140 square miles of Gaza, Hamas spent its years in power constructing over 350 miles of tunnels, with around 6,000 different tunnel entrances. Many of these were hidden in civilian houses, mosques, hospitals, and other nonmilitary buildings. Like storing weapons in such places, this is a breach of the Geneva Conventions, which are meant to preclude an army hiding military infrastructure in civilian buildings. Doing such a thing obviously puts civilians at risk. But this was one of Hamas's tools of war. Where most countries would seek to protect its civilians, Hamas always had a stated aim of using them as human shields. They knew that no country would be able to tolerate the buildup of rockets and other military infrastructure to be used against it, but they also knew that whenever Israel targeted a "civilian" facility in which Hamas had put its infrastructure, the world would condemn Israel.

I saw this myself in many places in Gaza. As the IDF were searching for Hamas terrorists and leaders and searching for the hostages, they found the same pattern time and again. Hamas had used its years in the Gaza to embed its military and terror infrastructure in every part of the Strip. While much of the world was condemning Israel, I spoke with a major in the IDF whose job it had been since the start of the conflict to go from building to building in Gaza looking for weapons and tunnel entrances.

An American by birth, Major "Y" went to Israel immediately after the 7th to use his expertise. What he had seen in the months since the IDF went into Gaza had shocked even him. Stories that had already emerged in the international press about Hamas explosives being found smuggled inside children's toys were just the start. By two months into the war his estimate was that somewhere between every two to every three civilian homes in Gaza had military weapons, including AK-47s, grenades, and rocket launchers, or tunnel entrances in them. From very early in the conflict he and his team had worked out where to search whenever they entered a civilian house. If they were looking for weapons, rockets, or tunnel entrances they no longer searched the main rooms, the kitchens, or the parents' bedroom. They now went straight to the children's bedrooms, since that was where tunnel entrances and weapons were generally located—including under kids' cots. While Israeli families built safe rooms to protect their children from rockets, these Gazan families actually used their families to protect their rockets.

A couple of days earlier Major "Y" had searched a house that the family had left. He had gone straight to the children's bedroom where there was a crib. He turned over the crib and underneath it was a rocket-propelled-grenade. Still, at this stage of the conflict he could be shocked. "It's hard to believe," he said. "Where in the world do you hide an RPG under a baby's crib?" Over the months I spoke with many soldiers who all relayed similar stories. And of the books they found inside the homes in Gaza. Those who had been inside before this latest conflict said that it was noticeable how radicalized the population had become. Copies of *Mein Kampf* in Arabic were one of the most common books they came across in civilian homes, as well as tracts like "How to Kill Jews."

It was the same in every UN school they went into. And every mosque and place of worship. While Hamas was claiming their members were devout Muslims, they had no problem at all putting tunnel entrances and hiding large stores of weaponry—again against every rule of war—inside Gaza's mosques. Whether schools, hospitals, or mosques, Hamas's cynical strategy turned out to work. If they could hide their armory in civilian buildings, then whenever the IDF even searched such a building Hamas could rely on the world condemning Israel for such a flagrant breach of etiquette.

As the major told me, "Every school and kindergarten we go into we find guns in the basement. In each one we found more than ten AK-47s, machine guns, and grenades." And this was when there weren't any Hamas terrorists in the buildings.

When there were, Hamas had other equally cynical tactics. In December 2023 there was a story that made headlines around the world. As the IDF was searching for Hamas and the hostages inside Gaza they were experiencing heavy fighting in the Shejaiya neighborhood of Gaza City. Civilians were emerging from buildings and at one point three men came out, one carrying a stick with a white cloth. One of the soldiers felt the men were a threat, and in a terrible moment at thirty feet away he thought the men were terrorists and opened fire. Two of the men were killed immediately and a third retreated wounded into the building they had come from. They turned out to be Yotam Haim, twenty-eight; Samer Talalka, twenty-two; and Alon Shamriz, twenty-six, all three of them Israeli hostages kidnapped by Hamas from the kibbutz of Kfar Aza on October 7.

The response of the world was, as usual, bizarre. Much of the international coverage reported the tragedy as though the Israelis were now so full of bloodlust that they were even deliberately killing their own. Open enemies of Israel of course rejoiced in the mistake, crowing with delight that the IDF, which had gone in to rescue the hostages, should have ended up killing three of them. As always, the lack of empathy was stunning—not least for the young soldier who had made such a fateful decision and would have to live with it. But there was also a complete ignorance of the kind of conditions that the IDF was operating in as it made its way through Gaza.

Outside Israel there was bewilderment about how such a terrible thing could have happened. But not inside the country. Hearing about how low morale was in the battalion that had made the mistake, Yotam's mother sent a message direct to the soldiers. "I am Yotam's mother. I wanted to tell you that I love you very much, and I hug you here from afar," she said. "I know that everything that happened is absolutely not your fault, and nobody's fault except that of Hamas. At the first opportunity," she continued, "you are invited to come to us, whoever wants to. And we want to see you with our own eyes and hug you and tell you that what you did—however hard it is to say this, and sad—it was apparently the right thing in that moment."

Later I spoke with a special forces soldier who had been with the division in which this terrible mistake had occurred. He described how he himself had not slept for two or three nights by this point. Shelling and incoming fire had been constant. "You start to smell colors" was one of the ways he tried to explain the disorientation you start to feel from sleeplessness. At one point Hamas mortar fire had been landing closer and closer to him, but he just stayed sitting on the remains of a street corner. He decided he was too tired to move simply to avoid landing shells, and it was only after the last of them landed that he realized he had been sitting beside a dead body all this time.

Among the many laws of war that Hamas blithely ignores is that members of its terror army dress as civilians. They operate in civilian areas, out of civilian buildings, and dress in civilian clothing. They do so in the knowledge that this makes it easier for their gunmen to operate and the certainty that if civilians are caught up in it, that will be an advantage to Hamas. I asked the major about some recent incidents he had been involved in. He described a recent occasion when his unit spotted an old woman in a wheelchair alone on a street corner in the south of Gaza. From a distance members of the unit approached the elderly lady, "who looked like my grandmother." As they approached her they were suddenly fired on by a Hamas terrorist who was lying flat on the ground underneath her wheelchair so that he could fire on the soldiers. It may seem strange to the Western way of war that anyone would even use an elderly, disabled woman as a human shield, but for Hamas it is normal operating procedure.

On another recent occasion the major's unit was beside an UNRWA school. The soldiers saw a thirteen-year-old boy running with a bag near one of the schools. He put the bag down and ran away. A few minutes later it detonated, badly wounding one of the Israeli soldiers nearby. As the major said, Hamas didn't think for a moment "about the Palestinian civilians" who were also nearby when the bomb went off.

And a tragedy like that of the shooting of the three Israeli hostages? I asked why Israeli troops have to treat even people coming toward them with white flags with suspicion. The major starts to list the many occasions just in recent weeks when he had seen Hamas use this tactic to carry out attacks. Recently, he said, "a group of old women and old men" came out of a building waving a white flag.

Suddenly someone came out from among them and started shooting at the soldiers. They knew that because of the civilians, the Israelis could not shoot back. Situations like this happen every day, according to the major and numerous other soldiers I spoke with on the battlefield. Add to this the rockets and grenades that the Israelis routinely uncover in UN bags, including UNRWA bags, plus the tunnel entrances and weapons stores everywhere. Another tunnel entrance had just been found in a school's playing fields. This is the Hamas way of war.

The search for the hostages was made more difficult not just by Hamas's tactics, but by the tactics that the Israelis used in response. In Gaza and Lebanon it was the Israeli way of war to drop leaflets, take over radio and television channels, and send millions of text messages to warn residents when a building was going to be hit. One special forces soldier whose job involved hostage rescue said that on a number of occasions he came across places where Israeli hostages had recently been held. He saw cages in which they had been kept as well as handcuffs and T-shirts from people from the kibbutz. He told me, "We always felt one step behind. Because we kept telling the Gazans when we were coming."

The summer after the war began, the *Wall Street Journal* got hold of a set of messages that Yahya Sinwar had sent to fellow members of Hamas since the beginning of the war. It seemed that early on, Sinwar managed to make his way south through the tunnel network, most likely surrounded by what he would regard as the "best" of the Israeli hostages, including the children and babies that he knew would be the ultimate "human shield" for him against Israel. Sinwar knew that it was not safe for him to communicate using phones and had gone "dark" since October 7. But a set of handwritten and hand-conveyed messages between him and members of the Hamas teams who were claiming to negotiate for him revealed his views about the loss of civilians on the Palestinian side. As the *Journal* wrote, his messages displayed "a cold disregard for human life and made clear he believes Israel has more to lose from the war than Hamas." In one of the messages, Sinwar described the deaths of civilians in Gaza as "necessary sacrifices." In a letter to his fellow Hamas leader Ismail Haniyeh, whose three adult Hamas sons had just been killed in an air strike, Sinwar said that their deaths would "infuse life into the veins of this nation."[62]

The question of how any army is meant to fight in such a situation is a terrible conundrum. How do you fight an enemy that wants you to wound and kill people on its own side? How would any army manage to do this without losing its own sense of morality?

From before the IDF went into Gaza in 2023, there were already worldwide claims that, as usual, the Israelis were committing genocide there. In the same way that many people had spent recent years being experts on global pandemics, Ukraine, Russia, and the Afghanistan withdrawal, the whole world suddenly claimed to know how to operate a hostage extraction strategy in the most densely built-up terrorist infrastructure on earth. The American battle for Fallujah, Iraq, in 2004 was often cited as a precedent, as was the wholly different counterinsurgency operation in Northern Ireland from the 1970s to 1990s. But the international condemnation over what Israel was and was not doing grew in part because the only casualty figures that were used came from the Gazan Health Ministry, which is part of the Hamas government. If the highest Hamas casualty figures that were lapped up by the international press were true, then by the end of the first year of the war, the casualty rate inside Gaza was some 42,000 people.

Hamas simultaneously claimed that such numbers consisted entirely of civilian casualties while frequently posting about the "martyrs" of their movement who had been killed in battle with the IDF. If the Hamas figures were true and the Israeli figures for Hamas operatives killed in Gaza are accurate, then at the very most this would mean a civilian-to-terrorist death toll of one-to-one. That is a terrible figure, to be sure, but it would also be the lowest civilian death toll per enemy combatant in military history. Both the British and American armed forces have in recent years operated on a rough

estimate of one enemy combatant killed for every three to four civilian deaths. Until the Gaza war this was regarded as a low level of
civilian casualties in a heavily built-up conflict zone. But when ISIS
was expelled from Mosul, or even when the Taliban and al-Qaeda
were in Afghanistan, there were no serious accusations that these
ratios counted as "genocide," "ethnic cleansing," or a "war crime."

In May 2024, human rights groups uncritically accepted the
latest Hamas death toll figures and drew their traditional conclusions. For example, one of the former executive directors of
Human Rights Watch, now running a group called Dawn, pro-
claimed that the Hamas figure of 32,000 civilian deaths meant
that "ISRAEL's daily death toll of Palestinians in Gaza surpasses
that of any other major conflict in the 21st century." Sarah Leah
Whitson pronounced that "Israel has murdered more children in
Gaza JUST in the past six months than the cumulative number of
children killed in GLOBAL conflicts around the world for the past
six years."[63]

Besides demonstrating that she had accepted Hamas numbers at
face value, such statements also showed absolutely no knowledge of
the non-Israel-related wars of the twenty-first century. It ignored
the more than 200,000 people killed in Ukraine, the 400,000 people
killed in Yemen, the 700,000 people killed in Syria, and the three-
quarters of a million people killed in the Tigray war in Ethiopia.
None of these conflicts had received the amount of coverage of the
Israel-Hamas war. One reason is that journalists and others were not
nearly as intent on covering any of these wars. After the killing of
American journalist Marie Colvin in Syria in 2012 it was extremely
hard for Western journalists to report from there, and so Bashar al-
Assad and his friends managed to oversee 40,000 or so deaths every
six months for over a decade. Although some journalists were able
to get into Yemen, very few were able to cover that war. Tigray was
on nobody's priority list.

Besides the old adage that "if it's Jews, it's news," in each of these
conflicts there was not a ready-made industry of journalists waiting

to cover the war as the propaganda wing of Hamas. Qatar, which helps fund and house Hamas, also funds and houses the Qatari media outlet Al Jazeera. Its journalists in Gaza turned out not just to be sympathetic to Hamas but actually part of the group.

Take Muhammad Washah, whom Al Jazeera presented as a stellar part of the press corps. Since 2022 he was in charge of research and development for aerial weapons for Hamas. Washah was able to present himself by day as a journalist, but in the evenings he'd get back to his job as a senior Hamas commander firing rockets at Israel. He might have gotten away with it if the IDF had not managed to find his laptop in Gaza.

In January 2024, two Al Jazeera "journalists" were killed in an air strike in Rafah. Al Jazeera and much of the Western press immediately presented this as an intolerable attack on the free press. Hamza al-Dahdouh was the son of Al Jazeera's Gaza correspondent Wael al-Dahdouh. And while the network complained that the Israelis had no right to hit the vehicle they were traveling in, they did not mention that these "journalists" were in a vehicle with a Hamas drone operator while it was targeting Israeli soldiers. Nor did they mention the fact that Wael was not in fact a "journalist," but was a member of Palestinian Islamic Jihad who was actively involved in attacks against the Israelis.[64] It was the same story the following month when another Al Jazeera "journalist," Ismail Abu Omar, was injured in Khan Younis. The network claimed that their "correspondent" had been subjected to a "deliberate targeting" by the Israelis and that this "intimidation" was done in order to prevent journalists from reporting the "heinous crimes" of the Zionists.[65]

What Omar's employers failed to note was that Omar was not simply one of their "correspondents." He was also the deputy commander of Hamas's eastern battalion in Khan Yunis. On October 7 he had gone into Israel with Hamas. In Kibbutz Nir Oz, Abu Omar could be seen screaming with joy that "the friends [Hamas] have progressed. May Allah bless," and boasting that Palestinian children would now be able to "play with the heads" of the massacred Israeli civilians. This was Al Jazeera's "journalist."

But perhaps even these cases did not come close to one of the most egregious examples of the world being duped. In June 2024, the IDF performed a daring and successful rescue mission for four of the Israeli hostages kidnapped on the 7th. They included Noa Argamani, a young woman who had been at the Nova party. Footage of her being driven off on the back of a Hamas motorcycle, screaming in terror, became one of the formative images of the day. When the IDF rescued her and the other three hostages they found out where they had been held. One of the people who had been holding them was one Abdallah Aljamal. During the war Aljamal had filed many articles about the humanitarian suffering inside Gaza. One of the news sites that he had contributed for was Al Jazeera. And it turned out that while filing these articles about the suffering of the people of Gaza he had failed to tell his readers that he was holding Israeli hostages in his own home, where they were being tortured daily.

Yet details like this were lost all the time. The world seemed so pleased to be able to throw its attentions onto the conflict in Gaza that any and every claim could be made about Israel's actions. Almost every time, these were presented in the worst possible light. If anyone pointed out that the death tolls in other conflicts in the twenty-first century were far larger than Gaza, they were told that they were trying to deflect attention from the latter. If they pointed out, as did Major John Spencer, the chair of urban warfare studies at West Point's Modern War Institute, that the IDF had implemented more precautions to prevent civilian deaths than any military in history—far beyond what international law requires—they were dismissed as mouthpieces of the Israelis.

It had been the same for years. When anyone pointed out any virtue of Israeli democracy they were accused of diverting attention from the "occupation," the "ethnic cleansing," or the always-ongoing "genocide." By the 2010s this had already reached such a pitch that anyone even pointing out that Israel has liberal rights in a region not known for the same was accused of diverting attention from the plight of the Palestinians.

Judith Butler and other "gender theorists" even came up with a term, *pinkwashing*, to describe anyone who even pointed out that Israel has equal rights for gay people. This allowed people like Butler (who identified as lesbian before identifying as nonbinary) to try to rationalize why they had openly landed on the side of people who would kill them if they actually lived under the governance of the groups they were supporting. At a teach-in at Berkeley during the 2006 Israel-Hezbollah war, Butler was asked whether the hesitation of some on the political left to support terrorist groups due to their violent actions risked harming international solidarity with the Palestinians. Butler responded: "Understanding Hamas, Hezbollah as social movements that are progressive, that are on the Left, that are parts of a global Left, is extremely important."[66]

If Butler herself ever lived under a regime run by Hamas or Hezbollah, she would be executed at worst, and made to cover her face from male attention at best. The fact that people like her and Western organizations such as "Queers for Palestine" can support groups that would kill them is often described as "cognitive dissonance," but that is not accurate. Such groups are not "confused." They are simply betraying a completely different agenda. For them the most important thing is to support the revolutionary left and the overthrow of Western liberal democracy. Supporting armed Islamic movements that rape and murder and execute is a necessary condition to achieve this goal.

This could, at best, be described as psychotic. But it is telling how effective this thinking has been, and how ardent they have been in pushing every argument and fact that runs against their campaign: to make reality a footnote in their far more important ideological struggle.

Watching Western would-be revolutionaries do this to everything involving Israel is like watching someone playing chess and trying to cut off any move their opponent can make. Every fact can be dis missed. When it comes to Israel the difference between "equal rights" and "hanging gays from cranes" is waved away as mere Israeli PR. Notice the difference between living and being hanged and you will be accused of "pinkwashing." Point out that Israel is a liberal democracy with all the benefits and complexities that that entails and you will be told that you are excusing "genocide." Notice that Israel is a pluralistic, multiracial, and multicultural society and you will be accused of being an apologist for "apartheid." It is a game set up for one side to lose.

***

Yet there is still such a thing as "reality." And the difference between those who recognize it and those who don't is as wide as the gulf between war and peace. And the two are, naturally, related.

Twenty-two years ago, in his book *Of Paradise and Power,* the American scholar Robert Kagan advanced a theory of why Europe and America seemed to have drifted apart. His argument was that after the world wars, Europe had gone into a different phase of history—a phase in which war was a thing of the past and the continent entered what Immanuel Kant conceived of as a state of permanent peace. Borders, which had once been the source of so many wars on the continent, were now settled and agreed upon. Even where they weren't, nobody in Europe wanted to open up that discussion again. The price was too high. In a similar way, Europe had for centuries torn itself apart with the wars of religion. Now Europe had entered a postreligious era in which the very idea of fighting, killing, or dying for your faith was anathema: something from a long-dead religious past. In Kagan's view Europe had even decided to draw down its defense spending because, in the most generous interpretation, they genuinely saw war as something that was no longer possible. A more cynical explanation was that European governments believed they could outsource their defense—including their defense spending—to the United States.

In Kagan's view, America was, by contrast, fated to be stuck in history. The world's superpower was not able to live in this Kantian peace or even dream these Kantian dreams. The US was destined to stay in a Hobbesian world in which might still mattered, and in which power needed to be exerted, not least because if it wasn't exerted by America it would be exerted by one of its rivals or enemies.

The thesis drew a lot of attention when it appeared. Today the war in Ukraine may have changed some European thinking. It has certainly led to a rush of European countries that were not under the umbrella of NATO to apply to become members. Perhaps, after the invasion of Ukraine, eastern and central Europe has had a reminder of the old way of doing things.

But if Kagan's view of America's position is accurate, it is an even starker description of the situation that Israel is forced to live in. America at least has the benefit of having friendly countries to its north and south and ocean everywhere else. Americans have the luxury of never having experienced the kind of attempted invasions or successful invasions that Europe had in centuries past. America has fought existential wars on behalf of its allies, but not since its founding has it had to fight an existential war for its very survival.

The impossibility of even imagining an invasion of the homeland is shown in polls that ask what members of the general public might do in such a situation. A month after the invasion of Ukraine, a poll asked people in the US how they believed they would act if America was invaded in the same way as Ukraine. Would they stay and fight—or would they flee? The results were not encouraging. Around 7 percent of the American public said they didn't know what they would do if the USA were invaded. But a larger number did.

In total just 55 percent of Americans said they would stay and fight. An astonishing 38 percent said they would flee—presumably to Canada, unless Canada was the country doing the invading. A full 52 percent of people who identified as Democrats said they would flee, as did a quarter of self-identified Republicans.[67] Of course, polls like this have to be looked at with a certain amount of caution, though at least two results can be extrapolated from it. The first is that people do not know what they would do, or misjudge themselves, because they cannot even imagine such a fantastical situation. Perhaps if such a thing ever did happen the American public would surprise themselves as much as the Ukrainian and Israeli publics have. After all, who knows how someone will behave in a time of trial until they are put in it?

Another consideration, though, is that the figures in America could be even worse than such a poll suggests. After all, many people give false feedback to pollsters, because they give the pollsters the answer they think they are expected to give and make themselves look better even to an anonymous pollster. So perhaps people said they would stay and fight when they would actually have no intention of doing so.

In early 2024, Britain's most senior army officer, General Sir Patrick Sanders, said that Britain may need to increase its preparedness for armed conflict and called for an increase in the size of the British Army. A poll by YouGov asked eighteen- to forty-year-olds whether they would be willing to fight in the event of a world war—including if the UK was under an imminent threat of invasion. That age group was selected because this was roughly the age range of the people conscripted to fight for their country in the two world wars.

Once again the results were not good. Almost a third said they would refuse to serve even if the UK was about to be invaded. In fact, the number of people who said they would refuse to serve was almost three times as high as the number who said they would actively volunteer.[68]

There was a certain amount of outcry about these figures. A follow-up poll asked young Brits why they would refuse to serve their country even in an existential conflict. One fifth of them said they were opposed to war or believed "that war doesn't solve anything." A fairly typical response was "I'm not interested in anything to do with war. It's pointless and destructive and I don't want any part of it." A further 9 percent said they felt they were too unfit to be a soldier. Curiously enough, 7 percent said they wouldn't be willing to fight because they had people to look after.[69]

Unfortunately for them, young Israelis do not have the luxury of deciding whether they like war or develop grand ideas such as "war doesn't solve anything." But that makes them unusual among young Westerners today. None of this is theoretical and none of it has to be imagined. Time and again in the months after October 7 I was struck by the young Israelis who went about work that their contemporaries in the West could never imagine.

One day I went to the site in the Gaza envelope where the cars and other vehicles that had been shot or burned out on the 7th had been collected together. The highways and forests around the Nova festival had been cleared of these vehicles and they had been brought to one huge site in the middle of the desert.

There were vast, towering piles of burned-out cars. At the far end there were also mountains of the motorcycles, jeeps, and cars that the Hamas terrorists had driven into Israel. In total there were thousands of vehicles at the site. Some were completely burned-out. Those that were not had bullet holes through the windshields, and huge dents where the hoods had caved in from crashing. It was a site of terrible desolation and destruction. At one point I came across the completely burned-out ambulance in which a dozen Israelis had hidden after escaping the Nova party and in which they imagined they might be safe. As the chief pathologist explained to me, the young people had run to the ambulance thinking no one would fire on an ambulance. "No one except Hamas," he went on to say. Hamas fired an RPG at the ambulance and all the young people inside were killed in the explosion or the ensuing inferno.

An important and vast task was underway at the site as I was there. The pathologists and religious authorities in Israel needed to make sure there were no remaining parts of the victims' bodies inside the cars in which they had died by the hundreds. Most of the obvious body parts had already been found, but the rabbis had said that the experts should use special instruments to make sure that remaining teeth, bones, and dried blood were sucked out of the wreckage and collected into big sacks, which could then be buried.

It was unpleasant work, and more unpleasant still to be shown the huge bags of ash that was all that was left of these young people. It was almost impossible to look into them—sack after sack of human remains. But there, helping out with a part of the task, was a unit of young women. They were first-year recruits in the IDF. They were not yet expert on anything, but they were there to help out with logistics where they could and help coordinate the task. I got the chance to speak to them—to this bright, sparkly, and vivacious group of young women. They were not enjoying their task, but they were going about it positively, knowing that they were making their difference, and in the knowledge that it was their honor to play their part.

"How old are you?" I eventually asked one of them. "Nineteen," she said. It nearly floored me. These girls were the same age as a student going to college in America or Britain. They were the same age as people in the West who are treated like—and often act like—children. But these Israelis were not children. They were young women. And young soldiers at that. And it struck me, not for the first time, that these women had already seen and gone through more in their lives than their contemporaries in the West would go through by the time they die. But this wasn't a curse for these young women. It was a blessing. To know something about life from its outset and to know what matters from the start of the journey.

Similar thoughts occurred many times. There was one evening in Jerusalem at the Friday-night dinner of friends. The whole extended, noisy Sephardic family was there. The children were all back from base and there were so many of us that we had to spread out over multiple tables. At one point in the evening I began speaking to a young woman in uniform who was sitting opposite me. I asked her how old she was. "Twenty-three," she replied. I asked about her service and what she did. "I'm an intelligence expert on Yemen," she replied. Again you could have floored me. As I looked at her I just got an image in my mind. It was of all the twenty-three-year-old girls I have known in the rest of the West. And though there are exceptions, by and large I would say that the ones I have met are, regardless of their economic status, not just privileged but entitled. They tend to expect that the world will revolve around them and should be endlessly interested in them. They have been told before they have even done anything that they are remarkable and special people. And I thought of the twenty-three-year-old American girls who have just left Stanford, or Yale or Columbia, and felt the absolute certainty that this girl sitting in front of me was not just already out in the world and way ahead of her contemporaries elsewhere, but was also already doing something useful and important with her life.

What she knew at twenty-three her contemporaries would be lucky to know at seventy-three. And then I wondered, who is likely to make the greater contribution? Her contemporaries in the West, or this girl who already just went about her work, without boasting?

***

Of course, the fate of the hostages was a subject which caused the concern of all Israelis just as much as it seemed to consume the fury of certain people outside Israel. Early in the conflict, while I was in Gaza, the world's attention turned to Shifa Hospital, located in the center of the Strip. When Israeli forces raided the hospital there was an outcry across the Western media. The media seemed intent on reporting, once again, that the Israelis were such barbarous people that they would even carry out a military raid on a hospital.

The fact that hostages had been taken there was disputed at every turn, even after closed-circuit footage emerged of Hamas taking them into the compound on the 7th. The IDF found the videos when they went into the hospital the following month. But Hamas's supporters and mouthpieces in the West speculated that it was possible they had been taken into the hospital for treatment. As if anyone rapes and wounds and kidnaps someone only to then take them to a hospital of their choice. When the IDF produced footage taken from the tunnels underneath the Shifa it showed vast reserves of Kalashnikovs, RPGs, sniper rifles, grenades, and other explosives. The BBC's resident Middle East expert, Jeremy Bowen, was asked live on-air by one of his colleagues what it meant in terms of the IDF's insistence that the Shifa was not a hospital but actually a command headquarters of Hamas.

"Wherever you go in the Middle East you see an awful lot of Kalashnikovs," he said. "And you know," he went on, "it's not inconceivable that, I don't know, perhaps the security department of the hospital might have them." He was not asked whether the grenades and RPGs might have belonged to the cardiology department. But he went on to insist that this wasn't the evidence the Israelis needed to show that the Shifa was being used for any nefarious purposes and that so far the Israelis hadn't proved any such thing. Forgotten was the fact that the BBC was just one of the networks that had interviewed Hamas operatives coming out from the tunnels under Shifa as long ago as 2014.

In the same month that the world was focused on Shifa, I spent an evening at another hospital—across the border in Israel. The Schneider Children's Medical Center is one of the foremost children's hospitals in Israel. In the weeks after October 7 the families of the hostages were desperate to get the world to pay attention to the plight of their loved ones. But much of the world, including many organizations that were meant to pay attention to just such situations, remained either cold or indifferent. More than a month after their children had been taken hostage I was at a meeting in Jerusalem where the parents of all the child hostages were finally granted a meeting with the heads of UNICEF, the UN agency that is meant to protect the rights of children around the world.

For more than a month UNICEF had ignored the situation of these Israeli children and ignored the requests of the families to meet. Eventually a meeting was set up in Jerusalem. Just beforehand we got word that the head of UNICEF had been in a car crash in

Egypt and would not be able to attend. So she sent her deputy. I have rarely seen such bare-faced internationalist bureaucracy at work. The representative calmly explained that he sympathized with the families for the loss of their children but that UNICEF was limited in what it could do. "Why could they not use their contacts in Gaza to speak with Hamas?" The representative explained that they had to be careful not to lose their leverage with Hamas. The fact that this might be just the moment to use any such leverage was lost on him. "You have one job," one of the mothers ended up saying, holding up a photo of her child. "Why can't you do it?" He had no answer. Instead, when someone pointed out that UNICEF could surely use its international presence to pressure the countries that sponsored Hamas, he took a couple of notes as though this were the first time he had heard of Qatar or Iran.

Eventually several of the mothers left the meeting weeping tears of frustration. Their children had been in an underground dungeon for weeks and here was a bureaucrat just taking notes. I didn't mention it to anyone, but during the meeting I got word that the head of UNICEF actually was well enough to attend meetings and that she was at the same time attending a meeting about the plight of Palestinian children.

But the Israelis and Hamas knew that the return of the child hostages was surely the easiest part of any hostage-return deal to pull off. The Israelis faced huge public pressure at home to do a deal, any deal, and at least get the children returned. Hamas knew that in terms of public opinion, even for them, stealing and holding children was a bad look.

Eventually, after many weeks, a deal was done. A pause in the fighting was agreed to, and in the first phase of the deal 50 Israeli hostages would be released in exchange for 150 Palestinian prisoners. Among the prisoners were terrorists, including a female Palestinian who had been imprisoned for stabbing her Jewish neighbor in East Jerusalem. As always the deal was not in Israel's favor in terms of numbers, and this confused parts of the media. Kay Burley of Sky News UK asked Israeli government spokesperson Eylon Levy whether the exchange didn't show that Israel valued Israeli lives over Palestinian lives. Levy's eyebrows said it all. The idea that Israel would want a swap so obviously disadvantageous to them in numbers terms seemed to escape Burley, among others. As did the fact that this swap was not a swap of equals—it was a swap of Israeli children for convicted terrorists.

Yet, however bad the deal, there was an extraordinary level of agreement inside Israel that releasing convicted terrorists was a necessary evil in order to leave no Israeli behind—let alone an Israeli child.

Hamas dragged out the negotiation for days. The list of names of hostages who might be handed over was being carefully managed by Hamas, as was their list of prisoners in Israeli jails whom they wanted freed. The release would include some but not all of the children, along with some of their mothers and some pensioners. If the children were going to be released they would be flown immediately to the handover point at the Rafah crossing between Gaza and Egypt, then flown to Tel Aviv by helicopter to area hospitals for immediate medical checkups.

For another agonizing night Hamas stretched out the deal. Then finally there was word that the handover had occurred. A group of us gathered at the children's medical center in Tel Aviv and waited for hours. Photos emerged of some of the mothers at the Rafah crossing—aged seemingly by years through their time in the tunnels. Then there was news that the helicopters had taken off. I stood on the rooftop of the hospital and waited for the sound of the first helicopter to break across the night sky. Much of Tel Aviv could be seen below me. Then the first of the two helicopters appeared. As they emerged, the city became aware of what was happening. Citizens started to gather on the pavements around the heavily cordoned-off landing area. Cars all across the city came to a stop as the IDF soldiers and others came out with screens to protect the children from the glare of the cameras as the first helicopter landed.

As the former hostages started to come out, I suddenly heard singing erupt from below—the citizens of Tel Aviv. "Havenu Shalom Aleichem" filled the air to help sing the children home: "We brought you peace." The returnees that night included twelve children and adults from Nir Oz. I later spoke to one of the helicopter pilots. He told me that there had been furious competition among the pilots for the honor of bringing home their precious cargo.

***

I thought that night on this difference. Whatever criticisms the world wanted to level at Israel, why could they not see this? The difference between a country that had built hospitals to care for its people and a death cult that had used its hospitals to protect itself and deliberately put its people in danger? The difference between a society that built bunkers for its people and a society that built bunkers for its rockets?

Within a year of the October 7 attacks, an emerita professor at Harvard, Ruth Wisse, made a point that was so searing, nobody else had dared raise it. Israel and Jews around the world had often pointed out that the massacres on October 7 had been the worst atrocity carried out against Jews since the Holocaust. But, Wisse pointed out, saying this puts the emphasis on the Jews—on the victims. Some had the courage to mention this and to note its significance, but what almost nobody had the courage to address was who the people are who had carried out this massacre. If the Jews were the victims of the 7th, then why did nobody want to dwell on just who the anti-Semites and Nazis were this time? Why was there so little concentration on the ideology that drives Hamas, Hezbollah, and the Islamic government in Tehran? Were people not interested?

Wisse raised another question: If people recognized the scale of the atrocities of Hamas—atrocities that Hezbollah joined—then why was there such large-scale support in the West not for the people who had suffered the massacre, but instead for the people who had perpetrated it? Some people had compared the outbreak of radicalism from October 2023 to the student protests of 1968. But while the protesters in the 1960s had their wilder aspects, they did not generally take the side of groups who wanted to massacre Jews. Nor were they in the main supporters of Nazism and genocide. What did it mean that on the streets of every major Western city, people who must have known what had been done on the 7th publicly took the side of the aggressors? As Wisse pointed out, perhaps the question wasn't raised because nobody wanted to face the fact that this time the Nazis were among us.

To even notice why the pro-death-cult movement had emerged and spread was to notice a fact that remains unmentionable in most Western democracies. There were patterns, to be sure. But nobody was meant to notice them, because they opened up questions too difficult to even ask.

A month after October 7, Britain's Labour Party was hardly calling the shots over the war in Gaza. But having been racked by years of scandal over anti-Semitism in the party, the new leadership of the party of opposition knew that it had to tread carefully. Show no support for Israel, and the party's reputation for pandering to Islamic extremism and its anti-Semitism scandal risked being reignited. But show too much—or perhaps any—support for Israel, and the party risked losing the support of many of its members. The party's internal debate ended up on whether the party should call for an immediate cease-fire. Such calls began just moments after Hamas had finished its massacre. But so intense was the internal party pressure that Labour representatives soon started to resign on the grounds that Labour leader Keir Starmer was not being sufficiently condemnatory of Israel.

In early November 2023, it was reported that Starmer's unwillingness to call off the IDF (as though this were in his power) had led to the resignation of the leader of Burnley Council and ten other councilors. Councilor Afrasiab Anwar and colleagues said in their letter of resignation that they were leaving the party because "the current party stance on Palestine does not align with the values we hold dear." They went on to attack Starmer for being unwilling to call out Israel on what they called its "indiscriminate bombing and collective punishment of innocent civilians." This was reported as though there were no story underneath it, and the few people who dared to point out that there might be a story were promptly castigated for doing so. But the list of councilors was interesting. As well as Anwar, the list included Ishtiaq Mohammed, Shah Hussain, Asif Raja, Sehrish Lone, Syeda Kazmi, Arif Khan, Lubna Khan, Saeed Chaudhary, and Nussrat Kazmi.[70]

This was presented as if it were just a group of random councilors from Burnley. Yet all were clearly Pakistani or Bangladeshi Muslims. Were people not meant to notice this? Or read anything at all into it? Wasn't it just racist to even notice that these councilors from Burnley seemed to have different names than councilors from the same area may have had even forty years ago? Apparently it was. It was something not to be even noted.

The same thing happened when the first minister (the leader) of Scotland seemed to divert all his attention from independence fights, or tackling poverty and drug overdoses in the East End of Glasgow, to campaign instead against the war in Gaza. Humza Yousaf had been much praised when he became the first Muslim first minister of Scotland. In the campaign to become Scottish National Party leader, his main rival was Kate Forbes. Throughout the campaign the fact that she was a believing Christian and a member of the Free Church of Scotland was widely used against her. The Free Church of Scotland holds some socially conservative views, and Forbes was hounded repeatedly by the media over whether these views were really compatible with being first minister of a "progressive," "tolerant," and "diverse" Scotland. The feeling seemed to be that they were not. But when Yousaf won the election he immediately led an Islamic prayer ceremony at the first minister's residence and this was praised by the media as yet another demonstration of diversity in Scotland.

Whatever Yousaf's views on social issues, when October 7 happened he condemned the Hamas attack and then spent all the succeeding months campaigning against Israel. He even held a one-on-one off-the-record private meeting with Turkish president Recep Tayyip Erdogan, receiving a rebuke from the British foreign secretary, who reminded him that Scotland is not meant to have a separate foreign policy from the rest of the UK. But nothing seemed to deter Yousaf. One reason might have been that he is married to a Palestinian and his in-laws were in Gaza at the start of the war. He also held private meetings with UNRWA, to whom he gave a 250,000-pound donation from Scottish government funds. When asked about this, and whether it had anything to do with his in-laws getting out of Gaza through the Rafah crossing, he attacked the questions as a "smear" and "Islamophobic."[71]

While there were certainly plenty of non-Muslim politicians in the West who decided to attack Israel from the moment the conflict started, it should also be noted that elected Muslim politicians across the West seemed to have a special beef with the Israelis and supported the Palestinian side in the conflict.

In Australia, the left-wing government of Anthony Albanese was widely congratulated in 2022 when Ed Husic was appointed as its first Muslim minister. It was welcomed as another milestone after the election in 2022 of Afghan Australian Fatima Payman as the first hijab-wearing Australian senator. Yet when the war in Gaza broke out, these and other Muslims in the Australian governing party also seemed to fall along distinctly sectarian lines.

In late October 2023, the United Nations voted to call for an immediate cease-fire in the region. The United States was among the countries voting against the motion. Australia abstained, ostensibly because the motion did not mention Hamas as the initiator of the war and the October 7 attacks. Breaking the concept of collective cabinet responsibility, Husic was outspoken in his attacks on Israel and his government's vote at the UN. He had called even the early phase of Israel's war "very disproportionate" and accused Israel of collective punishment in Gaza.[72] Shortly afterward the UN once again voted on a cease-fire motion, and while there were no meaningful changes to the resolution, this time Australia voted in favor of it. Later, when the Australian parliament voted on the issue of giving the Palestinians another state in the West Bank as well as Gaza, Payman crossed the floor and voted against her own governing party. Describing her crossing of the floor—breaking a protocol that had last been broken before her own birth—Payman said, "I walked with my Muslim brothers and sisters who told me they have felt unheard for far too long."[73]

In the US, the most vociferous anti-Israel opposition in Congress came from representatives Rashida Tlaib and Ilhan Omar. In every Western country it seemed to be the same. It was not simply immigration. In the UK, Prime Minister Rishi Sunak and Home Secretary Suella Braverman were both steadfast on the right of Israel to defend itself. Both of these politicians were the children of immigrants—but they were the children of Hindu parents. For some reason, Hindus in prominent positions in the West were less likely to take an instinctively anti-Israel stance, while the children of Muslim immigrants lined up in almost every country to take an anti-Israel line on the conflict.

Was this coincidence? Or was it because people are brought up with and educated into a particular ideology? One idea that is widespread across Muslim populations in the West is that Israel is always the aggressor in the region and Palestinians are always the victims. But might it, in fact, be worse than that? The visible dominance of Muslims at the protests in London and other Western cities suggested that this was very much falling along sectarian lines. And perhaps there were reasons for it.

In 2013, ten years before the outbreak of the latest war, the far-left anti-Israel commentator Mehdi Hasan made a rare admission in the pages of the *New Statesman*. Reacting to a Muslim peer who had recently blamed the Jews for a car crash in which he had run over and killed a Polish man while texting on his phone, Hasan observed one of the things that was actually going on. "It pains me

to have to admit this," he wrote, "but anti-Semitism isn't just toler-
ated in some sections of the British Muslim community; it's routine
and commonplace. Any Muslims reading this article—if they are
honest with themselves—will know instantly what I am referring to.
It's our dirty little secret." At any Muslim dinner table, he observed
from experience, Muslims could at any point break out into conspiracy theories about the Jews killing everyone from Diana, Prin-
cess of Wales to perpetrating the 9/11 attacks in America. The fact
that even a Muslim community so ostensibly unconnected with the
Middle East as Britain's Muslim community is was telling in itself.
As Hasan wrote, "The truth is that the virus of anti-Semitism has
infected members of the British Muslim community, both young and
old. No, the ongoing Israel-Palestine conflict hasn't helped matters.
But this goes beyond the Middle East. How else to explain why British Pakistanis are so often the most ardent advocates of anti-Semitic
conspiracies, even though there are so few Jews living in Pakistan?"[74]

How indeed?

***

One explanation is that the Muslim world is the one place where
the virus of Nazi anti-Semitism did not just continue unchallenged
after 1945, but actually flourished. Anyone who doubts that might
wonder why. There is actually a very clear reason.

After 1945, the people who committed the atrocities of the Nazi
era were either tried and hanged or escaped into anonymity and exile. The most prominent leaders were hanged or imprisoned after
the Nuremberg Trials. And the German public were famously forced
to accept the evil that had been committed among them, including
being shown the dead in the camps. Those Nazis who managed to
escape, like Adolf Eichmann and Josef Mengele, lived under pseud-
onyms in South America, fearing at any moment that their identities
would be discovered and they too would be brought to justice.

But there was one Nazi leader who managed to leave the inferno of Europe with his head held high. Haj Amin al-Husseini, the Grand Mufti of Jerusalem, distinguished himself in 1941 by actually going to Adolf Hitler and offering the services of his people. It was the Mufti's view that he and Hitler should be in alliance because they had a natural common enemy—the Jews. Newsreel footage from their meeting shows the Mufti doing a Nazi salute before shaking Hitler's hand, as well as inspecting Nazi troops. The official record of their meeting shows that Hitler agreed to have no territorial claim on Arab lands so long as the Mufti helped him with the extermination of the Jews in the Middle East. Al-Husseini was only too pleased to oblige and helped to set up a division of Germany's Waffen SS in his region to clear the Jews from the Middle East. Through his military and political leadership as well as his Arabic tirades on public radio, he repeatedly made it clear that his aim was to kill the Jews.

After the war the Mufti attempted to gain asylum in Switzerland, but the British and French authorities requested his extradition in order that he be tried for his collaboration with the Nazis. It took a year of back-and-forth in Europe (not least due to requests from the Yugoslav authorities to try him for war crimes there), but other politics were at play. The State of Israel was being prepared, as was a possible Palestinian state. Eventually, through a complex series of machinations, the Mufti was able to return to Egypt in June 1946.

As reported by the Egyptian media at the time, he was welcomed fulsomely. The Egyptian and Arab publics were fully aware of the Mufti and his achievements. The founder of the Muslim Brotherhood, Hassan al-Banna, was among those who welcomed him home. Al-Banna had also been an admirer of Hitler and Nazism ever since first reading *Mein Kampf*. In his open letter to the Mufti on his return to Egypt, al-Banna said, "The hearts of the Arabs palpitated with joy at hearing that the Mufti has succeeded in reaching an Arab country. The news sounded like thunder to the ears of some American, British and Jewish tyrants. The lion is at last free, and he will roam the Arabian jungle to clear it of wolves. The great leader is back."

Al-Banna went on: "Hitler's and Mussolini's defeat did not frighten you. Your hair did not turn grey of fright and you are still full of life and fight. What a hero, what a miracle of a man. We wish to know what the Arab youth, Cabinet Ministers, rich men, and princes of Palestine, Syria, Iraq, Tunis, Morocco, and Tripoli are going to do to be worthy of this hero. Yes, this hero who challenged an empire and fought Zionism, with the help of Hitler and Germany. Germany and Hitler are gone, but Amin Al-Husseini will continue the struggle."[75]

The importance of this moment and this sentiment cannot be overemphasized. There were many things that were remarkable about the Mufti. He was clearly a great leader of men, and a true fanatic and zealot. Such was his reputation that Yasser Arafat often played on the fact that he was a relative of the Mufti. Even a distant kinship with al-Husseini was a boon to Arafat's claim to be his successor. But the historical significance of the Mufti after the war and until his death in 1974 was singular. Everybody else who had led the way in the Nazi Holocaust of the Jews was either dead or in hiding. Al-Husseini was the only Nazi leader who returned to his home country after the war in triumph and as a hero. The bacillus of Nazi anti-Semitism returned, unmoderated, with him. That is why, from a Cairo train station to the houses of Gaza, the Middle East is the one region on earth where Nazi anti-Semitism is not seen as a strand of losing, toxic ideology, but as the stance of victors, and a hope for the future.

CHAPTER 5

FROM DEFEAT INTO VICTORY

There is something about war that heightens every human emotion. It is easier to hate in wartime, obviously. But all of life comes into a more vivid perspective. Most notoriously, it is easier to love. It is a cliché of wartime that young men and women return from the front and propose to their partners. Parents sometimes worry about this. Will it last when it started in this way? But it is unavoidable. When you see war up close, you cannot help but think about what matters most. The usual expectation that we will die in our eighth or ninth decade, quietly in our beds, surrounded by loved ones, is stripped away. When you are forced to wonder whether you will live to see tomorrow, everything today is different. It is one of the things that makes war so fascinating: because it feels like it is one of the few things on earth that has the ability to reveal the meaning of things. In war, you get the most vivid sense possible, that life itself might be understood.

At the beginning of her book on the Vietnam War, *Nothing and Amen*, the great Italian journalist and author Oriana Fallaci relates a conversation with her much younger adopted sister. During their chatter the child suddenly asks one of those questions that small children do: "Life, what is it?" Acknowledging that she has never been good with children, Fallaci tries to come up with a formula that will satisfy the child. "And death, what is it?" Elisabetta persists. Fallaci promises Elisabetta that if she falls asleep she will tell her about it all the next day. The next day Fallaci leaves for Vietnam.

By the time she returns home, Fallaci has not just witnessed the war in Vietnam but been shot three times and been left for dead among the bodies in the Tlatelolco massacre in Mexico City. Back with the family in the end, she says, "Come here, Elisabetta, my little sister. One day you asked me what life was. Do you still want to know?" "Yes, what is life?" "It is something you've got to fill up well, without wasting any time. Even if you break it by filling it too full."[76]

I thought about this question, and this answer, often during Israel's year of war. And I kept coming back to what Fallaci says: to fill it so full, you risk even breaking it. Amid all the heartbreak of war, that is certainly one answer: to fill life up.

In the days after the war began, I was given access to the Israeli pathologists who were working on identifying the bodies in the morgues. Bags were still being brought in, but with less and less in them to identify the victims. Many victims were being identified by bits of the mobile phones or other things on their bodies that had not burned fully. One of the skulls that had been put back together was small. Surely this was a child's skull, I said? Possibly, replied the expert, but it could also be the head of a young adult that had simply contracted in the fire.

These pathologists went about their task with unbelievable care, but I couldn't describe the sadness in their eyes. Nor the smell everywhere. If the thing you cannot communicate from a war zone is the noise, what cannot be identified from the aftermath of a massacre is the smell. One of the bodies in the morgue had been found near the site of the Nova festival, had been out in the open for days, and was badly decomposed. The bone structure showed that it was the body of a young man, but beyond that the pathologists were lost as to identifying him. They extracted a tooth from his skull to see if they could get a DNA sample from that, but as I looked at him and the two women going about their duty I suddenly thought of what Lord Byron said when he saw the body of his friend and fellow poet Shelley in the pit it had been temporarily buried in on the Italian coast. "Is that a human body?" the poet asked. "Why it's more like the carcass of a sheep, or any other animal, than a man: this is a satire on our pride and folly."[77]

And yet life, sometimes changed, altered for a time, continues. One evening I was having dinner with some friends in Tel Aviv. Suddenly someone stepped in from the balcony where they had been taking a call. It was one of the pathologists I had been with in the morgues. "Ah Douglas," he said, "how good to see you among the living." I sometimes asked these people how they cope with their job. And the answer of course is that they are used to it. But one of them once confided that there was something since the 7th that he had found especially hard. Many of the bodies, particularly the burned bodies of family members, had been commingled in the fire, or had been tied together. It is one thing to be surprised by death. But these people must all have known they were going to die, and often seen members of their family die already. "The knowledge that you are going to die," the pathologist said to me, shaking his head, "that is very difficult."

Perhaps it is why over all these months two lines kept going through my head. Unsurprisingly, perhaps, for someone in the Holy Land, they were both lines from scripture. One of the things that makes this region remarkable is that it is a place where the lines and the stories of the Bible live. On one of my first visits, in the 2000s, I spoke with members of an Arab Christian community who had just built a new church. What was the name? I asked. "The Church of the Transfiguration," one of the men replied. Beautiful, but why had they chosen that name? "Because it is our tradition to name any church after the name of the nearest religious event, and," he said, suddenly pointing to a nearby mountain, "the Transfiguration happened there." For him it was normal. For someone brought up only hearing these stories I was nearly floored. It is like the difference between asking directions in London or asking them in Jerusalem. "Turn left up the Edgware Road" is a very different command from "Turn right on the Via Dolorosa." It makes not just scripture come alive, but life come alive alongside it.

So throughout the year I kept finding the same lines coming back to me. First was the line from Deuteronomy when God says: "I have set before you life and death, blessing and cursing: therefore choose life, that thou and thy seed may live." I thought also of the Psalmist who says, "I shall not die, but live." I thought of these lines continuously, even in the moments when things could not have been darker. One evening, late into the night, I went to see a family who live in the town of Barkan in Samaria. The father was a local official, and he, his wife, and teenage son were all still up as though night and day no longer mattered. The house was filled with photos of their beautiful daughter, and pictures of sunflowers.

Their daughter, twenty-three-year-old Adi Baruch, was an aspiring photographer. She especially liked to photograph sunflowers, because she appreciated how whatever the time of day, they turn their faces toward the sun. She was a reservist on October 7 and didn't need to go back into the army. Her parents pleaded with her not to, but she knew she had a job to do and felt she was needed. On her first day back in uniform, October 12, she was in Sderot. Hamas were still firing rockets. When the sirens went off she got out of her car and lay on the ground beside it, but one of the rockets landed right alongside her, killing her instantly. Her mother described it all in terrible detail, but she had a comfort, she said, which was that the blast that killed her had also left her untouched. "She looked like she was just sleeping. Like an angel," her mother told me. They buried Adi three days later, and after the ceremony her fiancé approached the coffin alone and left on top of it a white box with the engagement ring that he bought for her. Afterward her parents shared with me the letter that her daughter had left for them before going back into the army. It was to be read in the case of her death. Her mother read it to me now. Among much else Adi had written to her parents to tell them how sorry she was. But toward the end she told them, "I wanted to live life, and now I want you to live it for me."

I thought of all the other people who wanted to live. Of Ben Shimoni, who was at the Nova party. His girlfriend, Jessica Miranda Elter, had called him that morning begging him to come back. "Something is happening, come back." "Yes, yes," he had tried to reassure her. "I'll come back, don't worry." In fact he did again and again, but he never got back to her. Ben managed to escape the party, taking four other terrified partygoers with him in his car. He drove them to safety in Beersheba, thirty minutes away. Then he headed back to the site of the party. On that trip he managed to save another group of five young people and also took them to safety. Each time, his passengers begged him not to go back into the firefight. But he had a mission. On the third attempt, carrying three more survivors in his car, the terrorists caught him and riddled the car with bullets until it crashed into another car, killing everyone.

I thought also of Omer Ohana and Sagi Golan, who woke up on the morning of the 7th just two weeks before they were due to marry. Both men were immediately recalled to their units. Omer was sent to the north and Sagi to the south. They both agreed that they would send each other a heart on WhatsApp every hour to let the other know they were okay. Thirty-year-old Sagi fought with his antiterrorism unit in Kibbutz Be'eri, among other sites, and saved many lives that day. Omer said, "On midnight, I got the last heart from Sagi." His fiancé was killed shortly afterward in the ongoing battle in Be'eri. The Israeli singer Ivri Lider, who was due to sing a song they had chosen for their wedding, performed it instead at Sagi's funeral.

***

All the time I thought too of the people who brought this death upon them. The people who seemed intent on death, not life. From the moment the massacre began, I decided that when I could get the chance I wanted to see some of the terrorists face-to-face: to look into the eyes of the people who had been so high on the thrill of death—who had demonstrated such ecstasy as they brought it on men, women, and children that morning.

Eventually, in the April after the massacre, I got permission to visit one of the world's most secure prisons. The facility, at an undisclosed location inside Israel, was where the Israeli prison service was holding some of the most dedicated and murderous people who had broken into Israel that day and been caught alive. Contact with the prisoners had to be exceptionally carefully managed. Everything that could have been used as a weapon had been used as a weapon by these prisoners. It was made clear to me that however defeated they looked now, every one of them had been someone who had wanted to die—who had expected to die and was still eager to die.

I had already seen the footage from the 7th from Netiv HaAsara, where the Taasa family lived. I saw it shortly after the 7th. The family's eldest son, who was seventeen, was on the beach when the terrorists came. He hid in a bomb shelter with friends but the terrorists came to the shelter and shot everyone inside and recorded it on camera before sending the footage out to the world. Shortly afterward Hamas found their way to the family house. Hearing them coming, the father, Gil, ran into a bomb shelter with his two young sons. Security cameras captured the moment when one of the terrorists threw a grenade after the family into the bomb shelter.

Gil threw himself on the grenade to save his young sons. Still, the youngest son, eight, had an eye blown out of its socket by the blast. The elder boy, Koren, twelve, seemed to have lost his hearing. Footage from inside the family house shows the boys clambering out of the shelter and staggering around the living room in their underwear. Koren asks his younger brother, "Can you see in this eye?" "No, no," says the eight-year-old, weeping.

Then one of the terrorists who had just killed their father calmly walks into the family room with an AK-47 around his shoulders.

He takes away the older boy's phone and insists he speak to him in Arabic. "What? I don't know. Please, please, let me go home. Call mama, my mum. Please. Where's my dad, my dad?" Eventually one of the terrorists comes back into the room, opens the family fridge in front of the boys, removes a bottle of the family's Coca-Cola, and calmly walks away drinking it.

The director of the prison had the video of this on his phone and he showed it to me again. It was even harder to watch and hear the second time around, particularly the cries of the boys as they staggered around in the deepest distress, each holding their heads, with the younger boy still denying that their father was dead. It was harder still, because one of the terrorists who committed this atrocity was only a few feet away from me in the prison.

Conditions in Israeli prisons used to be fairly relaxed for Palestinian prisoners. Palestinians I have spoken with who were in Israel's jails before the 7th related how they had semi-open-air markets where they could buy and eat chicken shawarma and other dishes. But after the 7th the minister in charge of prisons insisted on the strictest possible conditions for these terrorists. They were to be confined, with around eight people to a cell in the harshest maximum-security conditions. It was stressed to me repeatedly that although these men may now look beleaguered and poor, they were people who had done the most unimaginable things when they had the upper hand just a few months before.

As we entered the facilities I was allowed to go into the cells and see the terrorists for myself. I recognized one of the two men who had entered the Taasa family's home that morning. More startling was that in one of the cells I recognized someone who had become notorious in Israel since the 7th. He was a young Gazan with distinctive, bright ginger hair. Footage recorded by Hamas and others showed what he did on the morning of the 7th. He entered the Nova party with guns and grenades. From the evidence of the videos and survivor testimony, it seems that he may have killed as many as thirty or forty young people at the party that morning. And here he was in front of me, looking no different from any other person of his age. He didn't look evil—only pathetic.

I suppose that you look at people like this in the hope that you might see something in them. What is it? Remorse? Evil? I spent hours in the prison that day, and although I saw people I knew from the atrocity videos, there was nothing to learn from them. They had decided to live their lives with one ambition—to take away life. I thought not of Hannah Arendt, but of Gitta Sereny, who actually spent her life studying evil. I remembered something Sereny had said toward the end of her life: she had come to the conclusion that evil is a force that sometimes seems to just descend on the world. But the fact that it exists, and is a reality, was to her mind impossible to deny.

In October 2024, I was with my cameraman Moshe on our way to the Lebanon border. Hezbollah was firing large numbers of missiles at the north and center of Israel, but long before we got to the north, Moshe got an alert on his Hatzalah device. Something was happening in the town of Hadera. We happened to be exactly at the interchange and we drove right into the situation.

It seemed that three Israeli Arabs had gone on a terrorist stabbing spree in the city. We had the location for the first attack, which was still taking place. We arrived in time to find one of the first victims bleeding out in front of us in the doorway of his house. He had a set of knife wounds to his rib cage and was rolling on the floor as Moshe and another first responder tried to apply pressure to the wounds and stem the bleeding. We didn't know where the attacker was but there was blood all over the street and floor around us. Occasionally people peered out from their front doors and then locked them shut again fast. Everyone knew that the terrorists had gone on or were hiding somewhere around us, but where?

There was word that two of them had driven off on a scooter. Locals shouted that the attacker or attackers were heading to the local school. By now the police were on the scene too along with an ambulance. The man we had tended to was wheeled toward the ambulance, a look of extreme pain as well as amazement on his face.

He died shortly afterward. It turned out that he was a thirty-seven-year-old rabbi, and the father of seven children. Meanwhile the police managed to handcuff someone they thought was an accomplice of the terrorist—a young Arab man who was helping him on his spree. He was arrested a few feet away from me, and for a moment we looked directly at each other. There was a look of complete resignation on his face, as though all this was exactly as he expected. For my own part I was overcome with a single feeling: What a stupid, stupid thing to do with your life. Of all the things you could have done on this earth, why do this? Don't you know what a waste you have just made of your life?

Now there were alerts going off everywhere. We got to an intersection just after another victim had been attacked. It now seemed there was a single terrorist but he was hacking at people with an ax as well as a knife. Blood covered the middle of the road, and as panicked locals drove their cars to get away the blood and first-aid bandages were ground into the tarmac. Soon there were a group of us running, now with the police, to where the attacker was reported to be. Eventually they found him, standing at the end of an alley. He refused to take off his visor mask or padded jacket, and in a moment when it looked like he was about to reach for a weapon he was shot and fell to the floor.

It was a situation both surreal and ordinary, the sort that happens in a country at war. Terrible things happen, then rumors, panics, survival, and mourning. That day had only just begun and we still had to head north because the Israeli war on Hezbollah was now at full steam.

***

As the first anniversary of the war came around, Israel managed to shift the balance of the conflict in the most stunning fashion. For a year the tens of thousands of families who lived in the north of Israel had been displaced in their own country. I lived with the residents of one of the northern cities, Kiryat Shmona, for most of the year. And while the world didn't seem to care that these people were displaced, and their children's education disrupted for a second year in a row, I had come to care. And I had been to their hometown more often than they had during the year. Rockets landed there, as in other towns in the north, on a daily basis, but as with towns that had been close to the southern border this was a place where the sirens didn't work. If you were in a town some kilometers from the Gaza or Lebanon borders you got to hear the sirens when rockets and missiles came over. You had a few seconds to head to a shelter or throw yourself on the ground. But in places like this you heard the boom of the rocket and only then the siren.

From the start of the war, the Israeli government had said that they didn't want to fight a war on two fronts, but if they had to they would. Before the anniversary of the 7th, information gathered from Hamas in Gaza showed that the plans for October 7 had actually been even more ambitious than originally thought. Hamas had not informed their counterparts about the date of the attack, but Hezbollah and the Iranian regime were told of the Al-Aqsa Flood plans and Hezbollah were going to join in. Although Hamas did not communicate the date, the plan had been that what happened in the south that day would also happen in the north of Israel. There too the Hezbollah tunnels had been built right up to the Israeli border. There too there was meant to be missile fire followed by a ground invasion, with Israel being strangled from at least two directions in a nooselike maneuver. Hamas had hoped to come up through the center of the country and Hezbollah would come down the other way to meet in the middle and take it over completely.

Whether it was the discovery of this plan by the Israelis or the drawing down of the war in Gaza, military pressure could now be applied more to the north. And so in September 2024, Israel fully turned its attentions on Hezbollah in Lebanon, suddenly pulling off a set of stunning intelligence and military spectaculars.

It began in mid-September when news came out of thousands of pager devices exploding across Lebanon and Syria. The pagers had been acquired by Hezbollah in the past year because they had become as wary as their colleagues in Hamas were of using conventional communication devices. So the group acquired thousands of old-fashioned pagers, which they distributed among several thousand of their operatives. What they did not know was that the Israelis had got into the supply chain that Hezbollah was using and planted a tiny amount of explosive in each device, enough to cause serious harm or possibly death to the person who had a Hezbollah pager.

They went off in one go, at 3:30 p.m. local time, killing at least twelve people and injuring thousands more. Videos showed Hezbollah members getting a beep on the device and it then exploding like a gunshot. Operatives who were not killed were badly wounded in their groin, hands, or face. Hospitals in Lebanon and Syria were suddenly filling up with maimed Hezbollah terrorists.

It was probably the most discriminate strike against a terrorist network in history, even if, inevitably, much of the world condemned Israel for this "indiscriminate" act. One day later, having realized that their pagers had been compromised, Hezbollah resorted to walkie-talkies. Then these exploded too. In that attack some twenty people were killed and hundreds more were injured. At least one of the walkie-talkies went off at a funeral for one of the Hezbollah members killed in the pager attack the day before. The walkie-talkies had been purchased by Hezbollah five months earlier, and the Israelis had managed to get into that supply chain too.

In the aftermath of the pager and walkie-talkie explosions much of the senior leadership of Hezbollah met up in a building in Beirut. The Israeli Air Force then struck the building they were in, killing much of the leadership. Then, in perhaps the ultimate blow to the organization, the group's leader, Hassan Nasrallah, who had rarely appeared in public since the 2006 Lebanon War, thought that Benjamin Netanyahu's visit to speak at the United Nations in New York in late September was an opportunity to meet with Hezbollah's senior remaining leadership in Beirut. It appeared to have been a double bluff by the Israeli prime minister. He ordered an air strike on Nasrallah and the other Hezbollah leadership just before stepping onstage at the UN. By the end of the day it was confirmed that Nasrallah and most of the rest of the leadership of Hezbollah had been killed. The *New York Times* would go on to say in their obituary of the terrorist leader that he was "beloved," "a towering figure," and a "powerful orator."[78] America's president acknowledged that the death of a terrorist who had been behind the killing of 241 American service members at the Marine barracks in Beirut in October 1983, was a good thing.[79] Emmanuel Macron's thank-you for bringing the killers of fifty-eight French paratroopers to justice was to impose an arms embargo on Israel.[80]

Whatever his oratorical skills, Nasrallah and his group had waged war on the West for decades. They had fired rockets at Israel daily since October 8. And now, with a few strokes, the Lamborghini of Iran's terror network had been utterly wrecked.

***

This did not mean that Iran and Hezbollah's war against Israel was over. In the wake of Nasrallah's death the Iranian regime sent another barrage of missiles at Israel direct from Iran—the second such attack in a year. On October 1, the mullahs sent 180 missiles and other warheads directly into Israeli territory from Iran. Most of the missiles were intercepted but those that landed caused around $50 million in damage.

Some people saw this as a sign of Iranian strength, others of its weakness. During its first year of war the regime had been able to fire at Israel using its proxies in Gaza, Lebanon, and Yemen. Now they were reduced to this most dangerous of all strategies. No longer able to rely on their proxies, the Iranian regime was now out in the open, reduced to actually having to fight for themselves, and in the process risking all-out war with Israel.

Yet neither Hamas's nor Hezbollah's forces were entirely spent.

On the anniversary of October 7 there were sirens across Israel as Hamas managed to fire off a small barrage of rockets in the direction of Tel Aviv and other cities. But it was the increase of firing in the north that was more of a problem. In a matter of days Israeli air strikes had taken out an estimated 50 percent or more of the arsenal that Hezbollah had built up since 2006.[81] But that still meant Hezbollah had rockets to cover most of Israel. Haifa, one of the country's tech hubs, became the subject of daily rocket fire. Unmanned drones that were able to get through the Iron Dome defense by switching to battery power, thus becoming unidentifiable by the heat-seeking antimissile devices, started landing on Herzliya, at the home of the Israeli prime minister and, most fatally, on a military base in Binyamina.

On the same day as the attack in Hadera I continued to make my way north to the Lebanese border. Over the past year I had been there many times and seen many exchanges of fire on both sides. In towns like Shlomi I had watched Hezbollah missiles and Israel's interceptor missiles dance around each other in the skies in a game of catch that was at once both beautiful and terrible. This day I decided, among other places, to visit the town of Safed.

The hilltop town is about seven miles from the Lebanese border and many of its residents had stayed for the past year. I wanted to visit it for two reasons. One is that it is famous as a historic and religious site—perhaps most of all as the home of the Kabbalah tradition. The second reason was that it was here in 2006 that I first saw rockets land inside Israel. Back then I had been in the hospital in the town. Hezbollah had less precise missiles back then, but they had managed to hit the hospital, and a French journalist had broken the reporting restrictions that existed then against naming exactly what had been hit. So Hezbollah knew where to fire the rockets in order to keep hitting the hospital.

I thought now that I would revisit the hospital and see how it was doing. No sooner had Moshe and I arrived in Safed than we found one of the only food shops that was open. As we stood talking to the owner the sirens went off and then the sky started erupting with rockets. We took shelter in the cave beneath the shop. The floor started to shake with the impact of the explosives. Heading out into the street again, we watched the dance of missiles overhead. Hezbollah had fired several hundred rockets in a few minutes, and in the sky overhead the battle raged, with the interceptors struggling to catch up with the sheer volume of missiles that were coming over. Occasionally you would see one hit its target. Sometimes the sound from along the street told you that a rocket had hit.

After the barrage we went down to one of the houses that had been struck. Two women were rocking back and forth outside their bombed-out house. The older one was holding a piece of blood-covered cotton over one of her bleeding eyes. We made it to the hospital once the wounded were all there, and I met with the Druze head of the hospital. He asked if I had been to his hospital before. I told him that I had—in 2006. He showed me the footage of the hospital being rocketed again a few months earlier. "I hope you come in peacetime someday," he said. And so did I. But instantly my mind went back to that IDF soldier in Gaza the year before. It was eighteen years since I had been under a rocket barrage in Safed. And now eighteen years later, here I was, back again.

***

Among much else the thought brought me back to a conversation I had near the very start of the war. Late in the evening at a Friday-night dinner with a Sephardic family in Jerusalem, one of the fathers came over to the table I was at. He slammed down his vodka glass and suddenly said, "So. Iron Dome. Good idea or bad?" As I told him, it was a question that no one outside Israel would even understand.

Anyone outside Israel would say, "A good idea, obviously." But my friend's point was not that. What had Israel managed to do since the withdrawal from Gaza and the end of the 2006 Hezbollah war?

With the assistance mostly of the United States, it had managed to create a world-class system, of which everyone was very proud, to shoot down the regular rockets. But perhaps this had not been a good thing at all? If New Jersey had launched rockets at New York City constantly for a decade, would New York State find a way to shoot these down and learn to live with it? Or would it take out whatever infrastructure was launching the things?

Most people know the answer. But Israel had slipped into its own system of response and had seemed for a time to be consoled by it. Why did all these homes across the north and south of the country need safe rooms? In Safed I met a woman who was raising money to bring more bomb shelters to the town even now. It was necessary, but what a waste of resources. And what an answer to an attempt to wipe a country out. Why did every building in Tel Aviv have a bomb shelter in it or nearby? Why was the whole country so littered with bomb shelters that on the 7th people ran into them across the south and were promptly massacred inside them by Hamas? How was this a way to live? And who else would live like this?

Maybe the whole thing had been a bad idea. Perhaps the first time that Hamas sent rockets into Israel from Gaza, Israel or the international community should have gone in and stopped them immediately. But what was Israel to do? Its international allies had condemned them at every stage when they had tried to defend themselves; their best allies had simply helped them find more and more ingenious ways in which to cower.

There is no doubt that the young people of Gaza and Lebanon also know the fear of cowering from air strikes. But why should everyone I saw still living in the most dangerous areas have become accustomed to throwing themselves on the floor at any moment or running with a few seconds' notice to a bomb shelter? In Kiryat Shmona one day in October 2024, with no warning from the sirens, rockets started to land again from Lebanon. Two people were killed in the street. Later that day, as I sat outside the sole open cafe I saw a young teenager from the area—one of the very few people left—taking sup-

plies from a car to bring into the shop. This stockboy seemed different in his manner and behavior, and I realized why. The whole time
as he walked he was looking up at the sky, wondering what might
come out of it next and how to get cover when it did.

That is no way to live. But it was the death cults of Tehran that
made millions of people live like this in Israel, and as a consequence
of that, in Lebanon and Gaza too. Except that there the death cults
had built no bomb shelters for their people—only for their rockets.

It wasn't as though the leadership of Iran's groups hid what they
were doing. At the beginning of the war in Gaza, senior Hamas official Moussa Abu Marzouk was asked whether ordinary Gazan
civilians would be able to shelter in the tunnels. "These tunnels,"
he explained, "are meant to protect us from the airplanes. We are
fighting from inside the tunnels." Besides, he went on, the lives of
the people of Gaza were the responsibility of the UN, not Hamas.[82]

＊＊＊

There was one final trip to make. In all the months of war along the
northern border I had traveled everywhere. From Mount Hermon in
the winter, where we overlooked not just Israel but Syria and Lebanon too. From the town of Metula, surrounded on three sides by
Lebanon and where we could see Hezbollah outposts everywhere
around us. A lone hotel had just been rocketed. I went in to see the
damage only to have the IDF pull me out fast. Hezbollah could see
we were in the building and were likely to try to hit it again as a result. Later one of the soldiers in the Israeli observation post showed
me footage from their cameras the night before. Both sides were
watching each other intently. Between them was the border that was
meant to be patrolled by the UN peacekeeping force called UNIFIL,
which was established before the 2006 war.

The footage from the night before showed a UN peacekeeping
convoy setting off from their base to drive along the border. Shortly
after they had set out, Hezbollah fired a volley of several missiles

right over the UN vehicles and into Israel. The UN vehicles simply did a sharp U-turn and returned to base. It occurred to me that this was not peacekeeping. It was war-watching. But then what did the international community expect? The history of UN peacekeeping troops, from the former Yugoslavia to Rwanda, had always been the same. You might find a range of countries willing to deploy troops to the other side of the earth, but would those troops, or their countries, be remotely willing to risk or even lose their lives for this? What soldier from anywhere on earth would be prepared to tackle Hezbollah? And to what end? To enforce a resolution that the world didn't even intend to enforce?

By the anniversary of the war, the IDF were managing to make incursions into southern Lebanon. Their aim was to clear the Hezbollah infrastructure nearest to the Israeli border. I told them that as soon as it was possible for me to get into Lebanon I wanted to be there. Eventually, shortly after the ground war had begun, I managed to make it in a number of times.

The first time I headed in through two different locations on the Lebanese border to see the tunnels that Hezbollah had spent its time constructing. In recent years the group had taken in billions of dollars of support, including at least $1 billion a year from Iran. I got a chance to see what they had done with it. Right up near the border, I saw Israeli towns I now knew well, but from the other side. Here Hezbollah had spent years building a tunnel network like their colleagues in Gaza. These too had been built in the hope of carrying out a Hamas-style October 7 attack on Israel, as well as to store and fire rockets into northern Israel.

The ground in Lebanon is rocky, not sandy like Gaza, and so these deep tunnels require even more construction efforts and even heavier machinery. In the rock of Lebanon these are seriously difficult to construct. Yet these tunnel shafts opened not much more than three hundred feet from a giant UN peacekeeping base and observation point. How was it even possible that the kind of heavy digging needed to create these tunnels could have happened right under the noses of the UN? Were they not looking? Did they even care?

The answer seems to be an obvious no. They decided not to look. At this point the UN peacekeepers included Irish and Sri Lankan soldiers. Again, why would they put their lives on the line to enforce a mere UN resolution? The world might have expected them to, but at best what were they going to do? Go to Hezbollah and ask them what they were doing with all this heavy machinery and rocket apparatus in an area that was meant to be demilitarized?

The tunnels went deep into the ground and connected with each other, just as Hamas's tunnels do in Gaza. But these had even more deadly potential. IDF soldiers on the ground who had spent recent days clearing these areas told me that they had been astonished by the capabilities of Hezbollah they had found so far. In one square kilometer alone, they told me they had uncovered over one hundred tunnel shafts like these. All were filled with ammunition, blood units, and other medical gear, and much of it bore the label "Made in Iran."

We went farther along inside Lebanon—again only a few hundred yards from the Israeli border. There we went through an area of densely built-up forest that had not yet been cleared. We walked along a path that Hezbollah had made and been using until recent days. There were clear markers on the trees in green paint to guide the terrorists.

This narrow path had been cleared of the booby traps that Hezbollah, like Hamas, likes to leave. Then, in the middle of the forest, we came across one of many Hezbollah hiding places that had recently been abandoned. It was a camp with a bunker where a cell of perhaps ten Hezbollah terrorists had recently been living. They had left much of their kit on their way out. It included not just Hezbollah uniforms and vests, but all of the group's other necessities. There were mines, including ones that are used to blow open walls. Now it was known that Hezbollah was planning an October 7–style attack from the north; it was obvious this was going to be one of their ways to break into Israel, just as their friends in Hamas broke in from the south. They would have used these to blow open the border walls and fences between Lebanon and Israel and then move through the towns of northern Israel, massacring the citizens there just as Hamas had in the south.

The Hezbollah terrorists who had recently left this camp had left other things behind too, including pipe bombs, other explosives, and many rounds of bullets. The writing on these items showed clearly where they had come from, and how recently. There were items, including medical kits, whose expiration dates showed that they had been acquired in the last year from Iran. But there were other items that revealed how new weaponry had also arrived in the last year from a range of countries, most notably, apart from Iran, Russia and North Korea. Into the trunk of a tree a bored Hezbollah fighter had carved a swastika.

In this portion of Lebanon alone, the Israelis had already found more than seven hundred caches of weapons like this. All were a testament to the billions of dollars that Hezbollah might have used to improve the lives of the people of Lebanon but had instead used to try to destroy Israel.

With the same cynicism as Hamas, and in contravention once again of every law of war, the Hezbollah camp had water and electricity cable connections to two nearby Lebanese villages. Of course this could put the lives of these villagers at risk, but like Hamas in Gaza, Hezbollah knows that the lives of civilians do not matter. A strike by the Israelis that kills civilians is a win-win for Hezbollah, as it is for Hamas and their backers in Iran.

All this and more had been done under the noses of the United Nations, which at the very same moment was once again demanding a cease-fire. But seeing what they had allowed to go on for the past eighteen years, I wondered what might have happened if the UN had actually done their job. Also, if they were so keen on a cease-fire, could they ever take any responsibility for having overseen the rearmament that allowed Hezbollah to re-start the war?

Between two of my trips to Lebanon, the IDF captured a terrorist in one of the Hezbollah tunnels. Wadah Kamel Younis told investigators that he was captured in an underground Hezbollah compound and that in the previous days, after the deaths of almost all of Hezbollah's leadership, there had been a massive collapse in the organization. His comrades, field commanders, and others had left, he said, leaving him as one of the only people alone in the tunnels. For the previous four days he said he had been entirely alone. Hezbollah's feared Radwan Force had all run away. "They fled," he said, including the commander of the area and his deputy.

Wadah was asked why. He said that all year they had been having conflicts among themselves. But that "in Hezbollah's language" the people who fled had a "lack of faith." Asked what that meant he said, "People without religion. It's a person who comes to receive money and that's it." That's what they said in Hezbollah, anyway. He went on to describe how Hezbollah intimidates and kills the non-Hezbollah residents of southern Lebanon. "That's how Hezbollah is. Hezbollah kills us, our children, and want to destroy us and our homes." And what had he heard of the plans of the Radwan Force and Hezbollah in general? Why had they wanted to gather in the south of Lebanon? "They wanted to respond to an attack if there would be one." And then? "Maybe they will advance to the Galilee. . . . That was the plan." But, he added, "after the assassination of Mr. Hassan [Nasrallah], no one has seen any of them."[83]

When the scale of Hezbollah's plans became known, it made sense of something that Hamas's leadership had said a year earlier. What had sounded then like a grandiose boast was in fact advance notice of a very concerted plan.

Just over two weeks after October 7, 2023, Hamas official Ghazi Hamad had given an interview to Lebanese television channel LBC TV in which he laid out his views. "Israel is a country that has no place on our land," he began.

"We must remove that country, because it constitutes a security, military, and political catastrophe to the Arab and Islamic nation, and must be finished. We are not ashamed to say this, with full force.

We must teach Israel a lesson, and we will do this again and again. The Al-Aqsa Flood is just the first time, and there will be a second, a third, a fourth, because we have the determination, the resolve, and the capabilities to fight. Will we have to pay a price? Yes, and we are ready to pay it. We are called a nation of martyrs, and we are proud to sacrifice martyrs. . . . We are the victims of the occupation; therefore, nobody should blame us for the things we do. . . . Everything we do is justified."

He continued: "The occupation must come to an end."

"Occupation where?" asked the interviewer. "In the Gaza Strip?"

"No," Hamad replied. "I am talking about all the Palestinian lands."

"Does that mean the annihilation of Israel?" asked the interviewer.

"Yes, of course," Hamad replied, before continuing: "The existence of Israel is illogical. The existence of Israel is what causes all that pain, blood, and tears. It is Israel, not us. We are the victims of the occupation. Period. Therefore, nobody should blame us for the things we do. On October 7, October 10, October 1,000,000—everything we do is justified."[84]

That threat—that Hamas intended to do October 7 a million more times—might have sounded like empty rhetoric to some. It sounded like that to many people once they saw the destruction of Hamas in Gaza. But in fact this is what Iran's proxies across the region—and the government in Tehran—had been planning. October 7 again and again until the Jewish state was wiped from the pages of time. Which was exactly what the leaders in Tehran had said they would do for the past forty years.

✷✷✷

What can Western liberal societies do in the face of such movements? What can people who value life do in the face of those who worship death?

In April 2024, one of the leaders of Hamas confirmed that three of his four sons had been killed in an air strike in Gaza. All four were also Hamas leaders. Their vehicle was hit at a site near Gaza City. It was reported that four of Haniyeh's grandchildren were traveling in the same vehicle. Haniyeh's response to this news was caught live on camera while he was with colleagues in a luxury apartment in Doha, Qatar. To watch his reaction to the news you might think he had just heard of a minor alteration in his schedule. He is not upset, he is not even perturbed. If anything he is joyful. In a statement following the news, he thanked Allah for the "honor" bestowed on him for what he referred to as the "martyrdom of my three sons and some grandchildren."[85] Perhaps it should not be surprising. This was a man who had spent his life extolling the "martyrdom" of Palestinian children. To choose just one example among many, on January 17, 2017, he said, "Children are tools to be used against Israel. We will sacrifice them for the political support of the world."[86]

That is, of course, the reaction of a true fanatic, and not the kind who just wants to sacrifice other people's children, but one who is equally happy to sacrifice his own; someone who sees all Palestinian children as "tools"—including his own. All to use against the Jews. And while many military and political leaders have lost their children in wars, there is something completely inhuman about reacting in such a way to the death of your own children.

Gadi Eisenkot is a former chief of staff of the IDF, a member of the Knesset, and at the beginning of the war a member of Israel's emergency war cabinet. In December 2023 his family was struck by a double tragedy. First his son, Master Sergeant Gal Eisenkot, twenty-five, was killed in the north of Gaza after a booby-trapped Hamas tunnel shaft blew up. One day later Gal's cousin, Sergeant Maor Cohen Eisenkot, nineteen, was killed by an explosive detonated during a raid on a mosque in the city of Khan Younis in Gaza. Hamas forces had come out of a tunnel system in the mosque and gunmen from Hamas fired from the roof of the mosque. In a matter of one day Eisenkot had lost his son and his nephew to the war.

Unlike some Western democracies, in Israel military service is not something that other people do. It is something that everybody who can be conscripted does, and means that for people in the war cabinet or the Knesset, war is something that all of them know about, and deaths in battle are not something that only affects other people.

I happened to be in Jerusalem just after Gal's death was reported. I was due to meet a senior figure in the government to get background on the war and the international situation. When I entered the office, the man had his head in his hands. "We've just had the news about Gadi Eisenkot's son." I could see that he was about to have to call the minister and give his condolences. Through his grief he said simply to me, "I've known him since his bar mitzvah."

There seems to me to be all the difference in the world between these two griefs: the grief of a society that mourns for its sons and friends, and a society that is happy to hear of the deaths of their own family and other people's family.

This difference currently seems such a difficult concept for the Western mind to get its head around. Every college student and adult knows the banalities to trot out: that people around the world are the same everywhere and essentially want the same things; that everybody wants to just live in peace and bring up their family in safety. Yet some people do not. Not because they are born that way but because they have been raised that way.

My mind went back ten years earlier, to when I spent some time living in the Palestinian areas of the West Bank.

***

I had put myself up at a hotel in Ramallah and was traveling around having meetings with Palestinian leaders and officials. The meetings were disheartening, but not as much as one of the things I used to do between meetings, which was to check the street signs and names of the squares in this city that the US and EU had poured so much money into. Ramallah and the surrounding areas are ruled not by Hamas but by the Palestinian Authority, the successors of Yasser Arafat, who are always touted as the partners for peace in any final-status resolution of the Israeli-Palestinian dispute. Yet reliably, if you looked at a street sign, it would be named not after some great hero of the people who ought to be celebrated, but after the most appalling and bloodthirsty terrorists.

There was the street named after Yayha Abd-al-Latif Ayyash, a Palestinian bomb maker for Hamas who worked closely with Arafat. Ayyash was one of the pioneers of the use of suicide bombers against Israeli civilians. The street honoring him was right beside the presidential compound in Ramallah.

The Palestinian Authority and their supporters in the West constantly complained about the security fence that the Israelis had put up between the West Bank and the rest of Israel after the Second Intifada. Suicide bombings that had been constant swiftly fell away to nothing. Yet almost no one who subsequently criticized this barrier, including most recently the visiting American writer Ta-Nehisi Coates, made any mention of the reason why it had been erected in the first place: to stop the suicide bombings that caused the death and injury of hundreds of Israelis. If the Israelis didn't put up a barrier, they got suicide bombings. When they did put it up, and such attacks stopped, they were criticized for putting up a barrier. How dare the Israelis search people coming into Israel from the West Bank? Yet here in Ramallah the people who carried out such attacks and planned them were celebrated.

Dalal Mughrabi was a PLO terrorist and a member of the terrorist cell that carried out the Coastal Road massacre in 1978, in which thirty-eight Israeli citizens, including thirteen children, were murdered. Why does Mughrabi have a square, among other public places, named after her in the Palestinian Authority's territory? Mahmoud Abbas is occasionally careful about these things. In 2010 he postponed the naming of Dalal Mughrabi Square until just after Vice President Joe Biden had left Ramallah. But the question remains, why does even the PA in the West Bank oversee a society in which terrorism against Israelis is celebrated?

Not just celebrated, but rewarded. Everybody who has eyes can see the death cult that Hamas has instituted during its governorship of Gaza. But the PA, which European and American taxpayers support, also celebrates terror but financially incentivizes it.

Take the Palestinian Authority's own Amended Prisoners Law, signed in 2004 by Palestinian Authority chairman Rouhi Fatouh. As Article 1 says, a prisoner is "anyone incarcerated in the occupation's prisons for his participation in the struggle against the occupation." Article 6 says, "The National Authority will grant every incarcerated prisoner a monthly salary, without discrimination."[87] In 2018 the PA's own budget allocated $165 million to the Commission of Detainees and Ex-Detainees Affairs. In that same year approximately $197 million was given by the PA to "families of martyrs."[88]

These are the relatives of people who have carried out the murders of Israelis. And as though to add even more incentives to killing Jews, there is an increasing reward price whereby a prisoner or the family of a "martyr" gets more money depending on the number of Jews they or their relative has succeeded in killing.

Do Israelis have a similar mindset? It is the accusation of much of the world, which thinks that at the very least there is a six-of-one, half-a-dozen-of-the-other problem in the region. And it is certainly true that there are some Israelis at the furthest fringes of society who do mirror some of this behavior.

Some years ago I made a visit to the town of Hebron. Against stiff competition it is one of the most tense and unpleasant places I have ever been. The site of the Tomb of the Patriarchs is deep inside what the Palestinians call the West Bank. A small Jewish community continues to reside in the center of the city, surrounded on almost all sides by a far larger Arab population. In 1929, during the British Mandate, the city was the site of the notorious Hebron Massacre, when much of the city's Jewish population was massacred by the local Arabs. In what was seen as a double disaster, the Jews who survived were forcibly moved afterward by the British authorities. So there is a belligerence among the Jews who live in Hebron today. But in 1994 one of their number, Baruch Goldstein, took this to its illogical next step. Goldstein carried out a massacre of Muslim worshippers right at the disputed holy sites. Goldstein killed twenty-nine Muslims and wounded many more before being beaten to death by the surviving crowd.

Everyone from the Israeli prime minister down condemned Goldstein without caveat. Goldstein and other members of his group believed that the Israeli government was like the Nazi Party. The movement of which he was a part was swiftly designated a terrorist group by the Israeli government. But that day in Hebron I asked to see his grave. I had heard that some people in the Jewish community in the area viewed Goldstein as a hero and I asked to find a way to his grave to see whether it was a place of veneration or not. It was satisfyingly hard to find, and in the hills when we asked directions it was difficult to find anyone who knew of the site. We eventually found it in what was clearly a little-visited plot. A Hebrew-speaking friend laughed with disgust as he translated the epitaph on the grave, which suggested that Goldstein had been murdered in cold blood. "As though if you massacre people with a machine gun and are then killed then you are the innocent one," said my translator, shaking his head.

Do remnants of Goldstein's disgusting ideology linger on? Certainly. But is it a central part of Israeli or Jewish political life? No. There are no streets named after him in Tel Aviv, no squares named to his memory in Haifa. If all religions and ideologies can produce extremists and fanatics, which they can, then it is not just what they do but also how they are remembered, and whether they are widely venerated, that reveals the deeper truth about the society.

***

Nevertheless "both sides–ism" lingers in much of the international response to the conflict, even among those institutions that are meant to be a part of defending against such an absurdity.

Eight months after the start of the war, in May 2024, the International Criminal Court made an extraordinary intervention. In an unprecedented public pronouncement, with two solemn bureaucrats standing behind him, its chief prosecutor, Karim Khan, from the UK, announced that the ICC was looking into issuing arrest warrants on war-crimes charges against a number of individuals. These included Prime Minister Benjamin Netanyahu and Defense Minister Yoav Gallant. As though it were an afterthought, Khan also said that the court would look into arrest warrants for Yahya Sinwar, Mohammed al-Masri, and Ismail Haniyeh. It was the perfect example of mixing up victim and aggressor, firefighter and fire.

Of course there was no chance that Hamas or any government that protects Hamas would hand over any of the group's leaders for such a proceeding. But the ICC prosecutor knew that. What the world didn't immediately realize was that this was a massive overreach in international law. Neither America nor Israel is a signatory to the ICC. Although the court had threatened similar moves against Vladimir Putin over the war in Ukraine, threatening Netanyahu and Gallant constituted the first time the ICC had dared to threaten the elected leaders of a democracy. What is more, at the time of the announcement Khan had carried out no investigation and gathered no evidence. Still he allowed himself to level these charges and interfere in the workings of a democratic government for the first time, and not over what the relevant ministers had done, but over what Khan claimed they might have done.

In response, twelve US senators, including Tom Cotton, wrote to the ICC saying that they viewed issuing a warrant for the arrest of the Israeli leadership "not only as a threat to Israel's sovereignty but to the sovereignty of the United States." The letter went on, "The United States will not tolerate politicized attacks by the ICC on our allies. Target Israel and we will target you." Citing the US government's own Hague Invasion Act, the senators said that this targeting of American allies could lead to the US sanctioning and barring ICC officials, employees, associates, and their families from the United

States.[89] Anyone who doubted where the ICC and its associates were coming from could have noted that the court's former chief prosecutor, Luis Moreno Ocampo, had already praised the ICC warrants against Israeli officials and described the Hamas leadership that had organized the October 7 massacres as "victims."[90]

In response to this letter from the twelve senators, Khan threatened them in turn, saying in his reply, "When individuals threaten to retaliate against the Court or against Court personnel . . . [s]uch threats, even when not acted upon, may also constitute an offence against the administration of justice under Art. 70 of the Rome Statute."[91] So Karim Khan seemed to be acting under the belief that he could not only tell a democracy who should and should not lead the country, but that any elected official from another democracy who criticized him could themselves be claimed to be guilty of war crimes, even though the US is not a signatory to the Rome Statute either, having long believed that American officials and soldiers should not be able to be judged or prosecuted by a politicized foreign court. But with yet another international body pretending there is parity between Hamas and Israel, Netanyahu and Sinwar, it was a further sign of a world turning upside down.

⁕

Through the months after October 7 I managed to speak to almost every member of the Israeli government and war cabinet, as well as the leaders of all the main opposition parties. Each time I put to them the question that I had heard most from the survivors of the massacres: What had happened?

In the immediate aftermath of October 7 there was a rare unity in Israel. It reminded me of what happened in America after 9/11. The discussion up until September 11, 2001, had all been about George W. Bush being an "illegitimate president." People who had voted for Democrat Al Gore in 2000 insisted that the election had been stolen from them. The recounts in Florida, the hanging chads, and then the court-ordered stopping of the recounts festered on the American political system. Then America was attacked, three thousand people were murdered in a single morning, and the nation came together. Bush, who had seemed like one of the most divisive figures in recent American history, suddenly became a rallying point. In the months after 9/11 his approval ratings were consistently in the 80–90 percent range, which of course didn't last.

After October 7 in Israel, something similar happened. For over a year before the attacks Israeli society had been more divided than at almost any time in recent memory. The government had been attempting to introduce a set of judicial reforms. Part of the country approved of them but a significant portion did not. Week in, week out, those who were opposed to them took to the streets of Tel Aviv and other cities. They had almost daily demonstrations and blocked the highways; police in Israel had to work overtime. One Israeli friend remarked to me after the 7th, only half-jokingly, "Hamas were stupid. If they had left it another year we Israelis would have all killed each other."

Depending on who you spoke to in the months after the 7th you could get a different interpretation of what those demonstrations before the war had meant. Those on the left who were broadly against the judicial reforms complained that one reason Hamas had been able to attack was that the government's judicial reforms had visibly divided Israel and so the terrorists had noticed and seized the moment to strike. Those on the right, especially the pro–judicial reform, pro-Netanyahu right, pointed to the fact that the leftist protesters had spent the past year exhausting the country's police forces by making them work Israeli protests all the time. They also pointed to the fact that a large number of anti-Netanyahu figures in the IDF and other parts of the security establishment had spent the previous year threatening not to turn up to reserve duty, even if they were called upon.

In March and again in June 2023, hundreds of reservists in the Israeli Air Force said they would not turn up for reserve duty unless the Israeli government abandoned its judicial reform plans. In July, three hundred Israelis in the IDF's cyber and other tech arms signed a joint letter in which they said they would refuse to show up for reserve duty even if called. In total, thousands of soldiers in the Israeli military publicly refused to turn up for reserve duty. That month, IDF spokesman Rear Admiral Daniel Hagari assured the international press, "At the current point in time, the IDF is competent," which was not especially assuring. But he did admit that the country's ability to respond to military attack could well be affected by the refusals.[92]

Some of the claims made by those who were refusing to serve were especially noteworthy. In September one elite combat pilot publicly claimed, "For the first time, the greatest threat to Israel isn't from the Arabs, it's from other Jews."[93] A number of the most senior retired figures in the IDF agreed. In 2017, former chief of staff and vice prime minister Moshe Ya'alon said, "In the current situation there is no existential threat, neither from a conventional army, nor from rockets, nor from terrorism." Former Chief of the General Staff Dan Halutz agreed, saying that what was happening within parts of Israeli society "is a greater risk than any terrorist from Gaza, Lebanon or Syria."[94]

Given all of this, many people I spoke to in Israel after the 7th said that what happened was almost biblical. The Jews were all arguing among themselves and then something happened—perhaps the only thing that could happen—that would bring them to their senses: an existential threat. The potential of extinction.

***

This was on my mind in January 2024 when I had the chance to sit down with Benjamin Netanyahu. First I asked him the question that had been most on my mind in the months since the atrocities. I thought of all the people in the hospitals and the kibbutzim I had spoken with—all the parents who told me what they had told their children in the safe rooms or over their phones: "Don't worry—the IDF will be here in minutes." I wanted to know, "What went wrong that day."

"Quite a few things," he conceded, "and we'll examine it when the war is over." He compared the savagery of Hamas to the savagery of the Nazis during the Holocaust but pointed out that this time there was a difference. "In the death camps of the Nazis, they murdered thousands of Jews each day and we could do nothing. Here they murdered twelve hundred innocent people and the next day—even though we had these failings on that day, which will be examined—we rolled them back." Still, I wanted to know if he had any sense of how this had even happened. From the vulnerability of the border fence to the tech and intelligence failures, to parts of the IDF failing to scramble together in time. "All sorts of things just seem to have gone wrong," I said.

"Quite a few. Yes, I have an idea. But," he continued, "I think it's premature to talk about it. Operationally, we've reached quite a few conclusions, and we're putting them into effect. But remember, this war is ongoing. We're in the fourth month. It took the US and its allies nine months to vanquish ISIS and to vanquish the radical Islamic forces in Mosul. Mosul is smaller than Gaza, didn't have this vast terror, underground infrastructure, and fewer fighters. So, we're on course, but it's going to take some time. And in the meantime, yes, we have learned some lessons." But he insisted that he wouldn't go into them while the war was ongoing.

We talked about the wars in Lebanon and in Gaza, but also about the bigger picture—Iran. Even if he did manage to destroy Hamas in Gaza, how would that prevent Iran from developing a nuclear bomb and extending its regional ambitions?

"I didn't say that it would deflect it from the war," he said. "I said that these are twin goals. One is to defeat Hamas in Gaza, because it's trying to use its proxies and other means to conquer the Middle East. But secondly, and in parallel to that, act against Iran's attempt to develop nuclear weapons. You're quite right—there are two separate issues, but they're joined at the hip, and the hip is Iran's aggression and ideology, which has to be blocked." But, I suggested to him, none of this—stopping Hamas and Hezbollah, or the mullahs in Tehran from getting a nuclear weapon—could be fully achieved unless there was regime change in Tehran. "You're probably right," he said. "Does anyone agree with you?" I asked. "Well, I agree with me," he shot back. Which seemed to be enough.

I put it to him that of course October 7 had happened on his watch and that while a lot of the military and intelligence establishment in Israel had already accepted responsibility, he had not. Netanyahu's reply was characteristic: "Well, I think there is a responsibility and a mission of our government to protect the people and clearly, we failed in that. And all of us will have to answer questions at the end of the war when there will be investigations, there'll be systemic examination of what went wrong, and responsibilities will be assigned. That's fine. I'm not concentrating on that. No, I'm concentrating on one responsibility that I have, and that is to win this war and achieve total victory." He went on to reiterate that this was not about his reputation or what "the sands of time will wash away." It was about what he saw as his life's work, the defense of the State of Israel and the long-term future of the Jewish people. He said again that for that to be ensured "there is no substitute for total victory. And I think that's what we should all concentrate on."

***

It took more than a year of work by the IDF to start to get close to that ambition. But as a new year in the Jewish calendar approached it looked like the war had turned around too. The anniversary of Simchat Torah, the holiday that was being celebrated on the 7th, came along. As did Yom Kippur and then the festival of Sukkot. I was sitting in one of the outside tents that people put up to celebrate this holiday, at the home of some friends in Jaffa, when my phone pinged. It was a contact in the army. He was sending me two very graphic photos of the face of a dead man, a bullet wound clearly visible through the head. Big chances that this is it, he said. Who? I asked. Sinwar, he messaged back. They were waiting for confirmation. I thought back to a year earlier, when a friend in Jerusalem told me that when Sinwar was dead perhaps the war might be over.

Within an hour I got confirmation. One of the pathologists I had met a year ago in the morgues of Tel Aviv had identified the body of Sinwar. It was a perfect DNA match.

Sinwar had been killed in Rafah, in the south of Gaza, in the place where Vice President Kamala Harris and many other international observers had insisted the IDF should not go. It was a Friday when the news came out, and I knew I had to go to Gaza one more time. This time to the place of Sinwar's final stand.

Barely twenty-four hours later I was making my way into Gaza through the southernmost part of the border. We drove along the Philadelphi corridor, the border between Gaza and Egypt. In construction terms the Egyptian-Gaza border is a stronger, more formidable one than the fence between Israel and Gaza. But all the way underneath this border were tunnels that Hamas had spent years building and had used as their main route for bringing in weapons. At the northern border it was UN forces who had overseen this process; here Egyptian Army outposts were spread along the border. There is no way that all of the activity beneath ground at this border escaped their notice.

After less than an hour of driving we came to Rafah. The city was utterly destroyed. Hardly a building was left unmarked by the scars of war. The walls of many homes had been blown off, giving once again that obscene cross section of a family's life. Many of the buildings had the marks Hamas leaves on a building as a code to let other Hamas know it is now booby-trapped. Some of the multistory buildings had crumpled in, the floors all having fallen down on each other like a stack of cards from air strikes carried out after the IDF had told civilians to leave the area. It was a scene of unbelievably intense fighting.

Finally, after traveling through these now eerily empty streets, we reached Tel Sultan, where Sinwar had recently met his end.

For the past twelve months, the mastermind of October 7 had scurried like a rat through the tunnels beneath Gaza. Footage released after his death showed him just before October 7, 2023, guiding his family through part of the tunnel network with all the comforts they needed. Comforts he withheld from the people of Gaza. In the footage Sinwar's wife was even clutching a $32,000 luxury Birkin handbag.

Nobody knows how many times Sinwar had come aboveground during the past year. But as the IDF made his operating area smaller and smaller, he was obviously forced to abandon his last underground complex. This was soon uncovered and it became clear that Sinwar had been hiding with millions of dollars in cash in a range of currencies, as well as food and other UN supplies meant for the Palestinian people. But he was not with the remaining hostages.

Perhaps he knew that this was his last run. This part of Rafah is the deepest into Gaza that anyone can go. Army sources told me that in the past few days a number of Hamas battalions had tried to gather toward where Sinwar was, but those battalions were decimated in battles with the IDF along the way.

The collapse of his terror army probably came as a surprise for Sinwar. But as the IDF cut off one sector of Gaza after another, he most likely realized there was nowhere left for him to run.

Speaking to soldiers who had been there, I pieced together his final day. Four terrorists (one of whom turned out to include Sinwar) were spotted by a local battalion of the IDF. The area was meant to be cleared of civilians, so they immediately attracted attention. The Israeli troops exchanged fire with them and the men split off in different directions. Two were shot by the IDF shortly after. One briefly went missing. The other was Sinwar.

Soldiers saw him running into a building. Shots were fired and one seems to have hit him in the hand or arm. I followed the telltale blood spatter on the side of the staircase he had run up. This was

Sinwar's blood. He had run up the stairs and at first had tried to hide under some blankets in an upstairs room. He seems to have unsuccessfully tried to tie a tourniquet around his wounded arm. But an IDF observation drone was sent in to look for him and found the still-unidentified terrorist sitting in an armchair. A tank round was fired at the building but he seemed to have died from a machine-gun shot through the head. The pathologist who carried out the autopsy told me that it is likely that Sinwar actually bled out for many hours before he died. It was not until sometime later that the IDF found the body and then realized who it might be.

I stood in the same room a couple of days later and looked out at the final piece of this world that Sinwar saw.

Every window of every building in sight was blown out, including those in this final villa. What had once been a pleasant, even luxurious Gaza residence was now like every other building in sight—covered in rubble when not reduced to it altogether. As far as the eye could see were the consequences of the war that Sinwar and Hamas had started. I found the last chair that he had sat in and took a seat. There were bloodstains on the side. From here you could see nothing but destruction.

As I sat there I wondered whether, on this rare, maybe single, trip aboveground, Sinwar had recognized how much destruction he had wrought. Not just on the people of Israel—he would have been proud of having done that—but on the Palestinians of Gaza. As he was bleeding out—isolated, abandoned, and defeated—did he spend any of his final moments wondering whether this whole bloody, unnecessary war that he started had been worth it?

Perhaps he had decided on this last trip aboveground to abandon the Palestinian people and flee to Egypt. The cash, passports, and IDs (including UN IDs) found on his body certainly suggested as much. Perhaps he thought he could bribe his way out and become free on the other side of the nearby border? Either way it didn't work, and this wasteland he had created was where his life ended.

What did work was the IDF, its commanders, and the politicians who had directed them. Every expert who had kept telling Israel not to go deeper into Gaza, not to enter Rafah or to reach a cease-fire at the earliest opportunity had been proved wrong. Only military pressure had achieved the release of those hostages who had been freed, and only remorseless military pressure had now led to the death of the enemy. If Israel had followed the advice of the US president, vice president, and most Western leaders, Hamas would still be strong, half the hostages would never have been rescued, and Yahya Sinwar would have lived to breathe another day.

Some people claimed that killing Sinwar was "luck" or a "fluke." They were wrong. It wasn't "luck" that the IDF finished him off. It was the culmination of a year of hard, grueling work by young Israeli soldiers, and brave and careful decisions made by the country's politicians.

In the days that followed, many other details came out, including that the two other terrorists from whom Sinwar got separated were his bodyguards. One of them worked as a teacher and was employed by UNRWA.

The soldiers involved in the final firefight were from the IDF's Infantry Commanders and Combat Training School, known by its Hebrew acronym, Bislach. Two things stood out. The first was that these were the soldiers who made the fatal mistake in December when three Israeli hostages were shot by their own side inside Gaza. On that occasion, Iris, the mother of Yotam Haim, who was one of the hostages shot, sent an encouraging message to the soldiers. Now, hearing that these same soldiers were the ones who had killed Sinwar, she sent them another voice message. "Exactly ten months ago," she said, "I sent you a message and told you to keep fighting and not to think that you shot the kidnapped on purpose because we need you safe and sound and to keep taking care of yourselves. Today you did the thing we were all waiting for. You saved the people of Israel."

Another noteworthy aspect to the Bislach being there was that the young Israeli who killed the mastermind of October 7 was a nineteen-year-old serving his first year in the army. The soldier would not even have been in uniform when the atrocity was carried out. There was no way that Sinwar or anyone else could have known that the war he started produced a new generation of fighters—including the young man who would finally part him from this life.

***

Not everybody was pleased by the demise of the butcher. In Ramallah, Mahmoud Abbas' Palestinian Authority mourned Sinwar.[95] President Erdogan of Turkey, a NATO member state, said publicly that he mourned Sinwar and that he had been "martyred."[96] Meanwhile, the mother of the Emir of Qatar, Sheikha Moza, wrote in praise of Sinwar, saying, "The name Yahya means the one who lives. They thought him dead but he lives. Like his namesake, Yahya bin Zakariya, he will live on and they will be gone."[97]

Across America, numerous chapters of groups like Students for Justice in Palestine (SJP) posted memorials to Sinwar. Many of these student groups also portrayed him as a "martyr," often accompanied by pseudo-revolutionary slogans like "Rest in Power." When news of Sinwar's death reached the City University of New York, it landed badly with some students. One group called "CunyResists" ran a lengthy memorial for Sinwar. Among much else it said: "The news regarding the great commander has left our hearts heavy and out [sic] chests breathless. Today, we mourn the loss and celebrate the martyrdom of the lion of Al Quds, the beloved Commander, President, Fighter, his eminence, Yahya Sinwar."[98]

This was not unusual, but it was emblematic. On the first anniversary of October 7, students at British universities organized walkouts and protests against Israel. At the University of Edinburgh, a protest called for people to come out to celebrate October 7 with the slogan "Long Live the Student Intifada." At the School of Oriental and African Studies in London there was a vigil to honor the "martyrs."[99] It was no surprise when a poll published the day before found that

16 percent of young British people believed that the October 7 massacre was justified.[100]

Many of their American counterparts clearly felt the same. "From
Gaza to Beirut, all our martyrs we salute" was one of the chants
among the students at Yale.[101] And when a Jewish group in New
York held a memorial for six hostages, including an American, who
had just been murdered by Hamas, students chanted for more "intifada." Their contemporaries at Harvard likewise used the anniversary to chant for "intifada."[102] DNA evidence placed Sinwar himself
as having been at the spot where those six hostages were murdered.

Would there ever be any way to get into the heads of these students that this was not some kind of game? The same students who
had spent recent years saying "Believe all women" followed the dic-
tum right up until the moment that Israeli women were raped. Then,
even in the face of overwhelming testimony, the slogan was "Ignore
these women." And if they didn't care about Israeli women, what of
the pretense of caring about Palestinian women? Would anything
make them change the train they had got on?

While he was in prison in Israel, Sinwar had for a time shared a
cell with another Palestinian terrorist, Mohammed Sharatha. Sinwar's cellmate was in prison for helping to kidnap and kill two Israeli soldiers. This act didn't trouble him, of course, but something
else did. Sinwar later said of his cellmate that "I felt that he was sad
most of the time." One day Sharatha confided to Sinwar that the
problem was that his sister was bringing shame on the family. She
was having an extramarital affair. Was there anything Sinwar could
do to punish her appropriately for this? Sinwar agreed to help, and
got word out via his brother Mohammed Sinwar. Sharatha's sister
was found dead in Gaza shortly afterward.

It is quite a pathology someone must have fallen into to lionize a
rapist and murderer. But as Ruth Wisse pointed out, nobody seemed
to want to try to understand what it meant that there were people in
the West who had tried to make a hero out of this man. But that is exactly what happened. In New York, on the anniversary of October 7,

the Al-Aqsa Flood was celebrated by demonstrators on Wall Street who organized a "Flood New York City" event. The chants outside the New York Stock Exchange included "Long live the intifada." At a rally in Philadelphia, one of the speakers told the crowd, "On October 7th when I was watching those resistance fighters flying into Palestine on paragliders I was cheering."[103] In London students took the opportunity of the anniversary to mourn the "martyrs" and call for "intifada" and "resistance."

A bakery in Sydney was attacked by Hamas supporters for no other reason than that the owner was Jewish. It was daubed with Hamas signs.[104] Hamas supporters also broke into the office of a Jewish professor of physics at the University of Melbourne and scrawled the same pro-Hamas graffiti on his office. In each case the sign painted on the Jewish doors was the red sign that Hamas had used to designate a Jewish house. The same sign that the Islamists who carried out the Farhud massacre in Baghdad in 1941 and many other Islamists across the world had used before and since.

The Melbourne professor's crime, apart from being Jewish, was that protesters accused him of joint-hosting a PhD program with an Israeli university. The subject of study was the migratory patterns of birds.[105] Conspiracies and manias that had been spread across the Middle East by Hamas and the mullahs seemed to have gone far beyond the region. Spores of the virus were cropping up all across the Western world.

***

Throughout this year of war I often felt this strange disjunct. At first I worried that I might be doing what Oriana Fallaci had said life was about—filling it up, even if you break it by filling it too full. Friends and family occasionally remarked that I had changed. Readers sometimes noticed it too. In time I started to try to understand what it was.

First was living constantly between the realm of war and the realm of peace. I was sometimes reminded of a hotel I stayed in during the war in Ukraine. There was little electricity. The Ukrainian armed forces all smoked, as many soldiers do. And they obeyed the empty hotel's rules of no smoking inside. As we traipsed outside into the cold we laughed about this bit of etiquette from the land of peace. What did it matter whether people could get first- or secondhand smoke when a rocket could hit at any moment?

But it wasn't that disjunction that hit me this time. What struck me was that line from Deuteronomy. About choosing life.

Whenever I made brief trips back to America or Britain, I kept noticing the way these societies far from the front lines seemed to have been driven mad by war. Even the nonwar issues that dominated the public debate seemed obtuse. In America once again everybody was obsessing about the exact date at which you should be able to abort a child. In Britain the euthanasia debate had come around again, and the same moral issues were being rehearsed again. Is this really the highest moment of human achievement and peace, I wondered. To decide when you might kill an old person or a fetus?

In all this time, the place that felt least out of joint was Israel. And as the year went on readers started noting to me that I seemed to have lost some of my usual pessimism. I noticed it myself, and there was a reason for it: I was seeing answered a question that had always troubled me. What we would do if we came to a time of trial like our forebears did?

Like most people of my background, I grew up with the family stories of those who went away to war in 1914, and those who went to war again in 1939. On my father's side of the family alone, my grandmother lost her father at sea in World War I and her brother, also in the navy, in the 1940s. It was like that. The fight against tyranny had been real. It was not a subject to be entered into lightly. But all the time, the people who came after those generations asked themselves the same question, which was what would we do if our time came.

At one point in the early months of the conflict I was in a street in Tel Aviv and a taxi driver recognized me. We started talking and he said something that made my eyes prick. He explained to me that he was a veteran of the wars of 1967 and 1973. He said that there was something he wanted to tell me: "I owe the younger generation an apology." I was startled, but he continued. "I thought they had become weak," he said. "I thought they just wanted to party in Tel Aviv or be on TikTok or Instagram. But I was wrong. They have stepped up. They are magnificent."

Everything I saw in the wars around us confirmed this. And I thought of all the heroes—all the young men and women who were just like the people I knew outside of Israel, but who were having to do things these people couldn't imagine. There were enough tales of the horrors, but there were tales of unbelievable courage and resilience too. In the year after the October 7 attacks I went to weddings and bar mitzvahs and funerals in Israel. Sometimes on the same day. I heard tales of unbelievable suffering, but I also saw people grab for the light in the darkness.

When I spoke with Avida from Be'eri as he was recovering in the hospital, he said something that stuck with me. Even through his tears, telling me about seeing his wife and son die in front of him in their safe room, he still wanted to draw some light from it. He had had thirty-two years with his wife, he said, and he had had the good fortune to have fifteen years with his son. And this was what mattered. He wanted to tell me how he saw it. "All of us," he said. "All of us, we think that the time is going on until the end. But the time, it's really short. And I told my friends at work, there's no meeting after four o'clock in the afternoon. We're not going to stay at work. We go home to our friends and family to make a good time, and good memories. What we have, it's only people." He promised me he would be okay.

I saw also how people make each other and grow each other: how encouragement even in the face of the worst things gave encouragement in turn. When I met in the hospital with Harel, the badly wounded policeman from Sderot, I asked after his family. His face took on a look of great concern. "They took it hard," he said. "Very, very hard." He was concerned for their concern about him. After I thanked him for sharing his story, he suddenly said in his broken English, "I've watched your interviews. You warm my heart." In however small a way I had encouraged him, and now he had much more greatly encouraged me.

As the year of war came to a close I also saw one of those great acts of personal heroism that make you think that the age of heroes might have come around again. A friend in California had introduced me to a man in his thirties named Izzy. He was noticeable for being handsome and for having only one arm. His left arm was blown off by a bomb while he was serving in Gaza during the 2009 war. He doesn't remember the blast that took his arm off, only waking up in the hospital a long while later and trying to work out what had happened.

Izzy was a sharpshooter, and a very good one, but as he was recovering in the hospital most people acknowledged that his army days were over. Everyone except him. In the hospital he kept insisting that he could retrain as a one-armed sharpshooter. Most people dismissed him, but one man did listen—Yoav Gallant, who would later be defense minister. Gallant took Izzy seriously and he also took him under his wing, introduced him to his family, and even tended and dressed Izzy's wounds himself. Crucially Gallant said that if there was a way to get Izzy back in, he would make it happen. The IDF even had a special gun made that was adapted especially for their one-armed sharpshooter—and so he went back in. Before 2023, Izzy thought he was getting too old to keep doing his reserve duties and hung up his gun. He was in California on October 7, 2023, and the next day he was one of the thousands of reservists who paid to go back to Israel to reenlist and fight.

He went to his base, but because he was retired they wouldn't let him in. He refused to leave. For two weeks he stood outside the base every day, waiting for something to change. When rockets fell, he ducked for cover with everyone else. Eventually someone allowed him inside the base because they thought it was an insurance risk having him lingering outside. Once inside he was redrafted. His gun was exactly where he had left it, and soon Izzy was in Gaza. As defeat turned into victory and the land war in Lebanon began, I entered Lebanon one day with a unit of the IDF that included Izzy. He said he thought it could be useful for me to go in with him because he could be my one-man Iron Dome. Asked to explain, he said, "Well, I've already been hit by a rocket once. The odds of it happening twice are much smaller, so if you stick with me you'll be safe." Watching him walk ahead of me up the hills of Lebanon made me think again not just of how extraordinary some people are, but how it is that extraordinary events uncover extraordinary people. Some people never get a chance to be weighed in the balance. But people like Izzy did get a chance and they were found to be magnificent.

It struck me then as it had many times over the previous year, that everything was the wrong way around. Young people at institutions across the West were judging the actions of their contemporaries in Israel. They were throwing slur after slur at them and reigniting every blood libel of the past in a modern guise. Yet it was their contemporaries in Israel who were the ones they should have looked to not as a scapegoat but as an example. Whatever the years ahead hold for the West, I know that Canada, Britain, Europe, Australia, and America should be so lucky as to produce a generation of people like Israel has.

Finally, I also realized that I had found the answer to a question I had mulled over for almost a quarter of a century. All my adult life I had heard the taunt of the jihadists. "We love death more than you love life." I had heard it from al-Qaeda, from Hamas, from ISIS. From Europe to Afghanistan several of my friends and colleagues had heard such war cries in their last moments. And it had always seemed to me not just a necrophiliac utterance but one that appeared almost impossible to counter. How could anyone overcome a movement—a people—who welcomed death, who gloried in death, who worshipped death? Was it not inevitable that against such a force, a feeble and sybaritic West could not possibly win?

That is what I feared for many years. Yet this year I saw an answer to it. Of all the soldiers I saw in war, none took delight in their task. They could feel victorious on occasion, proud to have completed a mission and gotten their unit out alive. But from the south of Gaza to the south of Lebanon and the West Bank, none take a joy or pleasure in the task they have to do. They did it not because they loved death but exactly because they love life. They fought for life. For the survival of their families, their nation, and their people. Even the most secular of them knew that the lifestyle most of us take for granted cannot be taken so. They know that you won't have the ability to party in Tel Aviv, fall in love, grow a family, or live a meaningful life unless they are willing to fight for it.

"Choose life" is one of the most important commandments of the Jewish people. It is also one of the fundamental values of the West. They, and all of us, can win in spite of the enemy loving death. Because there is nothing wrong with loving life so much. It is the basis on which civilization can win.

ACKNOWLEDGMENTS

I would like to thank my agent, Matthew Hamilton, of The Hamilton Agency. Also Eric Nelson, James Neidhardt, Theresa Dooley, and Tom Hopke at HarperCollins in the US, and Joel Simons, Tom Hill, and Orlando Mowbray at HarperCollins UK.

I should also like to thank my manager, Evan Lowenstein, my chief of staff, Kennedy Lee, Daniel Samet, and all of the people I have been lucky enough to have around me during the writing of this book. Too many people to mention, but all dear to me. My gratitude to you is deep.

NOTES

1. Andrew Roberts, "What Makes Hamas Worse Than the Nazis," *Washington Free Beacon*, November 24, 2023, https://freebeacon.com/culture/what-makes -hamas-worse-than-the-nazis/.
2. Leo Tolstoy, *War and Peace*, trans. Richard Pevear and Larissa Volokhonsky (New York: Vintage Classics, 2008), 188.
3. See Paul Hollander, *From Benito Mussolini to Hugo Chavez: Intellectuals and a Century of Political Hero Worship* (Cambridge: Cambridge University Press, 2017), 276–277.
4. See Gal Hirsch, *Defensive Shield: An Israeli Special Forces Commander on the Front Line of Counterterrorism* (Jerusalem: Gefen, 2016), 71.
5. "Jewish & Non-Jewish Population of Israel/Palestine," *Jewish Virtual Library*, https://www.jewishvirtuallibrary.org/jewish-and-non-jewish -population-of-israel-palestine-1517-present.
6. "Demographics of Israel: Population of Jerusalem," *Jewish Virtual Library*, https://www.jewishvirtuallibrary.org/population-of-jerusalem-1844-2009.
7. "Farhud Memories: Baghdad's 1941 Slaughter of the Jews," BBC News, June 1, 2011, https://www.bbc.com/news/world-middle-east-13610702.
8. "At 34, This Israeli-Arab Surgeon Is an Expert in One of Medicine's Most Prestigious Spheres," *Haaretz*, October 3, 2021, https://www.haaretz.com /israel-news/2021-10-03/ty-article-magazine/at-34-this-israeli-arab-surgeon -is-an-expert-in-medicines-most-prestigious-spheres/0000017f-e1ac-d7b2 -a77f-e3affb230000.
9. "Evidence Points to Systematic Use of Rape and Sexual Violence by Hamas in 7 October Attacks," *Guardian*, January 18, 2024, https://www.theguardian .com/world/2024/jan/18/evidence-points-to-systematic-use-of-rape-by-hamas -in-7-october-attacks.
10. Ari Feldman, "The Killer Mossad Shark and 5 Other Animals That (Don't Really) Spy for Israel," *Forward*, July 9, 2016, https://forward.com/israel/344574 /the-killer-mossad-shark-and-5-other-animals-that-dont-really-spy-for/.
11. "Renegade Bird Accused of Being an Israeli Spy Cleared after Careful Exam-

ination in Turkey," *Hürriyet Daily News*, July 26, 2013, https://www.hurriye
tdailynews.com/renegade-bird-accused-of-being-an-israeli-spy-cleared-after
-careful-examination-in-turkey-51440.

12. "Rocket & Mortar Attacks Against Israel by Date," *Jewish Virtual Library*,
https://www.jewishvirtuallibrary.org/palestinian-rocket-and-mortar-attacks
-against-israel.

13. Seth G. Jones et al., "The Coming Conflict with Hezbollah," Center for
Strategic and International Studies, March 2024, https://csis-website-prod
.s3.amazonaws.com/s3fs-public/2024-03/240321_Jones_Coming_Hezbollah
.pdf?VersionId=m9pMWQNUFJr2g8opcaOpfJoNxQn8PMbf.

14. Naomi Klein, "How Israel Has Made Trauma a Weapon of War," *Guardian*,
October 5, 2024, https://www.theguardian.com/us-news/ng-interactive/2024
/oct/05/israel-gaza-october-7-memorials.

15. Jo Becker and Adam Sella, "The Hamas Chief and the Israeli Who Saved His
Life," *New York Times*, May 26, 2024, https://www.nytimes.com/2024/05/26
/world/middleeast/hamas-sinwar-israel-doctor-prison-swap.html.

16. Vasily Grossman, *A Writer at War: A Soviet Journalist with the Red Army,
1941–1945*, eds. and trans. Antony Beevor and Luba Vinogradova (New York:
Vintage Books, 2007), chap. 24, Kindle.

17. Ines de la Cuetara, "IDF Soldiers Say Repeated Warnings of Hamas Activity
Prior to Oct. 7 Attacks Were Ignored," ABC News, June 28, 2024, https://
abcnews.go.com/International/idf-soldiers-repeated-warnings-hamas-activity
-prior-oct/story?id=111312207.

18. Catherine Lough, "Pro-Palestine Group Tells Supporters to Break into Busi-
nesses Supplying Weapons to Israel," *Telegraph*, October 16, 2023, https://
www.telegraph.co.uk/news/2023/10/16/pro-palestine-protests-supply-israel
-business-hamas-war/.

19. Daniel Martin, Louisa Clarence-Smith, and Amy Gibbons, "Braverman to
Challenge Met Chief After Jihad Chant Allowed at Rally," *Telegraph*, October 22, 2023, https://www.telegraph.co.uk/politics/2023/10/22/braverman-met
ropolitan-police-palestine-rally-jihad-chant/.

20. "Some U.S. Professors Praise Hamas's October 7 Terror Attacks," Anti-
Defamation League, November 21, 2023, https://www.adl.org/resources/arti
cle/some-us-professors-praise-hamass-october-7-terror-attacks.

21. Chris Churchill, "Churchill: Professor's Support for Hamas Amid Atrocities Stokes Outrage," *Times-Union*, October 14, 2023, https://www.time
sunion.com/churchill/article/churchill-support-attacks-israel-brings-18424
004.php.

22. "CUNY Professor: Israeli Zionists Are 'Genocidal, Racist, Arrogant Bullies,'"
College Fix, October 21, 2023, https://www.thecollegefix.com/cuny-professor
-israeli-zionists-are-genocidal-racist-arrogant-bullies/.

23. Jesse O'Neill, "Cornell University Professor Calls Hamas Terror Attack

'Exhilarating' and 'Energizing,'" *New York Post*, October 16, 2023, https://nypost.com/2023/10/16/russell-rickford-says-hamas-terror-was-exhilarating-exciting/.

24. J. Sellers Hill and Nia L. Orakwue, "Harvard Student Groups Face Intense Backlash for Statement Calling Israel 'Entirely Responsible' for Hamas Attack," *Harvard Crimson*, October 10, 2023, https://www.thecrimson.com/article/2023/10/10/psc-statement-backlash/.

25. Haley Strack, "'Glory to Our Martyrs': Georgetown University Students Mourn Palestinian Deaths, Ignore Hamas Atrocities," *National Review*, October 13, 2023, https://www.nationalreview.com/news/glory-to-our-martyrs-georgetown-university-students-mourn-palestinian-deaths-ignore-hamas-atrocities/.

26. Andrew Lapin, "'Glory to Our Martyrs' Projected onto Building at George Washington University," *Times of Israel*, October 26, 2023, https://www.timesofisrael.com/glory-to-our-martyrs-protected-onto-building-at-george-washington-university/.

27. Statement from Director of National Intelligence Avril Haines on Recent Iranian Influence Efforts, Office of the Director of National Intelligence, July 9, 2024, https://www.dni.gov/index.php/newsroom/press-releases/press-releases-2024/3842-statement-from-director-of-national-intelligence-avril-haines-on-recent-iranian-influence-efforts.

28. @IsraelWarRoom, X, April 21, 2024, https://x.com/IsraelWarRoom/status/1781933305501212872.

29. @EFischberger, X, April 19, 2024, https://x.com/EFischberger/status/1781287784897991134.

30. "Our Campus. Our Crisis," *Columbia Daily Spectator* and *New York*, May 4, 2024, https://nymag.com/intelligencer/article/columbia-university-protests-israel-gaza-campus.html.

31. Mordechai I. Twersky, "Ten Years Later, Mothers of Hebrew U. Bombing Victims Look Back," *Haaretz*, July 27, 2012, https://www.haaretz.com/2012-07-27/ty-article/looking-back-at-hebrew-u-slaughter/0000017f-f037-dc28-a17f-fc37bf350000.

32. Chris McGreal, "Arafat Mourns Arab Shot in Error," *Guardian*, March 21, 2004, https://www.theguardian.com/world/2004/mar/22/israel.

33. Susie Coen, "Columbia Protester Mocked After Asking for Food for Occupiers," *Telegraph*, May 1, 2024, https://www.telegraph.co.uk/world-news/2024/05/01/columbia-protests-asking-for-food-humanitarian-aid/.

34. "Poll: Most Young Americans Think Israel Should Be 'Ended and Given to Hamas,'" *Times of Israel*, December 17, 2023, https://www.timesofisrael.com/poll-most-young-americans-back-ending-israel-many-find-jewish-genocide-calls-okay/.

35. Charles Hilu, "'Karma': Black Harvard Professor Demoted Under Claudine Gay Responds to Gay's Resignation," Washington Free Beacon, January 3,

2024, https://freebeacon.com/latest-news/karma-black-harvard-professor-de moted-under-claudine-gay-responds-to-gays-resignation/.

36. House Committee on Education and the Workforce, "Holding Campus Leaders Accountable and Confronting Antisemitism," YouTube, December 5, 2023, https://www.youtube.com/watch?v=3J0Nu9BN5Qk.

37. "Our Campus. Our Crisis."

38. "Our Campus. Our Crisis."

39. "Our Campus. Our Crisis."

40. "Palestinians: Special Dispatch No. 11342," Middle East Media Research Institute, May 21, 2024, https://www.memri.org/reports/hamas-leader -abroad-khaled-mashal-we-thank-great-student-flood-american-universities -we-want.

41. "DEAR YOUNG STUDENTS IN AMERICA, YOU NOW STAND ON THE RIGHT SIDE OF HISTORY," Office of the Supreme Leader, Iran, May 30, 2024, https://www.leader.ir/en/content/27338/Leader-s-Letter-to-American-Un iversity-Students-with-a-Conscience.

42. Paul Berman, *Power and the Idealists, or, the Passion of Joschka Fischer and Its Aftermath* (Brooklyn, NY: Soft Skull Press, 2005).

43. Jillian Becker, *Hitler's Children: The Story of the Baader-Meinhof Terrorist Gang* (Philadelphia: Lippincott, 1977), 18.

44. Vasily Grossman, *Life and Fate*, trans. Robert Chandler (New York: New York Review Books, 2006), 484–7.

45. Sana Noor Haq and Claire Calzonetti, "Queen Rania of Jordan Accuses West of 'Glaring Double Standard' as the Death Toll Rises in Besieged Gaza," CNN, October 25, 2023, https://www.cnn.com/2023/10/24/middleeast/queen -rania-jordan-amanpour-interview-intl/index.html.

46. Will Hazell, "Britain Was Founded on Racism, Say Almost Half of Young People in Poll," *Telegraph*, November 20, 2022, https://www.telegraph.co .uk/news/2022/11/19/teach-britain-founded-racism-say-almost-half-young -people-poll/.

47. Harvard Youth Poll, 43rd ed., Spring 2022, Harvard Institute of Politics, https://iop.harvard.edu/youth-poll/43rd-edition-spring-2022.

48. Sareen Habeshian, "Poll: Youth Sour on America," Axios, July 25, 2023, https://www.axios.com/2023/07/25/millennials-gen-z-american-pride-decline -patriotism.

49. "Modest Declines in Positive Views of 'Socialism' and 'Capitalism' in U.S.," Pew Research Center, September 19, 2022, https://www.pewresearch.org /politics/2022/09/19/modest-declines-in-positive-views-of-socialism-and -capitalism-in-u-s/.

50. "Fox News Poll," Fox News, July 19, 2020, https://static.foxnews.com/fox news.com/content/uploads/2020/07/Fox_July-12-15-2020_Complete_National _Topline_July-19-Release.pdf.

51. @AOC, X, June 11, 2024, https://x.com/AOC/status/1800599178424516934?l
ang=en.

52. Alexander Hurst, "Jean-Luc Mélenchon Is a Disaster for the French Left—
His Response to the Attack on Israel Proves It," *Guardian*, October 27, 2023,
https://www.theguardian.com/commentisfree/2023/oct/27/jean-luc-melenchon
-french-left-israel-france.

53. "Far-Left French Leader Slams Macron for Accepting French Complicity in
Holocaust," *Haaretz*, July 19, 2017, https://www.haaretz.com/world-news
/europe/2017-07-19/ty-article/melenchon-slams-macron-for-accepting-french
-complicity-in-holocaust/0000017f-f40e-d47e-a37f-fd3e04a60000.

54. "Gaza Program," United States Agency for International Development,
https://2017-2020.usaid.gov/west-bank-and-gaza/fact-sheets/gaza#:~:text
=Gaza%20Program,-Speeches%20Shim.

55. "USAID/West Bank and Gaza," United States Agency for International Development, https://www.usaid.gov/sites/default/files/2023-01/USAID_West%20
Bank%20and%20Gaza%20Profile%20%28December%202022%29_1_0.pdf.

56. "U.S. Announcement of Humanitarian Assistance to the Palestinian People," White House, October 18, 2023, https://www.whitehouse.gov/briefing
-room/statements-releases/2023/10/18/u-s-announcement-of-humanitarian
-assistance-to-the-palestinian-people/.

57. Jacopo Barigazzi, "Von der Leyen Announces Increase in Aid to Gaza,"
Politico, https://www.politico.eu/article/ursula-von-der-leyen-announce
-increase-aid-gaza/; "A Look at the Billions of Dollars in Foreign Aid to
Gaza," Associated Press, December 20, 2021, https://apnews.com/article
/business-middle-east-israel-foreign-aid-gaza-strip-611b2b90c3a211f21185d5
9f4fae6a90.

58. "How is UNRWA Funded?," United Nations Relief and Works Agency for
Palestine Refugees in the Near East, https://www.unrwa.org/how-unrwa
-funded.

59. Isabel Vincent and Benjamin Weinthal, "Hamas Leaders Worth Staggering
$11B Revel in Luxury—While Gaza's People Suffer," *New York Post*, Novem-
ber 7, 2023, https://nypost.com/2023/11/07/news/hamas-leaders-worth-11bn
-live-luxury-lives-in-qatar/.

60. "Fancy Restaurants and Olympic-Size Swim Pools: What the Media Won't
Report About Gaza," Tom Gross Mideast Media Analysis, May 25, 2010,
http://www.tomgrossmedia.com/mideastdispatches/archives/001114.html.

61. "Abd Al-Salam Haniyeh, Son of Slain Hamas Leader: People Who Came
to Gaza in Recent Years Couldn't Believe How Beautiful It Was," Middle
East Media Research Institute, August 15, 2024, https://www.memri.org/tv
/abd-al-salam-haniyeh-son-hamas-leader-ismail-gaza-beautiful-buildings
-promenades-restaurants.

62. Summer Said and Rory Jones, "Gaza Chief's Brutal Calculation: Civilian

Bloodshed Will Help Hamas," *Wall Street Journal*, June 10, 2024, https://www.wsj.com/world/middle-east/gaza-chiefs-brutal-calculation-civilian-blood shed-will-help-hamas-626720e7.

63. @sarahleah1, X, May 4, 2024, https://x.com/sarahleah1/status/1786785177 114493212.

64. Yonah Jeremy Bob, "Al Jazeera 'Journalists' in Gaza Were Terrorists: IDF Presents Evidence," *Jerusalem Post*, January 10, 2024, https://www.jpost.com /israel-hamas-war/article-781666.

65. "Al Jazeera's Ismail Abu Omar, Ahmad Matar Wounded in Israeli Strike on Gaza," Al Jazeera, February 13, 2024, https://www.aljazeera.com/news /2024/2/13/journalists-including-al-jazeera-reporter-injured-in-israel-gaza -strike; "Al Jazeera Rebukes Israel's Claim That Its Journalist Is Hamas Member," Middle East Eye, February 15, 2024, https://www.middleeasteye .net/live-blog/live-blog-update/al-jazeera-rebukes-israels-claim-its-journalist -hamas-member.

66. "Judith Butler and the Normalization of Hamas and Hezbollah within Progressive Social Movement," Institute for the Study of Global Antisemitism and Policy, October 18, 2023, https://isgap.org/post/2023/10/judith-butler-and -the-normalization-of-hamas-and-hezbollah-within-progressive-social-move ments/.

67. "Vast Majority of Americans Say Ban Russian Oil, Quinnipiac University National Poll Finds; Nearly 8 in 10 Support U.S. Military Response If Putin Attacks a NATO Country," Quinnipiac University, March 7, 2022, https://poll .qu.edu/poll-release?releaseid=3838.

68. Matthew Smith, "More than a Third of Under-40s Would Refuse Conscrip- tion in the Event of a World War," YouGov, January 26, 2024, https://yougov .co.uk/politics/articles/48473-more-than-a-third-of-under-40s-would-refuse -conscription-in-the-event-of-a-world-war.

69. Matthew Smith, "Why Won't Britons Serve in the Armed Forces If Called?," YouGov, February 26, 2024, https://yougov.co.uk/politics/articles/48749-why -wont-britons-serve-in-the-armed-forces-if-called.

70. Shuiab Khan, "Burnley Councillors and Leader Quit Labour Party over Gaza Stance," *Lancashire Telegraph*, November 5, 2023, https://www.lancashire telegraph.co.uk/news/23903217.burnley-councillors-leader-quit-labour-party -gaza-stance/.

71. "Yousaf Condemns 'Outrageous Smear' over Gaza Funding," BBC News, March 9, 2024, https://www.bbc.com/news/articles/cn0d2wnlek2o.

72. Daniel Hurst, "Ed Husic Says Israel Action in Gaza 'Very Disproportionate' and Children Shouldn't Bear Brunt of Conflict," *Guardian*, December 11, 2023, https://www.theguardian.com/australia-news/2023/dec/12/ed-husic-says -israel-action-in-gaza-very-disproportionate-and-children-shouldnt-bear-brunt -of-conflict.

73. Hannah Ritchie, "How a Gaza 'Stunt' Divided Australia's Parliament," BBC News, July 1, 2024, https://www.bbc.com/news/articles/c880l1ddpzgo.

74. Mehdi Hasan, "The Sorry Truth Is That the Virus of Anti-Semitism Has Infected the British Muslim Community," *New Statesman*, March 2013, https://www.newstatesman.com/politics/2013/03/sorry-truth-virus-anti-semitism-has-infected-british-muslim-community.

75. Jeffrey Herf, *Nazi Propaganda for the Arab World* (New Haven, CT: Yale University Press, 2009), chap. 8, Kindle.

76. Oriana Fallaci, *Nothing and Amen*, trans. Isabel Quigly (London: Michael Joseph, 1972), 1–2, 319–320.

77. E. J. Trelawny, *Recollections of the Last Days of Shelley and Byron* (Boston: Ticknor & Fields, 1858), 132.

78. "Protesters Mourn Nasrallah's Death Around the World," *New York Times*, September 28, 2024, https://www.nytimes.com/article/nasrallah-death-protests.html.

79. "Statement from President Joe Biden on the Death of Hassan Nasrallah," White House, September 28, 2024, https://www.whitehouse.gov/briefing-room/statements-releases/2024/09/28/statement-from-president-joe-biden-on-the-death-of-hassan-nasrallah/.

80. Laura Kayali, "Macron Faces Backlash After Demand for Israel Arms Embargo in Gaza," *Politico*, October 7, 2024, https://www.politico.eu/article/emmanuel-macron-france-backlash-call-israel-arms-embargo-gaza/.

81. Edward Wong, Julian E. Barnes, and Eric Schmitt, "Israel Has Destroyed Half of Hezbollah's Arsenal, U.S. and Israeli Officials Say," *New York Times*, October 1, 2024, https://www.nytimes.com/2024/10/01/us/politics/israel-lebanon-hezbollah-airstrikes.html.

82. "Hamas Official Mousa Abu Marzouk: The Tunnels in Gaza Were Built to Protect Hamas Fighters, Not Civilians; Protecting Gaza Civilians Is the Responsibility of the U.N. and Israel," Middle East Media Research Institute, October 27, 2023, https://www.memri.org/tv/hamas-official-mousa-abu-marzouk-tunnels-gaza-protect-fighters-%20not-civilians.

83. Yoav Zitun, "Radwan Force Fled After Nasrallah's Assassination, Captured Hezbollah Terrorist Says," ynetnews, October 15, 2024, https://www.ynetnews.com/article/h1hrqm2j1x.

84. "Hamas Official Ghazi Hamad: We Will Repeat the October 7 Attack, Time and Again, Until Israel Is Annihilated; We Are Victims—Everything We Do Is Justified," Middle East Media Research Institute, November 1, 2023, https://www.memri.org/reports/hamas-official-ghazi-hamad-we-will-repeat-october-7-attack-time-and-again-until-israel.

85. Jon Jackson, "Hamas Leader Reacts to 3 Sons Being Killed: 'Thank God,'" *Newsweek*, April 11, 2024, https://www.newsweek.com/hamas-leader-reacts-3-sons-killed-thank-god-1889074.

86. @EretzIsrael, X, March 3, 2023, https://x.com/EretzIsrael/status/1631632
865417936897.

87. "Amended Palestinian Prisoners Law No. 19 (2004)," in Yossi Kuperwasser,
*Incentivizing Terrorism: Palestinian Authority Allocations to Terrorists and
Their Families*, Jerusalem Center for Security and Foreign Affairs (Jerusalem,
2016), 36–7, https://jcpa.org/wp-content/uploads/pdf/salaries_kuperwasser
_12dec2016_nomarks_covers.pdf.

88. "Terror Funding by the Palestinian Authority: Mahmoud Abbas recently
approved the budget for 2018, about 7% of which is devoted to assisting
prisoners, released terrorists, and families of shahids," Meir Amit Intelligence
and Terrorism Information Center, March 29, 2018, https://www.terrorism
-info.org.il/app/uploads/2018/04/E_080_18.pdf.

89. Letter from Tom Cotton et al. to Karim A. A. Khan, April 24, 2024, https://
www.politico.com/f/?id=0000018f-4e0e-d759-a9ff-ff4ee9420000.

90. "Former ICC Chief Prosecutor Luis Moreno Ocampo on Possible Arrest Warrants for Netanyahu and Gallant: This Is a Game Changer; Hamas's Leaders
Are Victims, Their Families Were Attacked," Middle East Media Research
Institute, May 22, 2024, https://www.memri.org/tv/fmr-icc-chief-prosecutor
-ocampo-possible-arrest-netanyahu-gallant-hamas-leaders-victims.

91. @IntlCrimCourt, X, May 3, 2024, https://x.com/IntlCrimCourt/status/178631
6229688414518/photo/1.

92. Nadeen Ebrahim, Amir Tal, and Mick Krever, "Israel's Judicial Overhaul
Sparks Military Crisis as Number of Refusing Reservists Grows," CNN,
July 26, 2023, https://edition.cnn.com/2023/07/26/middleeast/israel-judicial
-overhaul-military-reservists-intl/index.html.

93. Josh Kaplan, "Why Elite Israeli Combat Pilots Are Refusing to Serve Until
Judicial Reforms Are Abandoned," *Jewish Chronicle*, September 21, 2023,
https://www.thejc.com/news/why-elite-israeli-combat-pilots-are-refusing-to
-serve-until-judicial-reforms-are-abandoned-hi81j9e1.

94. Danny Kushmaro, "Exclusive: 4 IDF Chiefs of Staff on Camera," N12 Israel
News, November 4, 2017, https://www.mako.co.il/news-israel/local-q4_2017
/Article-7304bf116038f51004.htm.

95. "Abbas's PLO Mourns 'Martyrdom' of Hamas Chief Sinwar, a 'Great National
Leader,'" *Times of Israel*, October 19, 2024, https://www.timesofisrael.com/ab
bass-plo-mourns-martyrdom-of-hamas-chief-sinwar-a-great-national-leader/.

96. Associated Press, "Turkey's Erdogan Offers Condolences for Yahya Sinwar
after Hamas Leader's Death," YouTube, October 19, 2024, https://www.you
tube.com/watch?v=lc6y10YRhaU.

97. @mozabintnasser, X, October 18, 2024, https://x.com/mozabintnasser/status
/1847276461671035391.

98. "Anti-Israel Activists Pay Tribute to 10/7 Architect Yahya Sinwar, Reflecting
Pattern of Glorifying 'Martyred' Terror Chiefs," Anti-Defamation League,

October 23, 2024, https://www.adl.org/resources/article/anti-israel-activists
-pay-tribute-107-architect-yahya-sinwar-reflecting-pattern.

99. Mathilda Heller, "Pro-Palestine Groups at UK Universities Stage Anti-Israel
Protests to Coincide with Oct 7 Memorials," *Jerusalem Post*, October 7, 2024,
https://www.jpost.com/international/article-823547.

100. Sabrina Miller and Natalie Lisbona, "Sickening Figures Reveal the Significant
Minority of British Youngsters Who Support Hamas, Believe Reports About
October 7 Are Exaggerated or Think the Massacre of Jews Was 'Justified,'"
Daily Mail, October 7, 2024, https://www.dailymail.co.uk/news/article
-13930881/youngster-sympathy-hamas-october-7-atrocity-israel.html.

101. Yolanda Wang, "Students March for Lebanon and Palestine, Block Traffic," *Yale Daily News*, September 30, 2024, https://yaledailynews.com
/blog/2024/09/30/students-march-for-lebanon-and-palestine-block-traffic/.

102. Abigail Anthony, "'Student Intifada': Anti-Israel Harvard Student Groups
Commemorate 'One Year of Genocide,'" *National Review*, October 8, 2024,
https://www.nationalreview.com/news/student-intifada-anti-israel-harvard-stu
dent-groups-commemorate-one-year-of-genocide/.

103. @EYakoby, X, October 6, 2024, https://x.com/EYakoby/status/1843078013
212352958.

104. "Jewish Bakery in Sydney Vandalized with Antisemitic Graffiti Amid Ten-
sions," *Jerusalem Post*, October 14, 2024, https://www.jpost.com/diaspora
/antisemitism/article-824468.

105. Noah Yim, "University of Melbourne Jewish Professor's Office Stormed by
Protesters Calling Him 'a War Criminal,'" *Australian*, October 10, 2024,
https://www.theaustralian.com.au/nation/university-of-melbourne-jewish-pro
fessors-office-invaded-by-protesters-calling-him-a-war-criminal/news-story/1e
f3661b22fe383c49aa2e01d760fb2f.

ABOUT THE AUTHOR

Douglas Murray is a journalist and the bestselling author of eight books, including *The War on the West* (2022), *The Madness of Crowds* (2019), and *The Strange Death of Europe* (2017). He has been a contributor to the *Spectator* since 2000 and an associate editor since 2012. He is a columnist at the *New York Post* and the *Free Press* and regularly writes for the *Telegraph* and the *Sun*. Mr. Murray is also a senior fellow at the Manhattan Institute and a contributing editor of *City Journal*.